Battle Orders • 2

Wellington's Army in the Peninsula 1809–14

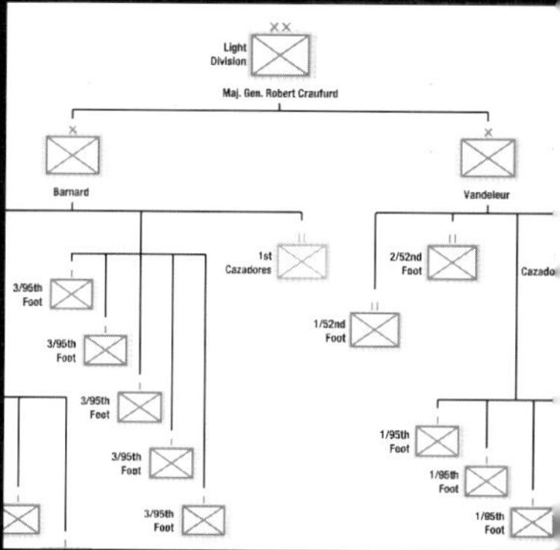

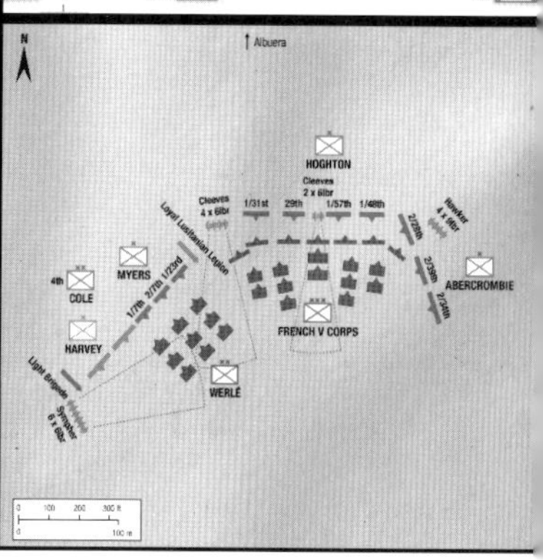

Stuart Reid • *Consultant editor Dr Duncan Anderson*

Series editors Marcus Cowper and Nikolai Bogdanovic

First published in Great Britain in 2004 by Osprey Publishing, Elms Court, Chapel Way, Botley, Oxford OX2 9LP, United Kingdom.
Email: info@ospreypublishing.com

ISBN 1 84176 517 1

Editorial by Ilios Publishing, Oxford, UK (www.iliospublishing.com)
Design: Bounford.com, Royston, UK
Maps by Bounford.com, Royston, UK
Index by David Worthington
Originated by Grasmere Digital Imaging, Leeds, UK
Printed and bound by L-Rex Printing Company Ltd.

04 05 06 07 08 10 9 8 7 6 5 4 3 2 1

A CIP catalogue record for this book is available from the British Library.

For a catalogue of all books published by Osprey Military and Aviation please contact:

Osprey Direct UK, P.O. Box 140, Wellingborough, Northants, NN8 2FA, UK
E-mail: info@ospreydirect.co.uk

Osprey Direct USA, c/o MBI Publishing, P.O. Box 1, 729 Prospect Ave, Osceola, WI 54020, USA
E-mail: info@ospreydirectusa.com

www.ospreypublishing.com

Dedication

To Maj. Gen. Viscount Barrington

Author's note

With the exception of the comparatively brief tenure of Sir John Moore the British Army was commanded throughout the Peninsular War by Sir Arthur Wellesley, successively ennobled as Viscount Wellington of Talavera, Marquis and then Duke of Wellington and a host of foreign titles as well. For the sake of clarity he is referred to in the text simply as the Duke of Wellington.

This book provides a complete order of battle for the cavalry, the seven regular infantry divisions, the Light Division and various Portuguese and Spanish units serving as a part of Wellington's field army during the Peninsular War. It does not include independent allied forces such as the Spanish Army proper, or those British and allied units engaged in secondary operations about Cadiz, or on the east coast of Spain, or serving in garrisons at Lisbon, Cadiz or Gibraltar.

This book also contains numerous biographical sidebars and boxes, which highlight key details of the lives and service careers of Wellington's commanders. Each commander appears in the section that deals with his unit of principal association.

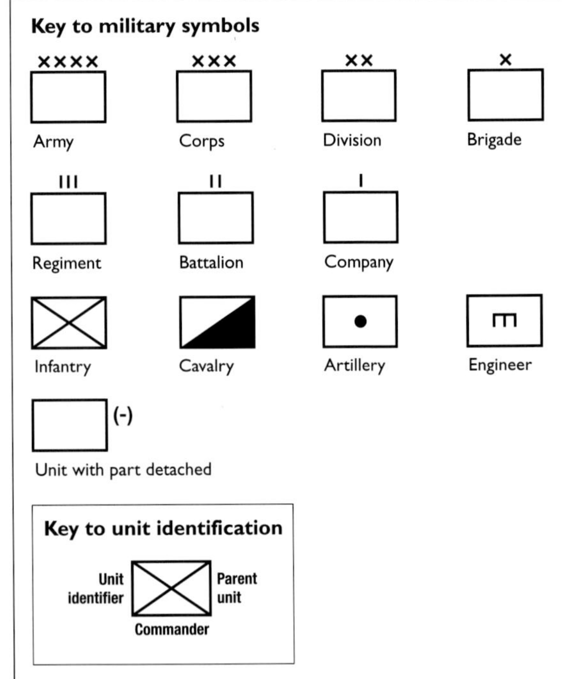

Contents

Introduction

At the outset of the Peninsular War in 1808 the British expeditionary force that landed at Mondego Bay near Lisbon was, to anticipate Kaiser Bill's rather unfortunate turn of phrase, a 'contemptible little army' which merely promised to be an irritant rather than a serious threat to the mighty armies of imperial France. Initially these gloomy expectations were confirmed. An isolated, small and rather lonely French army under Marshal Junot was defeated at Vimeiro and subsequently forced to evacuate Portugal. However, when the British expeditionary force then advanced into Spain it was very summarily chased out again by the Emperor himself and after a terrible retreat through the Galician mountains had in turn to be evacuated through La Coruña.

Were it to have ended at that point, British participation in the Peninsular campaign might now be remembered as just another in a very long succession of half-hearted and ultimately futile – if not downright disastrous – continental adventures, which merely nibbled ineffectually at the further fringes of the French empire. Instead, however, the British government took the extremely courageous political decision to send the army back to the Peninsula and to

The Iberian Peninsula.

Landing troops and guns, from a drawing by Rowlandson (1801) A very similar scene must have been witnessed at Mondego Bay when the British expeditionary force first landed in the Peninsula in 1808.

once more confide the command of it to a most remarkable general: Sir Arthur Wellesley, soon to become the Duke of Wellington.

Towards the end of the war, and with his army then on the point of invading France, Wellington famously declared it to be 'probably the most complete machine for its numbers now existing in Europe'. It is currently fashionable to attribute much of that perfection to the reforming zeal of the Duke of York, who, having been appointed Commander-in-Chief in 1795, supposedly eradicated all manner of abuses at every level and brought the army up to a remarkable pitch of efficiency just in time for Wellington to lead it to victory in the Peninsula.

In reality there was probably very little fundamentally wrong with the British Army at the outset of the great war with France in 1793, except that it was far too small. The Duke of York's real achievement was to bring order to the temporary, albeit very real, chaos caused by an over-hasty expansion of the army on a scale which would not be matched again until the creation of the 'Kitchener Army' in very similar circumstances a century later – a mobilisation which also produced similar problems.

Be that as it may, in 1808 the British Army was on the whole a reasonably efficient and professional force, but what really marked out the 'Peninsular' army from both its predecessors and from the other British forces serving elsewhere around the world, was the adoption in the following year of a divisional organisation which enabled it to operate independently in a major continental theatre of war.

During the 18th century the term 'division' had been widely used by soldiers, but only in a loose and usually a very literal sense. According to circumstances an army, a battalion or a company could be split or divided up into more manageable tactical divisions, but these simply reflected a given fraction or division (usually half or sometimes a quarter) of the troops in question, rather than any standard

Arthur Wellesley, Duke of Wellington (1769–1852)

Son of Garret Wellesley, 1st Earl of Mornington. Born 1 May 1769, probably in Dublin. Served Holland and North Germany June 1794 to spring 1795, latterly commanding brigade; October 1795 embarked 33rd for West Indies but storm-bound and destination changed to East Indies April 1796; arrived Bengal February 1797, transferred to Madras September 1798; appointed to command subsidiary force of Nizam of Hyderabad February 1799; fought at Malavelly 27 March; Sultanpetah Tope 5 and 6 April; storm of Seringapatam 4 May 1799; appointed Governor of Seringapatam 6 May and general command in Seringapatam and Mysore 9 July; campaign against Doodiagh Waugh July to 10 September 1800; assigned to Egyptian expedition 1801 but prevented by illness; served Mahratta War; siege and capture of Ahmednuggur 11 August 1803; siege and capture of Baroach 29 August; Battle of Assaye 23 September; siege and capture of Asseerghur 21 October; Battle of Argaum 29 November; siege and capture of Gawilghur 15 December; action at Munkaiseer 6 February 1804; embarked for England on HMS *Trident* March 1805; appointed to Staff Kent District 30 October 1805; commanded brigade, Hanover Expedition 30 November 1805; Colonel 33rd Foot 30 January 1806; command of brigade, Sussex District 25 February 1806; served Danish Expedition 1807, action at Kioge 29 August 1807, surrender of Copenhagen 5 September. Appointed to command Spanish expedition at Cork 14 June 1808; sailed 12 July, landed Mondego Bay 1–3 August; action at Obidos 15 August; Roleia 17 August, Battle of Vimeiro 21 August; signatory to Convention of Cintra 30 August; absolved by Cintra Inquiry November 1808. Appointed to command army in Portugal 2 April 1809, arrived Lisbon 22 April; Battle of Oporto 12 May; marshal-general, Portuguese Army 6 July 1809; Battle of Talavera 27/28 July; created Viscount Wellington 26 August 1809; Battle of Busaco 27 September 1810; entered Lines of Torres Vedras 10 October; followed French retreat commencing 16 November 1810; actions at Pombal 11 March 1811; Redinha 12 March; Cazal Nova 14 March; Foz d'Arouce 15 March; Sabugal 3 April; Battle of Fuentes de Oñoro 3–5 May; action at El Bodon 25 September; action at Aldea da Ponte 27 September 1811; storming of Ciudad Rodrigo 19 January 1812; created Earl of Wellington 18 February 1812; storming of Badajoz 6 April; capture of Salamanca forts 27 June; Battle of Salamanca 22 July; entered Madrid 12 August; created Marquis of Wellington 18 August 1812; unsuccessful siege of Burgos in October and retreat to Portugal November 1812; *generalissimo* of Spanish armies 4 December 1812; colonel Royal Regiment of Horse Guards 1 January 1813; advance into Spain 6 May; Battle of Vittoria 21 June 1813 and in consequence promoted field marshal (*Gazette* 3 July); Pyrenees July 1813; passage of Bidassoa 7 October; Battle of Nivelle 10 November; passage of Nive 9 December 1813; Battle of Orthez 27 February 1814; passage of Adour 1 March; Battle of Toulouse 10 April 1814; made Duke of Wellington 3 May 1814; returned to England 23 June 1814; ambassador to Court of France 5 July; to Congress of Vienna 1 November 1814; appointed commander of British Forces on Continent and joined army at Brussels 11 April 1815; Battle of Quatre Bras 16 June; Battle of Waterloo 18 June; capture of Cambrai 25 June; capture of Peronne 26 June; capitulation of Paris 3 July 1815; appointed commander-in-chief Allied Army of Occupation 22 October 1815; evacuation of France 21 November 1818; master general of the Ordnance 26 December 1818; Governor of Plymouth 9 December 1819; colonel-in-chief Rifle Brigade 19 February 1820; Constable of Tower of London 29 December 1826; colonel Grenadier Guards and commander-in-chief British Army 22 January 1827; resigned 30 April but re-appointed 27 August and then resigned again 15 February 1828 on being appointed prime minister; commander-in-chief British Army 10 August 1842. Married Katherine Pakenham, with issue. Died at Walmer Castle 14 September 1852.

Commissions: ensign 73rd Highlanders 7 March 1787; lieutenant 76th Foot 25 December 1787, exchanged to 41st Foot 23 January 1788, exchanged to 18th Light Dragoons 25 June 1789; captain 58th Foot 20 September 1791, exchanged back to 18th Light Dragoons 31 October 1792; major 33rd Foot 30 April 1793; lieutenant-colonel 30 September 1793; colonel (brevet) 3 May 1796; major-general 29 April 1802; lieutenant-general 25 April 1808; general (Spain and Portugal) 31 July 1811; field marshal 3 July 1813.

unit of measurement or of organisation. An army, for example, could be divided into two wings or corps, which could either be formally referred to as such or colloquially described as divisions. Similarly within an infantry battalion the drill book normally called for it to be broken down into either two wings or four grand divisions for manoeuvring and fire control, while a company could also in its turn be split into two divisions if required.

Indeed, although invariably loose, these terms continued to be used in the drill book both throughout and long after the period in question; but the infantry division as introduced by Wellington in 1809 was a discrete formation, with a fairly standardised organisation and strength, and which superseded the brigade as the major tactical unit.

In part this innovation sprang from the sensible realisation that given the near unprecedented size of the forces involved, an intermediate command level was required somewhere between brigade and army headquarters. In itself this was not of course a particularly revolutionary step since most other large continental armies had already adopted some kind of divisional structure, but it did reflect the British Army's very significant transition from a supporting role to a principal role in the conflict.

A French print depicting two British officers in Paris after Waterloo. The gentleman on the right would appear to belong to either the 42nd or 79th Highlanders and is identified as a light-company officer by his sabre. However, while his uniform is more or less in accordance with the regulations, his companion appears to be flouting them entirely. His 1812-pattern cap identifies him as an infantryman, but he wears a braided jacket quite unknown in any set of dress regulations, carries a sabre and sabretache, and wears a long braided pelisse coat. He can only be a staff officer.

Wellington's qualification that his army was the most complete 'for its size' was an honest acknowledgement of the fact that notwithstanding the enormous resources in men, money and *matériel* habitually expended by the government in wartime, the British Army was still a rather small one by comparison with those of its major continental rivals. Moreover, once its own very extensive defensive and colonial commitments had been met, the disposable portion of the army that was actually available for major operations on the continent was even smaller still. Consequently, throughout the 18th century coalition warfare had been the rule and, except for some very minor adventures, British troops had normally taken the field in continental Europe merely as one contingent amongst many in a patchwork Allied army. This had invariably proved unsatisfactory and often downright destructive even when comparatively substantial numbers of British troops were present, since the various allies naturally had their own agendas and priorities which were not always in accord (and sometimes downright incompatible) with each other. The Duke of York's campaign in Flanders at the outset of the war had been a very salutary case in point, and in 1808 not only had Wellington's operations been hampered by poor co-operation with his very independent Portuguese allies, but his successor, Sir John Moore, had fared even more disastrously with his Spanish ones.

Wellington too was to make one final and unhappy attempt at joint operations with the Spanish Army during the Talavera campaign in 1809, but the divisional organisation he had introduced for that particular operation was judged a success and thereafter the British Army under Wellington's personal command was able to operate entirely independently.

Organisation

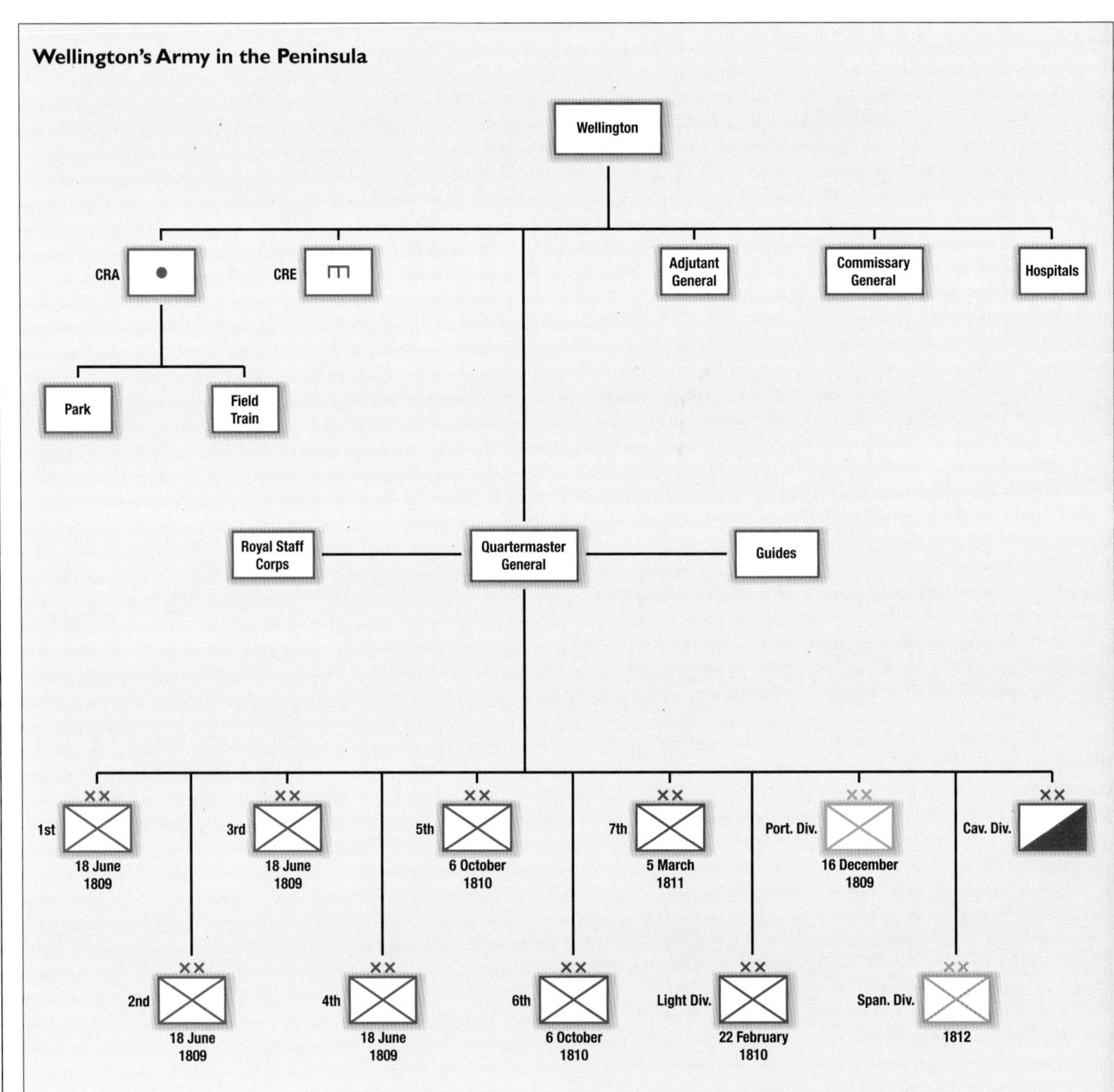

The composition and organisation of a British infantry division was by no means rigid, particularly since it was something of an innovation and therefore evolved to some extent during the course of the five-year-long campaign. At the very outset of the war in 1808 the British Army in Portugal comprised simply eight more or less independent infantry brigades, each in turn made up of two to three battalions plus detachments of riflemen. In the following year for the operations against Oporto, Wellington initially fielded nine brigades, each commanded by a major-general and comprising between two and four battalions apiece with a single company of riflemen. Significantly, five of those brigades included a Portuguese battalion – an innovation undoubtedly inspired by Wellington's previous service in India where it was customary to brigade European and the supposedly less effective Sepoy battalions together rather than deploying them in discrete contingents. However, for the subsequent advance into Spain for what became the Talavera campaign, Wellington left the Portuguese behind, and grouped his British brigades into four divisions and an independent Light Brigade.

Divisional organisation

The 1st Division usually had four brigades, each of two battalions, while the others initially had only two brigades each of two or three battalions. In addition each division normally had at least one artillery battery (usually referred to as a brigade) and its own staff and commissariat. Over the next two years as the Peninsular army expanded, three new divisions were added, besides expanding the Light Brigade into a full division, and their internal organisation was also altered from time to time.

Most divisions, for example, were reinforced by the addition of a complete Portuguese brigade, normally comprising two regiments of line infantry and one regiment of cazadores or light infantry. Although some discrete Portuguese formations remained, including a complete division under Hamilton, this measure, while understandably unpopular with the Portuguese government, effectively increased the overall strength of the British Army in the Peninsula by about 50 per cent and at the same time avoided most of the traditional operational problems associated with co-ordinating independent allied forces.

The integration of the Portuguese units into British divisions was considerably aided by the interlarding of British and native officers in the Portuguese service. In theory these alternated through the ranks so that battalions commanded by Portuguese officers had a British brigade commander, and vice versa. Predictably enough this arrangement rarely survived contact with the enemy, but it remained an important principle throughout the war and avoided a great deal of resentment and friction. Indeed for a time the 'British' 7th Division was actually commanded by the Portuguese general Le Cor.

British divisions did not, however, have an organic cavalry element. The organisation and employment of the cavalry will be separately discussed in due course, but at this stage it is sufficient to note that cavalry units were only assigned to support divisions as and when required for a particular operation, although the nature of the Light Division's employment on the outposts meant that it enjoyed the almost permanent attachment of the 1st Hussars King's German Legion (KGL).

Typical divisional administrative organisation, 1812. This is the basic 'template' or matrix employed for 'British' infantry divisions after the integration of the Portuguese brigades in 1811. It is important to appreciate, however, that a quite different table of organisation came into use when the division was in action.

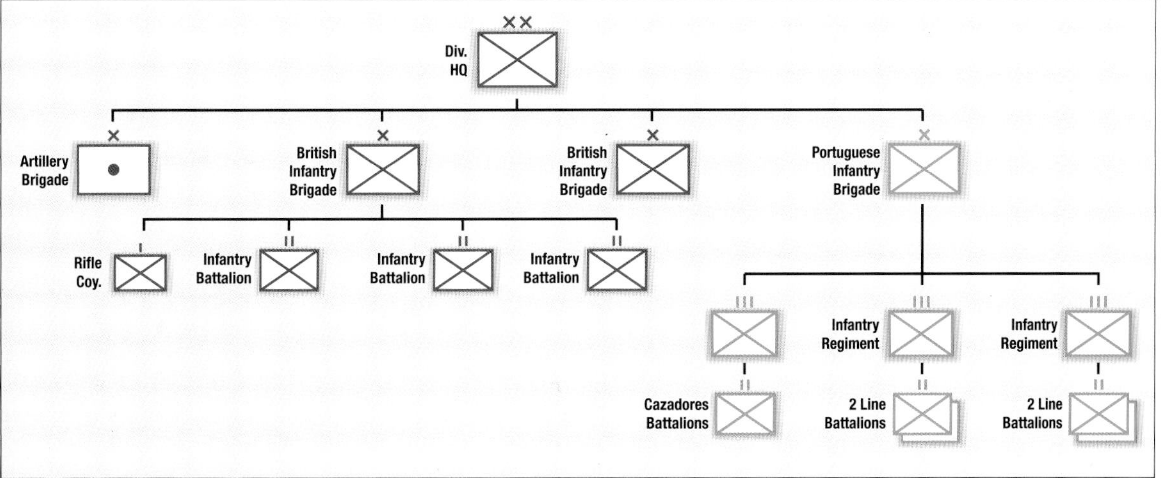

Brigade and battalion organisation

A brigade normally comprised three battalions, but its organisation was by no means as straightforward as it might at first appear: to understand why, it is necessary to first look at its basic component unit, the infantry regiment.

With certain exceptions, such as the Footguards, the terms regiment and battalion had been synonymous in British service throughout the 18th century, and notwithstanding the introduction of Second Battalions for most regiments in the early 1800s this very largely continued to be the case during the Napoleonic Wars. Each infantry battalion had a theoretical wartime establishment of about 1,000 men organised in ten companies, commanded by a lieutenant-colonel. Whilst two lieutenant-colonels and two majors appeared on the establishment of an infantry battalion it was very rare for all four of them to actually be present. Illness and casualties aside they could be assigned to command provisional light infantry battalions or other ad hoc units, detachments or posts, or to serve upon the staff in one capacity or another.

Wastage and replacements

Moreover wastage very quickly reduced the number of men in the ranks. In theory this wastage should have been repaired by drafts sent out from the regiment's Second Battalion, which was originally conceived as a reserve formation with the dual purpose of home defence and at the same time serving as a depot for the First Battalion. In practice it was a lot less straightforward. A number of units sent to the Peninsula, such as the 68th (Durham) Regiment, had no Second Battalion. In other cases the Second Battalion went out to the Peninsula while the First Battalion was either deployed elsewhere around the globe or at least recovering at home after some arduous service abroad. In either case the sheer distance and slow pace of communications ensured that it was very difficult to supply regular reinforcement drafts to the unit actually in theatre, which consequently dwindled away quite dramatically.

The ideal solution in this case was to build up the battalion at home and then send it out entire to replace the one in theatre – which would then turn over all its remaining effectives to the newly arrived battalion before returning home to recruit itself afresh. When this did occur, however, the handover was by no means slick or instantaneous and Wellington sometimes tried to hang on

Typical divisional battle organisation, 1812. This is the different matrix actually employed in combat. Instead of three brigades of infantry each with an integral skirmishing element, the division actually fielded three brigades of line infantry and a fourth brigade of light infantry.

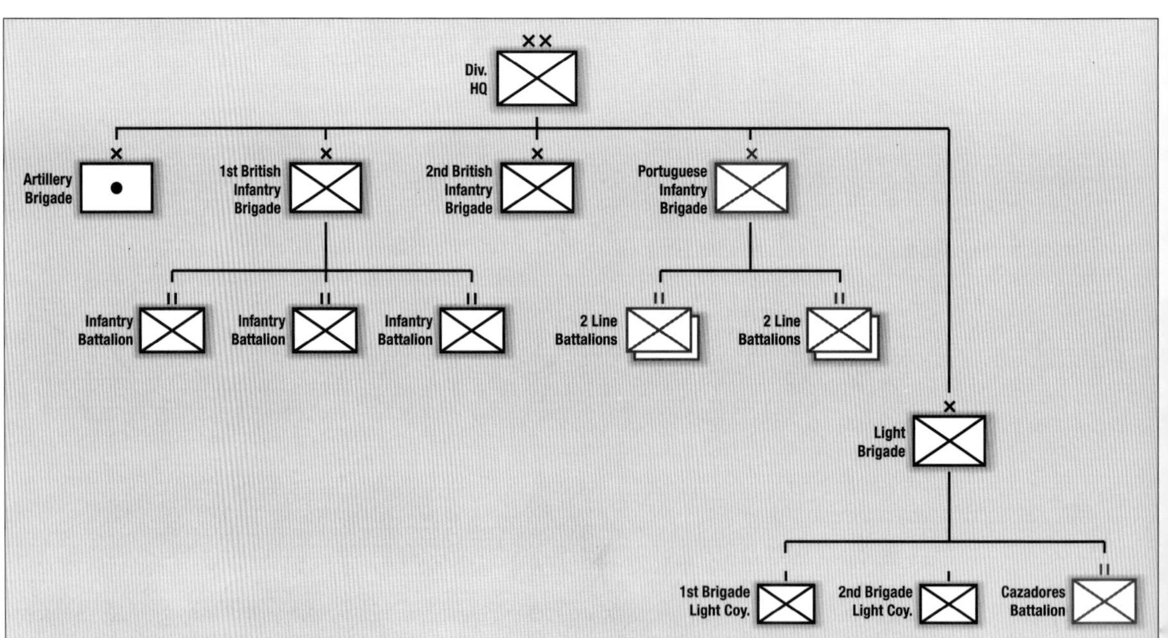

Battalion strength

When fully recruited up to its establishment an infantry battalion ought to have had 100 rank and file in each of its ten companies to make 1,000 in all exclusive of officers (four per company) besides the regimental staff. If ordered overseas, authorisation would usually be given to recruit slightly over this number to allow for the inevitable casualties from all causes. The shrinkage which followed could be quite dramatic. At Salamanca in 1812 there were 43 British battalions present (exclusive of the 60th and 95th Rifles) ranging in strength from the 1,039 rank and file in 1/42nd Highlanders to a mere 231 rank and file in 2/44th Foot. In all just three battalions had over 900 rank and file; one (1/5th) had 870 rank and file; four had between 708 and 771; eight had 606 to 686; six had 517 to 576; nine had 404 to 485; seven had 316 to 381, and five had less.

The fate of those five is interesting. On 27 July, five days after the battle, the 289-strong 2/5th Foot turned over its effectives to 1/5th Foot and went home. In contrast, 2/38th Foot who had mustered 281 rank and file on 22 July, soldiered on until 6 December before being drafted into 1/38th and sent home, while 2/44th although ordered home formed a part of 4/Provisional Battalion on the same date. The two remaining regiments, the 280-strong 51st Foot and 295-strong 2/83rd Foot, remained until the end of the war.

Naturally enough the losses from all causes sustained by infantry companies within a battalion fluctuated just as widely. An unlucky blast of canister fire could decimate one company while leaving another untouched. Consequently it was standard practice constantly to 'level' all the companies by temporarily drafting men from one into another in order to ensure that all ten companies were approximately the same size. This was essential for manoeuvring the battalion efficiently since uneven numbers would quite literally unbalance the unit – most dramatically perhaps in forming a square.

to both battalions for as long as possible. The most famous example was the two battalions of the 7th (Royal Fusiliers) who fought together in Myers' Fusilier Brigade at Albuera in 1811; but at Salamanca in 1812 Campbell's Brigade in the 3rd Division had four battalions including both the newly arrived and very strong 1/5th Foot and the very weak and rather worn out

The 71st (Glasgow) Regiment in action at Vimeiro, as depicted in a print by Dubourg. Although the Highlanders are inexplicably depicted in the uniform of the 42nd Regiment, this illustration is not without interest. Note the folding knapsacks worn by the Highlanders and the light marching order of knapsacks with rolled blankets in place worn by the riflemen of 5/60th on the left.

Col. Hon. Francis William Grant of Grant. Although he is a militia officer, this print provides a good illustration of the uniform of a field officer commanding a battalion, and some notion of what a battalion looked like.

2/5th Foot. Conversely where a regiment had but a single battalion or at least had no sister battalion available to replace it, the official policy, insisted upon by the Duke of York (the army's administrative commander-in-chief) was that once it became too weak to operate effectively it should be sent home and replaced by a completely different corps. Wellington, however, was unwilling to lose 'salted' units that, however weak, he regarded as being more useful and serviceable than unacclimatised and inexperienced ones, no matter how large they might be. He therefore resisted this policy as far as possible, preferring instead – when he could get away with it – to join weak units together in provisional battalions in order to maintain a working strength of between 1,500 and 2,000 men to a brigade.

Skirmishers

The internal organisation of most British infantry brigades was further complicated by its skirmishing element, which primarily consisted of one attached company of riflemen and the light company from each of the constituent battalions. The evidence clearly indicates that these companies did not operate independently, but were formed into provisional battalions as a matter of course. It would in fact be rather more surprising if the reverse were the case, for the 1792 *Rules and Regulations for the Formations, Field Exercise and Movements of his Majesty's Forces* clearly state that 'When two or more companies are together they are to consider themselves a battalion, the senior officer is to take the command, leaving the immediate command of his own company to the next officer belonging to it' (p.332). This particular rule had very little to do with specific tactical precepts or doctrines and everything to do with simple common sense. If a typical three-regiment brigade deployed its three light companies (and an independent company of rifles from either the 60th or the Brunswick Jäger) out in front it would clearly be sensible if not downright essential for someone to take charge of the whole skirmish line and run it as a single battalion. Were this to be a purely temporary arrangement which was only entered into on the day of the battle, then one would expect that, just as the *Regulations* laid down, the officer in command would simply be the senior captain of the four. Hopefully he would also be well enough known to his colleagues to avoid the need for standing around comparing commission dates while bullets were whistling about them. In reality of course the arrangement was a touch more permanent than that and it is common to find captains specifically recording in their post-war returns of service that they had commanded the light companies of their brigade.

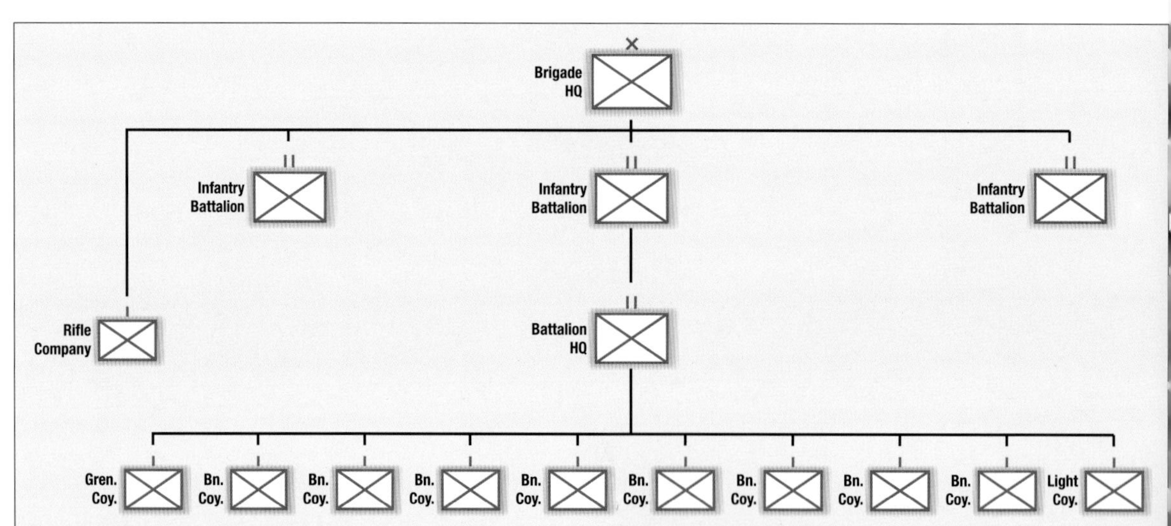

A typical British infantry brigade. This was the standard administrative matrix for a brigade, comprising three battalions each of ten companies, plus an additional independent company of riflemen.

This process did not end at brigade level, and a surprising number of field officers – majors and lieutenant-colonels – recorded their having commanded the divisional light battalion or 'brigade'. Moreover, the fact that these composite formations were not casual groupings, but semi-permanent formations, is graphically underlined by the fact that the field officers commanding them also had adjutants to assist them with the day-to-day administration of the 'brigade'.

Essentially therefore, although on paper a British infantry brigade might normally consist of three ten-company battalions of the line and one rifle company, in actual practice at a tactical level a brigade actually fielded three nine-company battalions of the line and a four-company light battalion. At a divisional level these small light battalions, together with the Cazadores battalion belonging to its Portuguese brigade, were then in turn grouped together as a fourth 'brigade' co-ordinated by a permanently assigned field officer and adjutant. While these temporary formations obviously differed from 18th-century flank battalions which preceded them in that they were not detached at any distance from their parent brigades and divisions, the employment of this higher organisational structure clearly points to a much more sophisticated degree of tactical control being exercised over 'ordinary' light companies in the Peninsula than may previously have been recognised.

Foreign corps in British pay

A number of Wellington's infantry brigades included units which although a part of the British Army were actually officially termed 'foreign corps in British pay'. The 1st Division always included at least one brigade, and sometimes two brigades, of KGL infantry, and the 7th Division was so cosmopolitan in its makeup to be nicknamed 'The Mongrels'.

The quality of these foreign units, often recruited in customary fashion from prisoners of war and the other side's deserters, was extremely variable, but with the exception of the Brunswick Oels contingent they all wore British uniforms and followed British tactical doctrine. Their organisation was also exactly the same, other than the fact that a half company in each KGL Line Battalion was equipped with Baker rifles and designated as sharpshooters. While this might at first sight appear to be a unique German innovation, it was actually of no especial significance since ordinary British units had for

A British infantry brigade in combat. In this typical matrix, the light companies of the three battalions have been brigaded with the rifle company to form a fourth, light, battalion. On paper this four-company battalion appears much smaller than the nine-company line battalions, but this was not necessarily the case. While it was standard practice to level the size of companies before going on service, it was equally customary to draft men into the light company in order to keep it as closely up to strength as possible, and the discrepancy between the light and line battalions may have been more apparent than real.

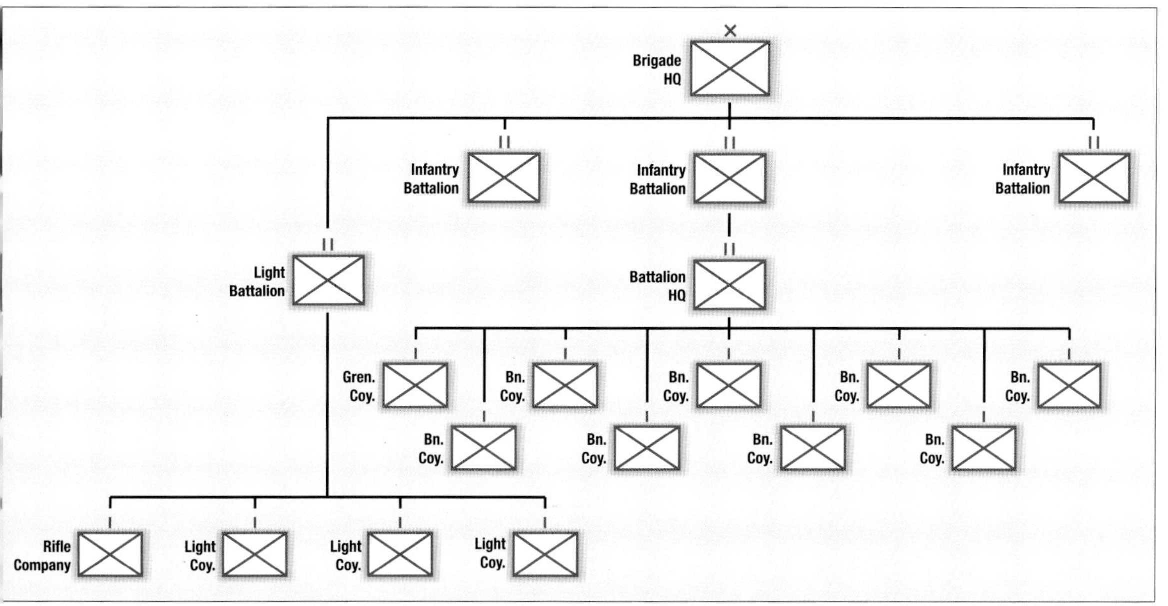

some time been in the habit of informally designating a number of men in each battalion company as 'flankers' or 'marksmen' – and perhaps even in some cases equally informally arming them with rifles. It did, however, mean that it was unnecessary to attach a rifle company of 5/60th or of Brunswick Oels Jäger to KGL infantry brigades.

The Brunswick Oels contingent in fact occupied a fairly unique position in that whilst wholly in British pay, it was actually a subsidiary allied force rather than an integral part of the British Army like the Kings German Legion. Its independent status was most readily apparent from the fact that unlike the other foreign corps its men did not wear British uniform or carry British colours – however disguised.

The Brunswickers' internal organisation was also slightly different. Although all 12 infantry companies were officially designated as jäger, only three of them were actually dressed in green, equipped with rifles and employed as sharpshooters. These companies, like the 5/60th Rifles, were dispersed singly amongst various infantry brigades, in this case belonging to the 4th and 5th Divisions. The remaining nine companies, dressed in rather shabby black jackets and equipped with common firelocks, served as an ordinary infantry battalion, which after some shuffling around eventually found a natural home in the 7th Division.

Portuguese brigades

At the outset of the war, Portuguese infantry regiments had an official establishment of 1,500 men organised in two battalions each of five very large companies. When the army was re-organised in the wake of the French occupation in the summer of 1808, it was initially planned that all ten companies should be consolidated in a single battalion, although in the end the old two-battalion organisation seems to have been retained throughout. Thanks to an efficient conscription system and the fact that unlike their British counterparts they were serving comparatively close to home, these regiments were maintained at a reasonable strength throughout the war. Consequently Portuguese brigades, comprising two regiments of line infantry and a single-battalion regiment of cazadores, seem to have had an average strength of 2,000–2,500 bayonets, in contrast to the 1,500–2,000 usually found in a British one. In practice, once both the cazadores and the two regimental light companies had been claimed by the divisional light infantry brigade, the strength of the main fighting line will have been broadly similar.

A Portuguese infantry brigade. This comprised two regiments of line infantry and one of cazadores. Some sources suggest that the line regiments each comprised a single battalion of ten companies patterned after the British model, but the evidence actually points to their retaining a two-battalion organisation, with only five companies in each. One company in the first battalion was designated as grenadiers and one company as cazadores or light infantry. The cazadores regiment on the other hand had a single battalion of five companies, one of which was designated as tiradores or sharpshooters and armed with rifles.

All in all, one third of a Portuguese brigade was formally designated as light infantry. It is unclear whether the two cazadores companies belonging to the line regiments remained with their parent units in action, or joined the brigade cazadores battalion, but as the latter was in line with British practice it would seem more likely.

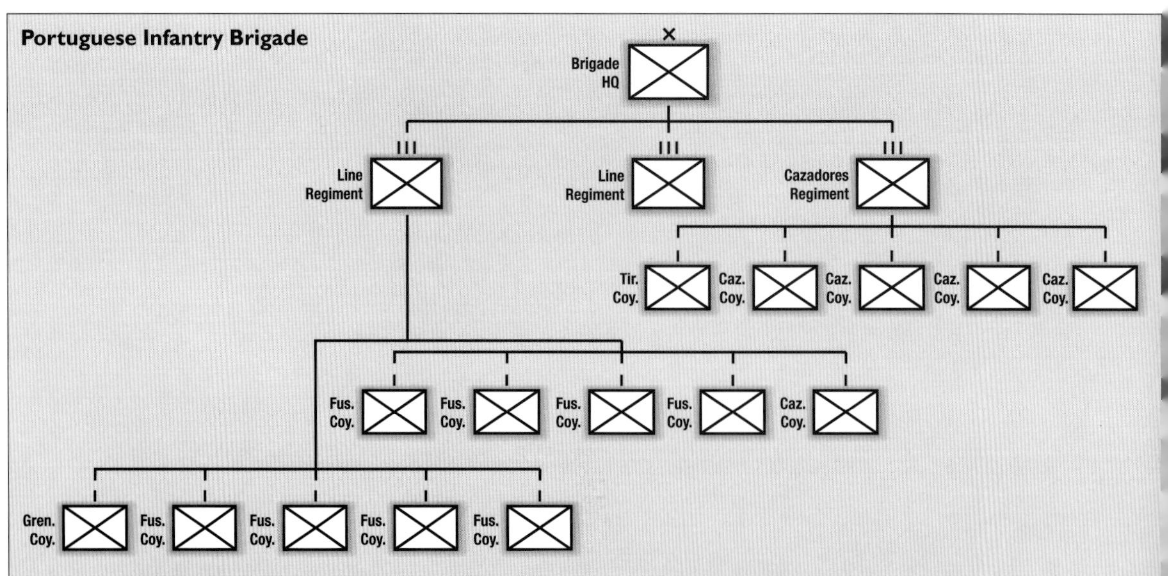

Command and control

General staff

Wellington's staff appeared to most continental, and not a few British, observers to be small, under-resourced and incorrigibly scruffy.

The army's administrative staff, as distinct from the personal staff of general officers including Wellington himself, was divided between two principal departments, those of the Adjutant General and the Quartermaster General, although there was also a third major department, that of the Commissary General, which was ultimately answerable to an ever suspicious Treasury rather than to the military authorities at Horse Guards.

The precise parameters of the departmental responsibilities and indeed the primacy of the two departments were to a very considerable extent dependent on the personalities and abilities of the men actually running them. However, broadly speaking, in Wellington's Peninsular army the Adjutant General's department was only responsible for routine matters such as discipline, the collection of returns and the issue and implementation of regulations and standing orders. The Quartermaster General's department on the other hand was presided over for most of the war by the very capable George Murray and under his direction it was given, or abrogated to itself, responsibility for the actual conduct of operations and everything that went with them, including (obviously) the quartering of the army, its movements and transport. Accordingly the department also needed to concern itself with reconnoitring and, where necessary, improving the routes along which the army would move, and as a further logical extension of this particular function the department also assumed responsibility for reconnoitring the enemy as well and gathering and collating the resulting intelligence. Consequently its officers not only went out

George Murray (1772–1846)
Second son of Sir William Murray of Ochtertyre. Served Flanders and Holland 1793–95; ADC to Maj. Gen. Alexander Campbell for Quiberon Expedition. A-QMG Helder Expedition, wounded. A-QMG Egypt 1801; Adjutant General West Indies; A-QMG Hanover and Denmark 1807; QMG for abortive Swedish Expedition 1808, and Corunna 1809; appointed QMG in Peninsula 1 April 1809; struck off strength in consequence of promotion to major-general 7 May 1812, but resumed appointment 26 December 1812. QMG Army of Occupation 1815–18. Governor RMC Sandhurst 1819–24. Colonel 42nd Highlanders 6 September 1823. C-in-C Ireland 1825–28. Colonial Secretary (pc) 1828–30. Master General of the Ordnance 1834–35 and again Master General of the Ordnance 1841 until his death in 1846.

Commissions: ensign 71st Highlanders 12 March 1789, transferred to 3rd Footguards 1790; lieutenant and captain 16 January 1794; captain and lieutenant-colonel 5 August 1799; colonel 9 March 1809; brigadier-general 4 June 1811; major-general 1 January 1812; lieutenant-general (North America) 1814; lieutenant-general 27 May 1825; general 1841.

Wellington often took a hands-on approach to command, which although suitably inspiring to those directly involved, made life very difficult for other commanders – and even his own ADCs trying to find his 'headquarters'.

Toulouse, the last battle, 10 April 1814; a print by T. Sutherland after W. Heath. Note the very long blue greatcoats worn by all the staff officers.

Sir William Howe De Lancey (1781–1815)
Only son of Stephen De Lancy, American Loyalist and Governor of Tobago. Served Peninsula: DQMG 1 April 1809. Acting QMG December 1811 to August 1812 and December 1812 to March 1813. Acted as Head of Department under Hope, May 1813 to April 1814. Quartermaster General in Netherlands May to June 1815. Married Magdalen Hall 4 April 1815. Died of wounds ten days after Waterloo.

Commissions: cornet 16th Light Dragoons 7 July 1792; lieutenant 26 February 1793; captain Independent Company 25 March 1794, transferred to 80th Foot; captain 17th Light Dragoons 20 October 1796; major 45th Foot 17 October 1799; lieutenant-colonel (permanent staff) 1 April 1809.

looking for the enemy and liaising with allied forces, including the ubiquitous guerrillas, but also became involved with cryptography, prisoner interrogation and the preparation of intelligence summaries, which were, properly speaking, the preserve of the Adjutant General's department.

To help the Adjutant General and the Quartermaster General in the execution of their duties they normally had two assistants apiece, conventionally designated simply by the initials of their appointment as AAG (Assistant Adjutant General) or AQMG (Assistant Quartermaster General) respectively. The officers appointed to these posts were normally lieutenant-colonels or majors. At the next level down came a couple of deputies, again by convention referred to by their initials as DAAG (Deputy Assistant Adjutant General) and DAQMG (Deputy Assistant Quartermaster General). These officers were usually captains or even subalterns. There was in addition a final substratum of non-commissioned officers and enlisted men serving as clerks and orderlies.

For the most part only the more senior appointments were held by permanent staff officers, the majority being only temporarily seconded to the staff from their regiments. Any distinction between them was, however, outwardly obliterated by the wearing of what amounted to an unofficial staff uniform. Permanent staff officers were prescribed a scarlet uniform coat very similar to that worn by general officers, except for wearing silver lace instead of gold. This uniform was unpopular, since it was both expensive and far from being a practical working dress. Gleig indeed recounts a story of how when Wellington was commanding the Army of Occupation in France after Waterloo he had occasion to order his staff to parade in their proper departmental uniforms by way of punishment for some unruly behaviour – an order which produced absolute consternation since none of the officers concerned possessed such things. Instead both they and the regimental officers seconded to the staff or serving as ADCs or brigade majors almost invariably wore slouch greatcoats (normally either dark blue or occasionally grey in colour) hence their reputation for scruffiness, particularly by comparison with their continental counterparts.

Other departments

The Commissary General – for much of the war Robert Hugh Kennedy – ultimately reported to the Treasury and was responsible for organising all the food, forage, non-military transport (including the mule-trains) and non-military stores required by the army, and, together with the Deputy Paymaster General, acted as its banker.

The Commander Royal Artillery (CRA) and Commander Royal Engineers (CRE) with their respective staffs also formed a part of Headquarters, but as specialists were independent of both the Adjutant General and the Quartermaster General and in any case both answered to the Board of Ordnance rather than to Horse Guards. As such the CRA was responsible for provision of all arms and ammunition as well as acting as Wellington's artillery advisor. It should be emphasised, however, that this was primarily an administrative rather than a command post. Similarly the CRE not only provided supposedly expert advice on fortifications (and how to demolish them) but was also a storekeeper of engineering tools. Both of these officers, not the Commissary General, were also responsible for the transporting of their guns, ammunition, bridging pontoons and other stores.

The Inspector-General of Hospitals, Sir James Murray McGrigor, was in sole charge of the army's medical arrangements and its supplies. Similarly the Deputy Judge Advocate General (DJAG), Francis Larpent, and his staff were also pretty well independent, since their role was to act as Official Solicitors. The day-to-day maintenance of law and order was the direct responsibility of the Provost Marshal, who in turn reported to the Adjutant General.

Divisional staff

In outline, tactical command and control was straightforward enough. Divisions were supposed to be led by lieutenant-generals, brigades by major-generals and battalions by lieutenant-colonels. In practice of course it was a good deal less straightforward, especially in the early years of the Peninsular War when Wellington was short of general officers. There was a great deal of 'acting up' usually as the result of senior officers becoming casualties and it was not uncommon to find divisions temporarily commanded by major-generals, although there were even a couple of occasions when divisions were briefly commanded by lieutenant-colonels. When this occurred the officer's brigade was in turn temporarily commanded by its senior lieutenant-colonel (usually holding the brevet rank of colonel or even brigadier-general), who left his own battalion to be run by the junior lieutenant-colonel, or more commonly one of the majors – or even the senior captain.

Major-generals were officially allowed one aide-de-camp (ADC) or personal assistant at public expense, while lieutenant-generals had two and full generals were allowed three. The regulation was necessary because like other permanent staff officers, ADCs (normally captains) were supposed to transfer on to the half-pay, and an allowance was therefore made (through the employing general) to cover the difference. In addition senior officers holding independent commands were also allowed a military secretary to handle confidential paperwork and look after both his own finances and the public funds with which he was entrusted. In addition most generals also took on 'extra' ADCs, who were regarded as being on temporary attachments and, although serving on the staff, still remained on the books of their parent regiments.

Each division also had a small administrative staff, normally comprising an Assistant Adjutant General, and an Assistant Quartermaster General with a Deputy apiece. Assistant Commissaries and Assistant Provost Marshals also served on the staff of a division. In the ordinary course of events those appointed to divisional staffs had previously served at general headquarters rather than simply being thrown in at the deep end.

Brigade staff

Brigadier-generals and colonels commanding brigades were not officially allowed ADCs, but instead had the assistance of a Brigade Major. Strictly speaking he was not a personal staff officer since it was a permanent staff appointment and his first loyalty was to his brigade. Thus while ADCs came and went with their generals, he remained with his brigade through its various changes of commander and his role was rather that of an adjutant, although it was not unknown for the brigade commander to remain prudently in the rear, where of course he could assess the situation coolly and deliberately, while the brigade major flourished his sword and actually led it forward.

The only other staff officer serving at brigade, unless as often happened the brigadier got himself an unofficial ADC, was an Assistant Commissary.

Staff troops

Being ultimately responsible for the maintenance of discipline, the Adjutant General had direct control over those detachments serving as provosts or military police – an organisation which did not exist as a separate corps at this time, but which was made up of suitable individuals, usually seconded from cavalry regiments.

The Quartermaster General on the other hand had some troops of his very own, namely the Royal Staff Corps, and the Corps of Guides and its successor, the Cavalry Staff Corps. The first of these units was primarily concerned with certain aspects of military engineering. Its officers were indeed trained as engineers, while the rank and file were intended to act as overseers for working parties drawn from the infantry or even the local peasantry. Inevitably there was a certain scope for overlap between the respective duties of the Staff Corps and the Royal Engineers, but broadly speaking the Staff Corps, as an extension of the Quartermaster General's department, was primarily responsible for the building, repair, maintenance and improvement of the many roads and bridges over which the army would march, or transport its supplies. Much of the work was consequently a matter of navvying (hence the requirement for skilled overseers or gangers) rather than the construction of field works and fortifications, which properly belonged to the Royal Engineers.

The Corps of Guides was originally raised by Murray in Portugal in September 1808 'to act as guides and orderlies', although most of the personnel were in fact a pretty cosmopolitan mixture of local recruits and foreign deserters, with a distinct preponderance of Italians. Their commander, Capt George Scovell, took considerable pains to ensure their evacuation at Corunna since capture (or recapture) would have been attended with unfortunate results. In April 1809 the Corps was again reformed under Scovell's command initially with a large Portuguese element, although many of his former troopers evidently turned up again, as did more 'foreign deserters' and a fair number of Spaniards also subsequently joined. Once again they served individually as guides, despatch riders and interpreters.

In April 1813 Scovell, who by then was a brevet lieutenant-colonel – and the resident cryptographer at headquarters – passed command of the Guides to Lt. Col. Henry Sturgeon of the Royal Staff Corps, on being appointed major commandant of the newly created Cavalry Staff Corps. Made up from volunteers 'of good character and exemplary service' taken from existing mounted units, the Cavalry Staff Corps was primarily intended to serve as a military police force answering to the Provost and should therefore by rights have come under the aegis of the Adjutant General. However, Scovell remained attached to the Quartermaster General's department and during the Vittoria campaign his Cavalry Staff Corps was employed on reconnaissance duties with the Light Division.

Sir George Scovell (1774–1861)

Son of George Scovell, of Cirencester. Attended RM College 1808. Served throughout Peninsular War and appointed DAQMG 1 April 1809; initially attached to Cotton's cavalry brigade but then placed in charge of Corps of Staff Guides 23 May 1809. AQMG 30 May 1811. Placed in charge of 'all military communications' 14 August 1811. Specialised in Intelligence work and cyphers. Commandant Cavalry Staff Corps 13 March 1813 and struck off strength 25 June. AQMG at Waterloo. Governor of Royal Military College. Died Henley Park nr. Guilford 17 January 1861.

Commissions: adjutant 4th Dragoons 5 April 1798; cornet 20 June 1798; lieutenant 4 May 1800; captain 4th Dragoons 10 March 1804; captain 57th Foot 12 March 1807; major (brevet) 30 May 1811; lieutenant-colonel (brevet) 17 August 1812; major commandant Royal Staff Corps 15 April 1813, half-pay 25 October 1814; returned to full pay 10 August 1815; lieutenant-colonel commandant Staff Corps Cavalry 22 February 1816; colonel (brevet) 17 May 1825; major-general 10 January 1837.

Intelligence

As indicated above, the collection, collation and interpretation of intelligence fell in the Peninsula to the Quartermaster General's department, largely because of the importance of ascertaining as much as possible about the countryside over which the army was expected to operate. All officers (and not just those serving on the staff) were routinely required to pass back any useful information on the state of roads, bridges, accommodation and anything else that might conceivably be of use in planning future operations. Rather more pro-actively the so-called 'exploring officers' were sent out to gather similar information from behind the enemy lines as well as information on enemy movements.

Most information on the enemy, however, other than casual reports from allied forces (including captured despatches), spies and friendly civilians, came from conventional armed reconnaissance patrols and even from the picquet lines. It is hard to say just how much useful information came from the latter, who were notorious for fraternising with their French counterparts, but by the end of the war it was considered sufficiently valuable for battalions to designate their own intelligence officers to debrief incoming picquets and pass back anything interesting.

Command and control in action

So much for the organisation of the staff, but how did it actually function on the battlefield? It was of course in many respects a highly personal and often frighteningly unsophisticated process.

As is well known Wellington was a very firm believer in the dictum mockingly laid down for 'General Officers, Commanding-in-Chief' in Francis Grose's satirical *Advice to the Officers of the British Army*:

> As no other person in your army is allowed to be possessed of a single idea, it would be ridiculous, on any occasion, to assemble a council of war, or, at least, to be guided by their opinion: for in opposition to yours, they must not trust to the most evident perception of their senses. It would be equally absurd and unmilitary to consult their convenience; even when it may be done without any detriment to the service: that would be taking away the most effectual method of exercising their obedience, and of perfecting them in a very considerable branch of military discipline.

Not only was he disinclined to consult with his colleagues except informally and on points of technical detail, but also any tendency towards independent behaviour was savagely quashed. Nevertheless, although this autocratic style of management evidently came naturally to him, it was no less necessary for that and it was also a recognition of the fact that since the size of the army precluded his personal supervision at every point, he had to ensure that those parts of it which were not under his eye were where they ought to be and doing exactly what they had been ordered to do.

Some Peninsular veterans never forgave him for the punishment of Norman Ramsay for his alleged disobedience of orders at Vittoria, yet the facts were clear enough: Wellington ordered him to hold his battery at a particular point until called for and then was furious to learn that he had in fact left it and moved somewhere else at the behest of another officer. Consequently when Wellington did want him he was nowhere to be found. Although this particular dereliction was not apparently attended by any serious

Staff and field officers were required to be mounted, in order both to move rapidly about the battlefield, and also to see over the heads of their own troops. The 28th Foot, shown here at Waterloo, served in the 2nd Division during the Peninsular War.

consequences, an exactly similar case arose at Gettysburg exactly 50 years later. The artillery batteries detailed to provide close support for Pickett's charge signally failed to do so because they were ordered away by another officer without reference to either the corps commander or even his chief of artillery.

Having decided what he wanted to do the next day, Wellington would then brief his Quartermaster General, who would proceed to draw up formal orders for each division or discrete detachment. Once personally approved by Wellington these would be copied – invariably by an officer – and delivered by 'staff dragoons' or orderlies. Such formal orders were normally extremely comprehensive and would form the basis for the divisional commanders' own orders which would in turn be transmitted down the line in the same way. Normally it worked well enough, making due allowance for the ordinary hazards of the road, but on at least one occasion important orders were lost when the messenger got drunk; and Brennier's breakout from Almeida in 1811 was successful largely because Maj. Gen. Erskine simply stuck the orders directing him to block the escape route in his pocket unread – since he was about to dine.

Once operations were actually in progress a much more direct system had to be employed and there were in effect three ways in which a general could transmit his orders.

In the first place he could do so in person, by simply turning up on the spot and orally instructing the subordinate concerned. This was something which Wellington was very prone to doing throughout his career, as for example when ordering Pakenham to take the 3rd Division forward at Salamanca, or most famously when he took personal charge of a battalion of Footguards at Waterloo. This method certainly had the very obvious advantage of allowing the commander to fully explain what he required and reassure himself that those orders were pertinent to the situation at that precise time, were properly understood – and would be carried out. It suited Wellington's autocratic command style very well, and there is no doubt that it also encouraged the troops to see him taking a close interest in their operations.

On the other hand it very blatantly violated the important principle that the location of headquarters should be fixed and known to all the subordinate commanders in order that they themselves could efficiently communicate with headquarters and pass back reports and requests for reinforcements and or assistance.

It might also be added that a very mobile headquarters made it extremely difficult for a general's own staff to find him again after delivering messages or orders. This was particularly marked at Waterloo where Wellington quite literally 'lost' so many ADCs through hurrying back and forth across the battlefield that at one point he was reduced to seeking the highly improbable (but authenticated) assistance of a passing button salesman from Birmingham.

Rather more conventionally, orders would be delivered by orderlies or the general's own ADCs. Although formal movement orders were, as we have seen, normally carried by orderlies, they were apparently little employed on the battlefield since the trooper or NCO concerned was quite literally no more than a messenger charged with handing over a written note.

Instead it was far better therefore to send important orders by means of an officer, one of the general's ADCs, who had the authority to ensure that the orders were carried out and just as importantly could explain or emphasise any part of them which might be unclear, either by rote or in response to questioning, and generally provide a much fuller picture of what was required to an extent which was quite impractical to write down in the heat of battle. On the whole this means of transmission worked pretty well, especially as the ADC could carry back any necessary response, and indeed add his own observations on the developing situation. Nevertheless it was of course far from an infallible method as the Light Brigade discovered to its cost at Balaklava in 1854.

Infantry

Infantry tactical doctrine and practice

British tactical doctrine in the Peninsular War is frequently dismissed as simply a question of line versus column. The hoary old tale of Wellington remarking at Waterloo that the French were coming on 'in the same old style' is frequently used to bolster this view, but in fact he was really commenting on the fact that the French were blindly mounting poorly prepared frontal assaults. British commanders certainly endeavoured to fight in line as a matter of course – as did the French in the appropriate circumstances – but tactical doctrines were actually a touch more sophisticated than this stereotype would suggest.

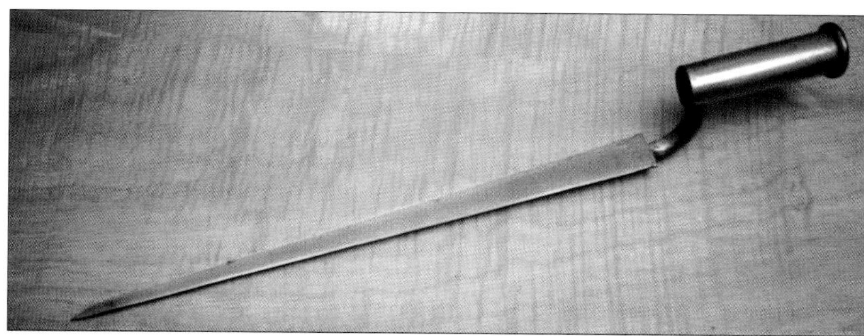

LEFT The bayonet; useful for a variety of domestic tasks, as well as being a potent weapon.

BELOW The Short Land Pattern Firelock (left) and the India Pattern Firelock (right). Production of the former ceased in 1797. Some may still have been in use in the early stages of the Peninsular War, but the India Pattern will have been in almost universal use by the end.

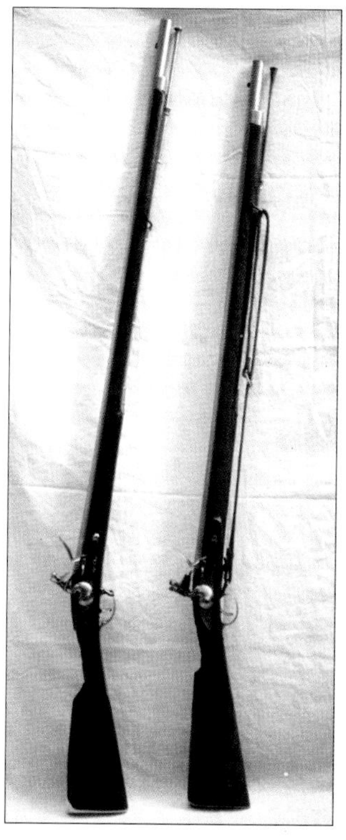

Infantry weapons

The basic infantry weapon of the period was the smooth-bored flintlock musket, which appeared in a variety of models collectively referred to as firelocks. The commonest variant in British service was the India Pattern, with a 39in. barrel in .75 calibre (14 bore). Originally designed by the East India Company in the 1760s it was adopted by the British Army in 1793 and in 1797 completely superseded the 42in.-barrel Short Land Pattern. Since firelocks were reckoned to have a useful life of 12 years it is likely that some Short Land Pattern weapons were still in use at the outset of the Peninsular War, but must have been replaced shortly afterwards.

On the whole the flintlock was robust and relatively reliable. Whilst all manner of statistics are quoted on misfire rates, the reality is that they only became marked after prolonged firing wore down the flint, and powder residues clogged the gun, especially in damp weather. Even in relatively wet weather it was possible to keep a gun firing providing the barrel remained warm. So long as the soldier went into battle with a weapon in good condition and a new flint fitted, he could usually count on getting through an individual firefight without a serious misfire.

As always, the soldiers on both sides grumbled that their opponents' weapons were superior to their own. The French Charleville was certainly better designed and lighter in construction, but this was offset by a longer barrel (42in.) which may have given British troops a slight advantage in reloading. Similarly (thanks to the use of Indian saltpetre) British gunpowder was widely recognised to be far superior to the charcoal-like French product: however, any advantage obtained thereby in terms of reliability was offset by the equally widely admitted superiority of French flints.

The only real technological advantage enjoyed by some British troops came in the form of the famous Baker Rifle, accepted for service in 1800 and produced with a 30in. barrel in 0.625 calibre (20 bore). It had a practical accurate range of 100m, occasionally more: it should be stressed though that whilst a rifled weapon could provide an advantage to a good shot, it could not turn a mediocre one into a marksman.

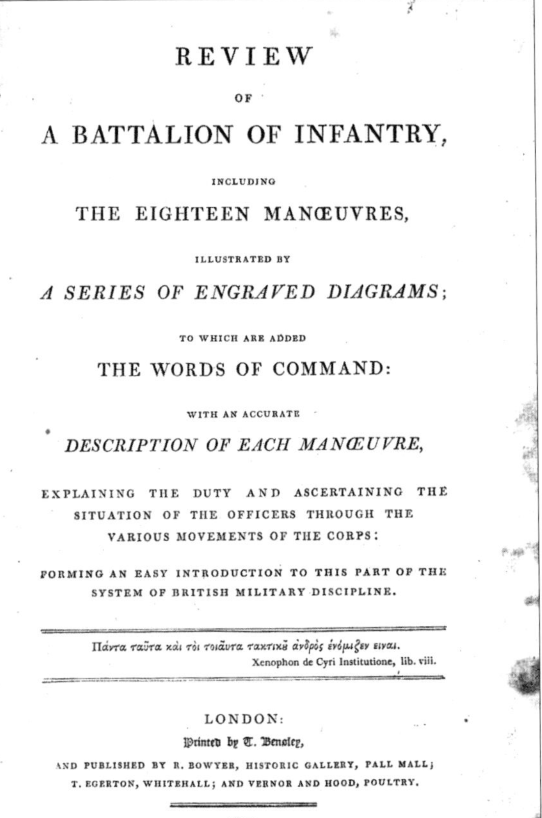

REVIEW

OF

A BATTALION OF INFANTRY,

INCLUDING

THE EIGHTEEN MANŒUVRES,

ILLUSTRATED BY

A SERIES OF ENGRAVED DIAGRAMS;

TO WHICH ARE ADDED

THE WORDS OF COMMAND:

WITH AN ACCURATE

DESCRIPTION OF EACH MANŒUVRE,

EXPLAINING THE DUTY AND ASCERTAINING THE SITUATION OF THE OFFICERS THROUGH THE VARIOUS MOVEMENTS OF THE CORPS:

FORMING AN EASY INTRODUCTION TO THIS PART OF THE SYSTEM OF BRITISH MILITARY DISCIPLINE.

Πάντα ταῦτα καὶ τὸι τοιᾶυτα ταχτικῦ ἀνδρὸς ἐνόμιζεν ειναι.
Xenophon de Cyri Institutione, lib. viii.

LONDON:

Printed by T. Bensley,

AND PUBLISHED BY R. BOWYER, HISTORIC GALLERY, PALL MALL; T. EGERTON, WHITEHALL; AND VERNOR AND HOOD, POULTRY.

1799.

ABOVE The title page from a popular and useful crammer produced by Thomas Smirke for officers preparing their regiments for the annual review, at which they would be expected to demonstrate their proficiency in a standard series of 'manoeuvres' or exercises.

While David Dundas was frequently criticised for reducing the art of war into the notorious '18 Manoeuvres', the 1792 *Rules and Regulations for the Formations Field Exercise and Movements of His Majesty's Forces* were actually a remarkably comprehensive and useful set of instructions covering most eventualities. Far from representing the sum total of the military art as prescribed for the British Army, the 18 Manoeuvres were simply a series of set proficiency tests used each year by reviewing generals to determine whether a battalion was fit for active service overseas. Ultimately a commanding officer's skill lay not simply in performing those set manoeuvres, but in judging which particular combination of the many manoeuvres available to him was appropriate to the tactical situation in which he found himself.

It does need to be strongly emphasised, however, that whilst the manner of performing weapon-handling drills and tactical 'evolutions' were closely prescribed by the regulations, there were no published tactical instructions or recommendations as such, other than some privately published treatises on light infantry work, and there was nothing to say when and under what circumstances a particular drill or evolution should be performed. The British Army's actual fighting methods were therefore both empirical and learned by officers on the job.

In any case, once in the field the opportunities for training were naturally limited, and unlike the French system of forming 'march battalions' which engaged in a continuous training programme all the way from the depot to the front, the officers in charge of British replacement drafts (often newly commissioned subalterns) considered their duty done if they simply managed to deliver their men without losing too many of them on the way.

The standard of training therefore varied from battalion to battalion and while most units arrived capable of efficiently performing a wide variety of

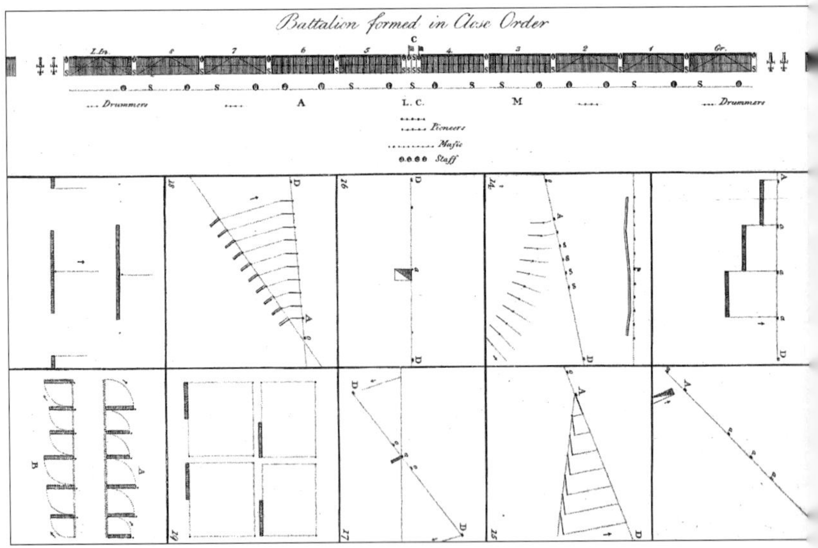

RIGHT A battalion formed in Close Order as illustrated in the official 1792 Regulations, which remained in force with only very minor revisions throughout the Revolutionary and Napoleonic wars.

manoeuvres, veterans soon learned to concentrate on the basics. Lieutenant William Grattan recalled that 'It was the fashion with some to think that the 88th were a parcel of wild rattling rascals, ready for a row, but loosely officered. The direct contrary was the fact. Perhaps in the whole British army there was not one regiment so severely drilled.' On the other hand Sgt. Anton of the 42nd Highlanders no doubt spoke for the majority of units when he commented that on his joining the regiment in northern Spain he found its discipline lax by comparison with that of his old militia regiment. This was because, firstly, 'the ruggedness of the mountains prevented precision of movements; secondly the weather had become so unfavourable that every fair day was dedicated to some other necessary purpose about the camp, and instead of [Col. Macara] acquiring practical knowledge himself, even his regiment was losing that part which it had perhaps previously possessed; thirdly, draughts of undisciplined recruits were occasionally joining and mixing in the ranks, and being unaccustomed to field movements, occasioned a sort of awkwardness in the performance of them.'

While it would of course be easy to say that the truth probably lay somewhere between the two, it would be rather more accurate to say that while a high standard of individual training in what was then called the Platoon Exercise was maintained in most units, at a higher level officers concentrated on excelling at a comparatively limited tactical repertoire. Indeed, Grattan notes: 'At drill our manoeuvres were chiefly confined to line marching, echelon movements, and formation of the square in every possible way; and in all these we excelled.'

How a division and its constituent brigades manoeuvred up to the point of contact obviously varied considerably according to the peculiar notions of its commander, the terrain and the tactical situation, but so far as possible divisions were manoeuvred and fought as a single tactical unit. It is worth

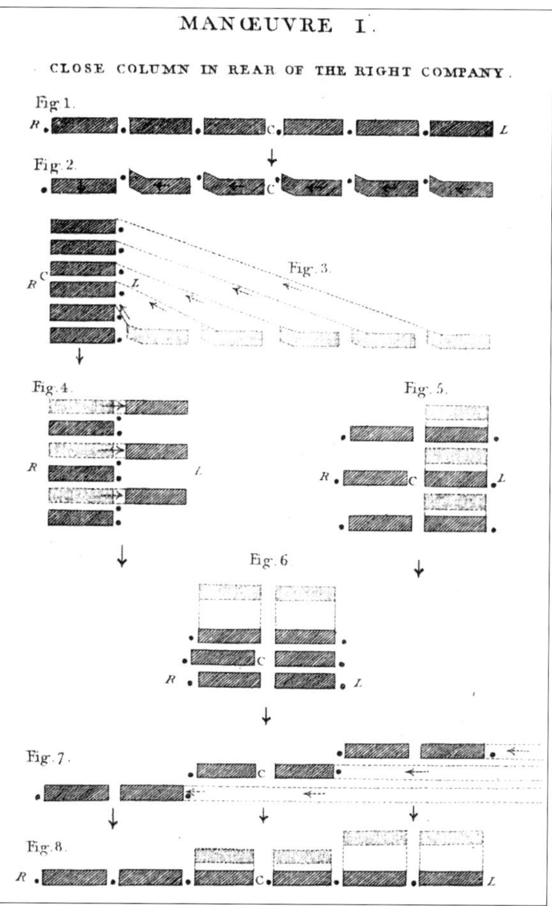

ABOVE Manoeuvre I from Smirke's crammer, forming close column of companies in rear of the right company – and deploying again into line. For the sake of simplicity, Smirke depicted a battalion as having just six companies, rather than nine plus a frequently detached light company.

LEFT The French counter-attack at Roliça; although not contemporary, this illustration by Philipotteau provides a useful reminder that early-19th-century battlefields and fighting tactics were by no means as neat and tidy as the drill books tried to suggest.

The two-deep file, meticulously recreated here by members of the 68th (Durham) Regiment, was invariably used by Wellington's army in preference to the three-deep file still officially prescribed by the drill-book. These two are closed up and charging their bayonets to receive cavalry.

remarking that while the infantry battalion was the basic building block, it was very rare for a battalion to be deployed on its own, although it did of course happen from time to time if the circumstances demanded. Perhaps the most striking example was the fight at Maya in 1813 when a half battalion of the 92nd Highlanders, deployed athwart a narrow ridge, fought an entire French division to a standstill, but this was quite exceptional and normally the primary tactical unit was the brigade.

The normal procedure was for brigades to manoeuvre in columns of battalions, with the battalions in turn moving in open column of companies, before deploying into line in good time to fight. At this point all three

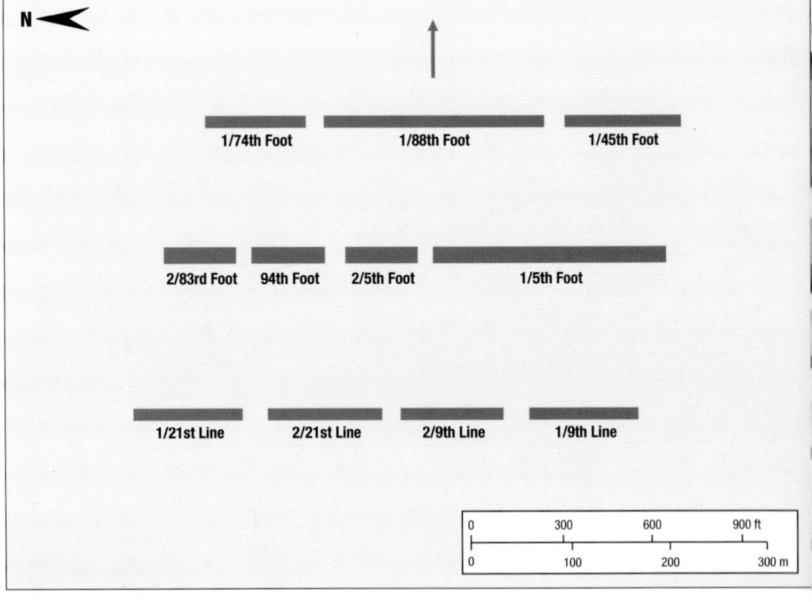

Pakenham's 3rd Division at Salamanca, 1812. Skirmishers are omitted for the sake of clarity. Immediately prior to deploying as shown here, the division had been marching due south in three columns of companies in order to place itself on the French flank.

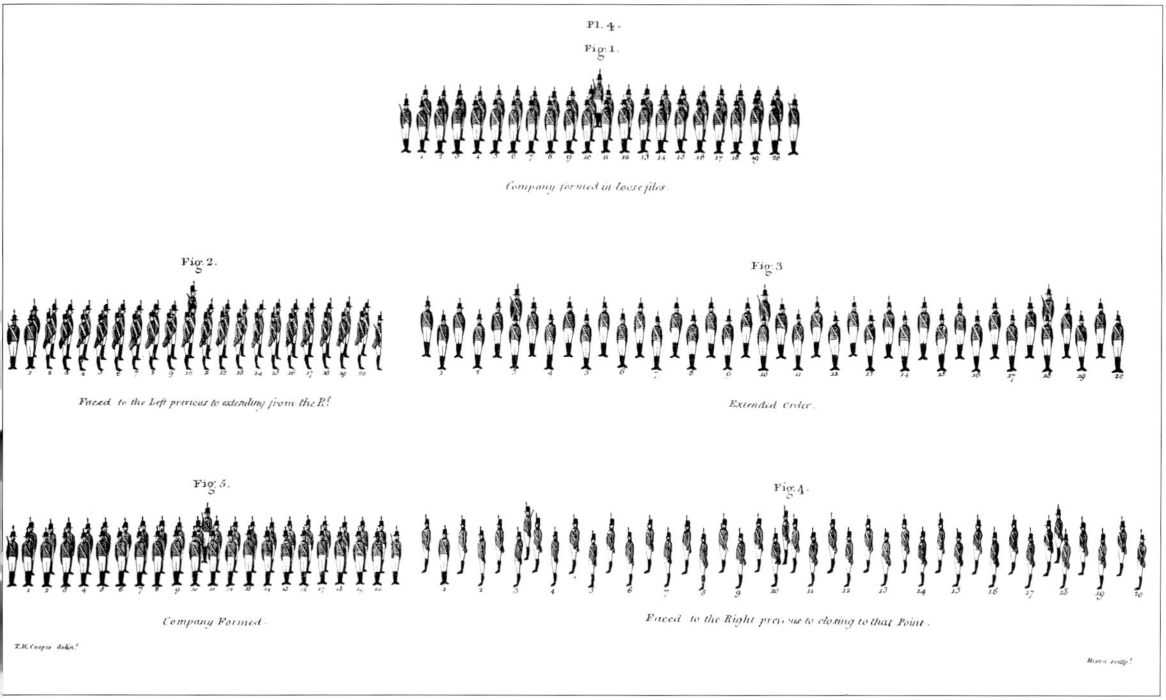

Basic light infantry drill; a company as originally formed, extending from the right and closing again to the right.

battalions of a brigade formed up in line abreast. Another brigade would then be deployed to the rear to act as its supports. Depending on the state of the ground, divisions were normally formed with two brigades forward and one back, although it was also quite common to find all three brigades stacked one behind the other. Less common was for all three brigades of a division to deploy in line abreast, but it did happen if another division was available to be deployed in close support.

Once formed in line and more or less facing the enemy a single battalion, or a brigade of two or more battalions, could either hold a given position or more commonly advance into contact before halting and engaging in a firefight. It is

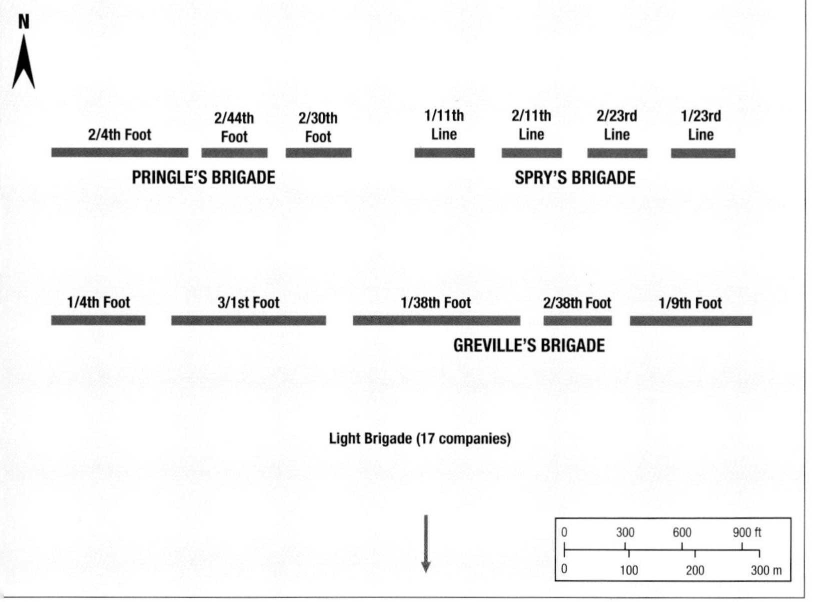

Like Pakenham's 3rd Division, Leith's 5th Division went into action at Salamanca on a frontage of one brigade. In this case however the other two brigades were formed in a single line, although it was necessary to bring up 1/4th from Pringle's brigade to extend the front of Greville's brigade and thus equalise the first and second lines.

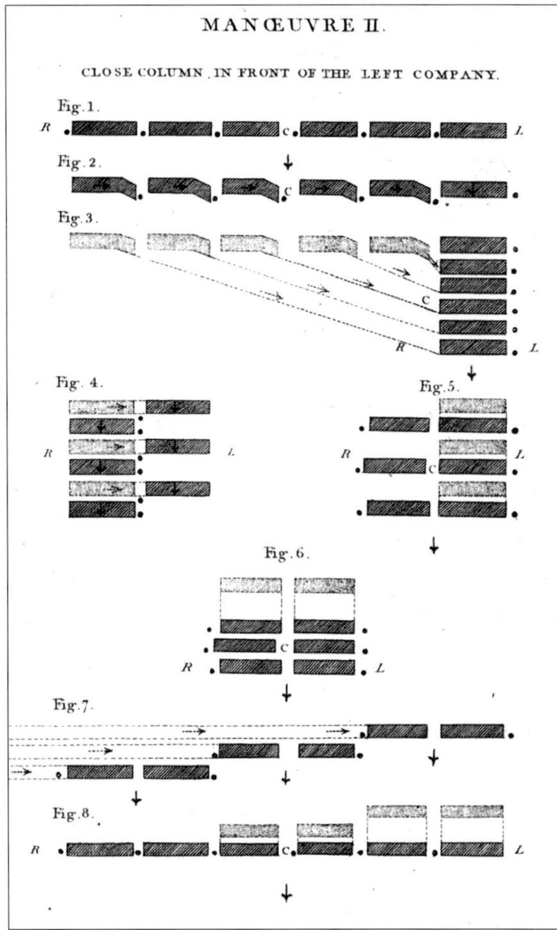

Manoeuvre II from Thomas Smirke's crammer for officers, forming close column of companies in front of the left company. This manoeuvre was perhaps one of the most basic of all.

perhaps the precise nature of this firefight that is least understood. Traditional historians, wedded to the entirely erroneous notion that British infantry still practised the old platoon firing system, are apt to count the number of firelocks in those two ranks and smugly contrast them with the comparatively small number of men at the head of a French column who were actually able to fire, before pronouncing the inevitable result.

In considering what actually tended to happen on the battlefield rather than on the training grounds of Hyde Park or Phoenix Park, a number of important factors should be borne in mind. In the first place the French were not so stupid as to be unable to comprehend the simple arithmetic of a firefight in which a single battalion column was pitted against another battalion of equal size deployed in line.

There were essentially two ways of using an infantry column. The first was simply to move and manoeuvre in column rapidly up to the point of contact before deploying into line and engaging in a firefight. While this was indeed done on a number of occasions – including the controversial Battle of Maida in 1806 – the British Army still enjoyed a formidable reputation for its musketry and French officers were often wary of entering into firefights unless acting on the defensive. Consequently, and demonstrating the second way, when attacking they were prone to attempt to carry the position at a rush, without stopping to deploy into line, or to fire at all.

That both variations ultimately proved unsuccessful was down to two main factors. The first was Wellington's predilection, particularly when acting on the defensive, for positioning his men in dead ground. Naturally enough this made it very difficult for French officers to time either their deployment into line or the alternative gallant rush. All too often they seem to have stumbled unawares into the killing ground before being brought to a halt by the first close-range volley. The second factor was the increasingly strong emphasis placed on skirmishing tactics by the British Army. Well aware of the column's inherent firepower limitations, French tactical doctrine called for any advance to be screened by a thick screen of skirmishers. In the early campaigns of the Revolutionary Wars this had proved very effective, but in Spain the British response was to counter it by deploying an even heavier screen of skirmishers.

At this point therefore it is perhaps worth making clear the distinction between light infantry and skirmishers. It was a distinction that had been far from clear during the 18th century and a failure to appreciate it had hampered in some degree the development of British skirmishing tactics prior to the Peninsular War.

Although the nature of their service inevitably requires a certain proficiency in skirmishing tactics, light infantry are primarily intended to be used in a fast-moving strategic role rather than a tactical role. Consequently the principal distinction between light infantry and so-called 'heavy' infantry is that the former sacrifice comfort (and ultimately their health) for speed, carry everything on their backs and operate with a minimal 'tail', while the latter remain heavily dependent on their trains. Ironically therefore this often means that the individual light infantryman is much more heavily laden than his 'heavy' infantry counterpart in the line.

When faced with an operational requirement for light infantry during the 18th century the British Army's standard response had been to form provisional battalions from regimental light companies. This worked well enough up to a point but its greatest drawback was that it removed the organic skirmishing element from ordinary infantry battalions, particularly since the battalions tended in their turn to be brigaded together as a *corps d'élite* for detached operations. As an interim solution regimental commanders therefore took to informally designating certain of the men in the ordinary battalion companies as 'flankers' or 'marksmen', but in the longer term the problem was only solved by the permanent conversion of certain units into designated Light Infantry regiments. With what became the famous Light Division at his disposal Wellington then had no need to cull the regimental light companies for detached operations, such as Craufurd's defence of the Coa, and instead they remained with their parent units to form the core element of the increasingly all-important skirmish line, thus bringing about a remarkable tactical revolution.

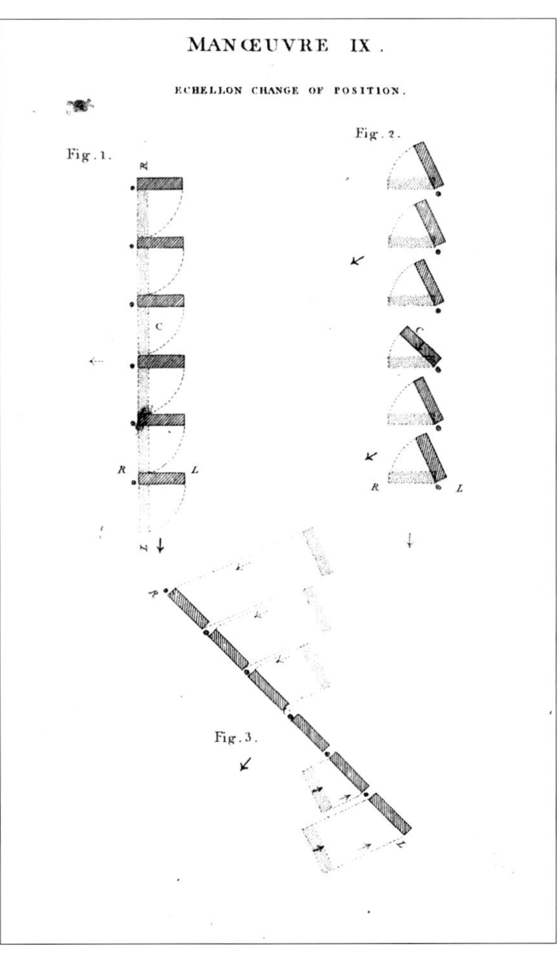

Manoeuvre IX from Smirke's crammer, echelon change of position. Grattan commented that echelon movements were amongst the manoeuvres most frequently practised by the 88th Foot in the Peninsula.

Throughout the 18th century, European infantry tactics had been governed by the technical limitations of the firelock musket. In theory it could be fired as often as five times in a minute but even when this could be achieved, in the excitement of doing so most rounds went high in the air. Perhaps a little paradoxically, officers and NCOs therefore did their best not to speed up the rate of fire, and on the contrary endeavoured to control it, trying to maintain a steady rate of no more than two or occasionally three properly aimed rounds per minute. Accordingly 18th-century military theoreticians became obsessed with devising methods of maintaining that steady rolling fire. Essentially there had always been two ways of doing this. One was by firing each rank successively as originally favoured by the French; and the other was by dividing the firing line into a number of blocks or platoons which then fired in a pre-arranged sequence. By the Napoleonic Wars a third and much simpler method, known as file firing, had been introduced. As its name implies each individual file initially fired in sequence down the line and then thereafter in its own time.

So long as both sides played the game, the British platoon firing is generally held by historians to have been superior, but judgement on this point tends to be highly subjective and largely dependent on who was on the receiving end. It is extremely interesting to note Andrew Leith Hay's account of Salamanca in which he remarked:

> The 6th (Division) suffered very much having been halted when advanced about half way – which is a system that never will answer, the only way is to get at them at once with the Bayonet, that they can never stand, but as to firing that [the French] will do as long as you like, and fire much better than we do.

While supported by other testimony on the subject, this statement is not of itself sufficient reason to turn conventional wisdom about the relative effectiveness of British platooning and French file-firing on its head, although the latter eventually became the norm in most armies – even including the

The following sequence of five maps (the final two appear on page 32) shows the British Army in action, at the Battle of Albuera, 1811.

Phase one: at the outset of the battle Beresford had his army deployed on a north-south alignment facing east, but the French commander, Marshal Soult, succeeded in turning his right flank. Colborne's brigade of the 2nd Division was all but destroyed and disaster was only averted by the determined stand of a Spanish brigade commanded by Gen. Zayas. This map shows the situation immediately after Zayas' brigade had been relieved by the rest of 2nd Division – including the sole surviving battalion of Colborne's brigade.

As a result of this relief in place the intervals between the battalions of Hoghton's brigade were greater than normal and an officer of 1/57th afterwards complained that each of them was left to fight the battle on its own.

Artillery support was provided by Cleeve's Brigade KGA. Two sections were positioned on the right flank of 1/31st and the third section between 29th and 1/57th. In addition Abercrombie's brigade was supported by two more sections under Hawker. It is likely that at this point all of the British artillery was concentrating on the central column of the French V Corps.

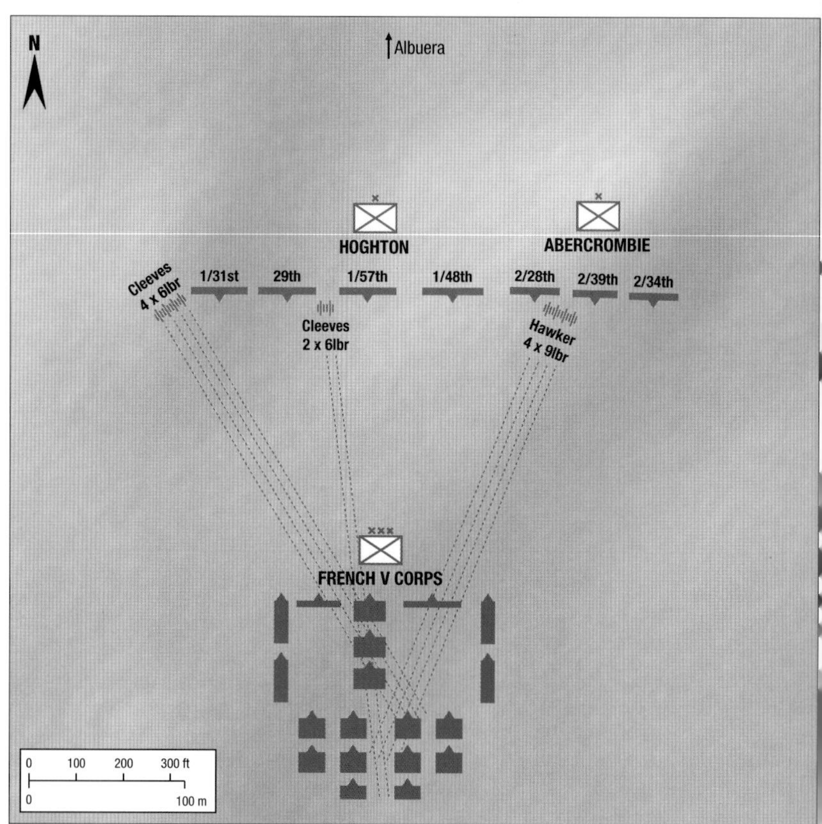

Phase two: V Corps has been halted by the musketry of Hoghton's brigade and is now being thoroughly raked by canister fire.

Werlé's Division is coming up into the fight only to be countered by the advance of Cole's 4th Division – less Kemmis' brigade, stranded on the wrong side of the flooded River Guadiana.

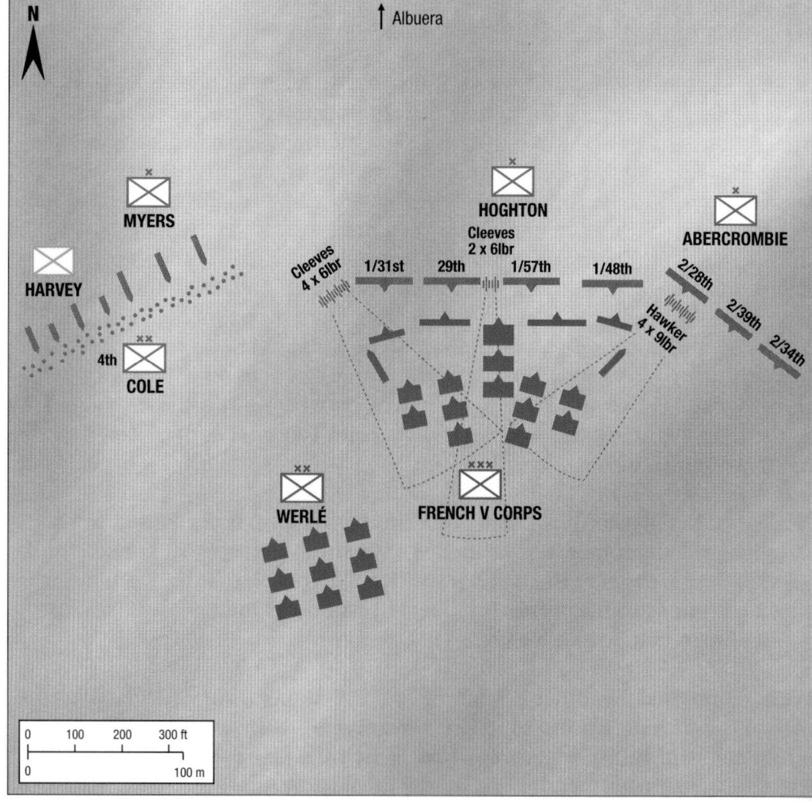

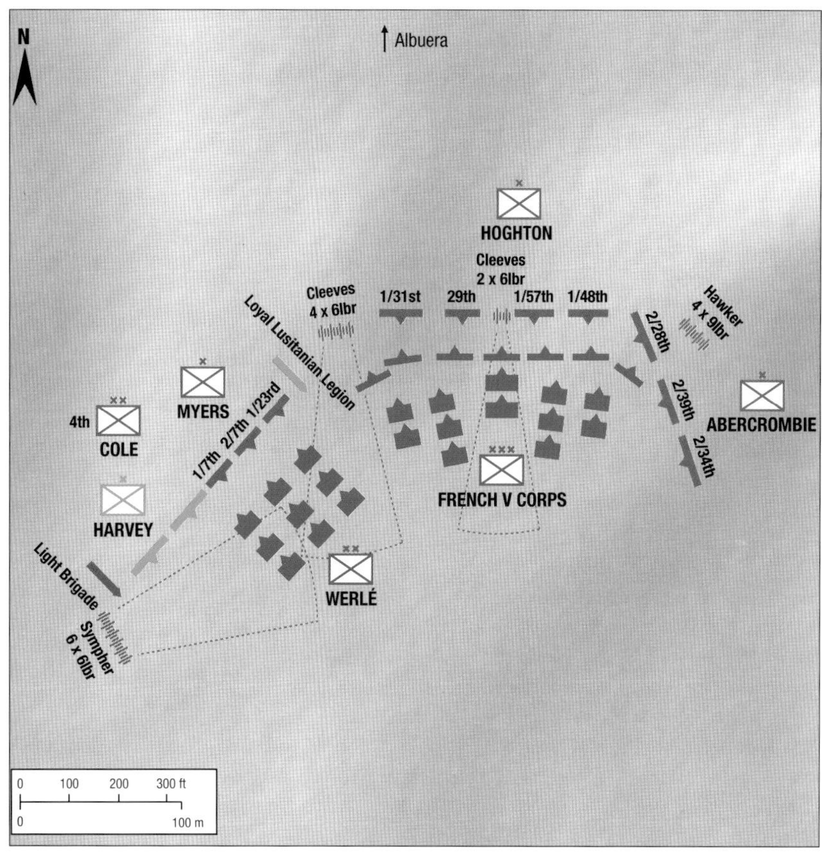

Phase three: 4th Division has deployed into line to attack Werlé's Division accompanied by Sympher's Brigade KGA. Abercrombie's brigade has now swung around on to the flank of V Corps. It is uncertain whether Hawker advanced with the infantry in order to continue firing canister, or remained on the higher ground to provide overhead fire with roundshot and spherical case.

Note that once attacking infantry came within 100m of the British battleline the artillery could only fire effectively into the flank and deep rear of the attacking formation. The resulting 'dead' zone was covered only by musketry. (See the phases four and five maps on page 32 for further details of this action.)

British one. What it does very clearly illustrate is the growing and well-founded perception on the ground that static firefights were ineffective and indecisive, often costing heavy casualties to little effect.

There was moreover another factor. Although the common smooth-bored firelock was a good deal more accurate in ideal conditions than armchair critics allow, its effective range on the battlefield was only about 50 metres. Beyond (and even well within) that range both sides might indeed fire away all day long by whichever means they chose. On the other hand if one side had sufficient resolution to keep on coming instead of stopping and engaging in the firefight, those troops being attacked simply could not kill enough of their assailants quickly enough to stop them, whether they were firing by platoons, by whole ranks or by individual files.

This in turn goes a long way to explaining why both sides not only advocated pressing forward with the bayonet, but also loudly professed it to be their country's natural weapon. 'The whole business was performed by the Bayonet,' wrote one officer in an absolutely typical example, '& the most sceptical must now be surely convinced how superior in the use of it is the British Soldier to every other in the world.'

Nevertheless, however it was conducted, the traditional, static firefight was still very much a feature of the Peninsular battlefields, most notably perhaps at Albuera in 1811 and at Maya in 1813. However, it is very important to appreciate that it actually tended to occur in circumstances that militated against rather more decisive manoeuvres, such as broken or otherwise unfavourable ground, or once the troops had become disorganised or had lost their momentum. Otherwise the British Army increasingly employed a much more aggressive infantry fighting doctrine known as 'volley and bayonet', which was equally effective in attack or defence.

Manoeuvre XIII (marching to a flank in echelon), and Manoevre XIV (the hollow square and its movements). Both are taken from Smirke's crammer for officers.

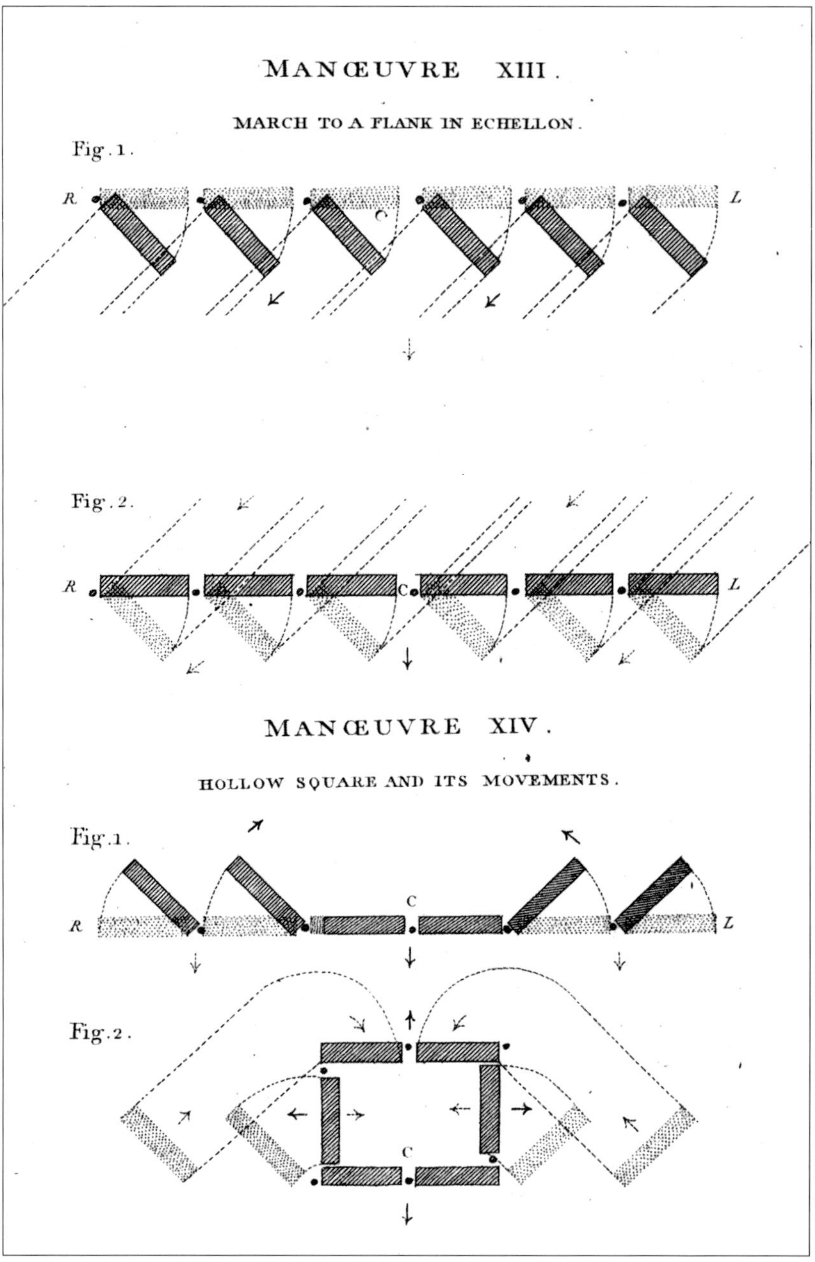

This entailed the burden of the preliminary firefight being carried on not by the main fighting line, but by the very considerable body of skirmishers deployed in front. Only if this thick skirmish line was dispersed or forced back did the main line come forward, not to engage in a firefight, but in the volley and bayonet tactics first introduced by James Wolfe in the 1750s and then developed against American rebels during the Revolution.

Depending on the tactical situation, or more commonly the individual preference of the commanding officer, the initial volley would be fired either by wings or occasionally by grand divisions or even in a single heavy battalion volley aimed at causing the maximum number of casualties in the shortest possible time. Delivered at short range this heavy volley is almost invariably described as having 'staggered' the opposition, bringing them to an abrupt halt, at which point the volley fire was immediately followed up by one of

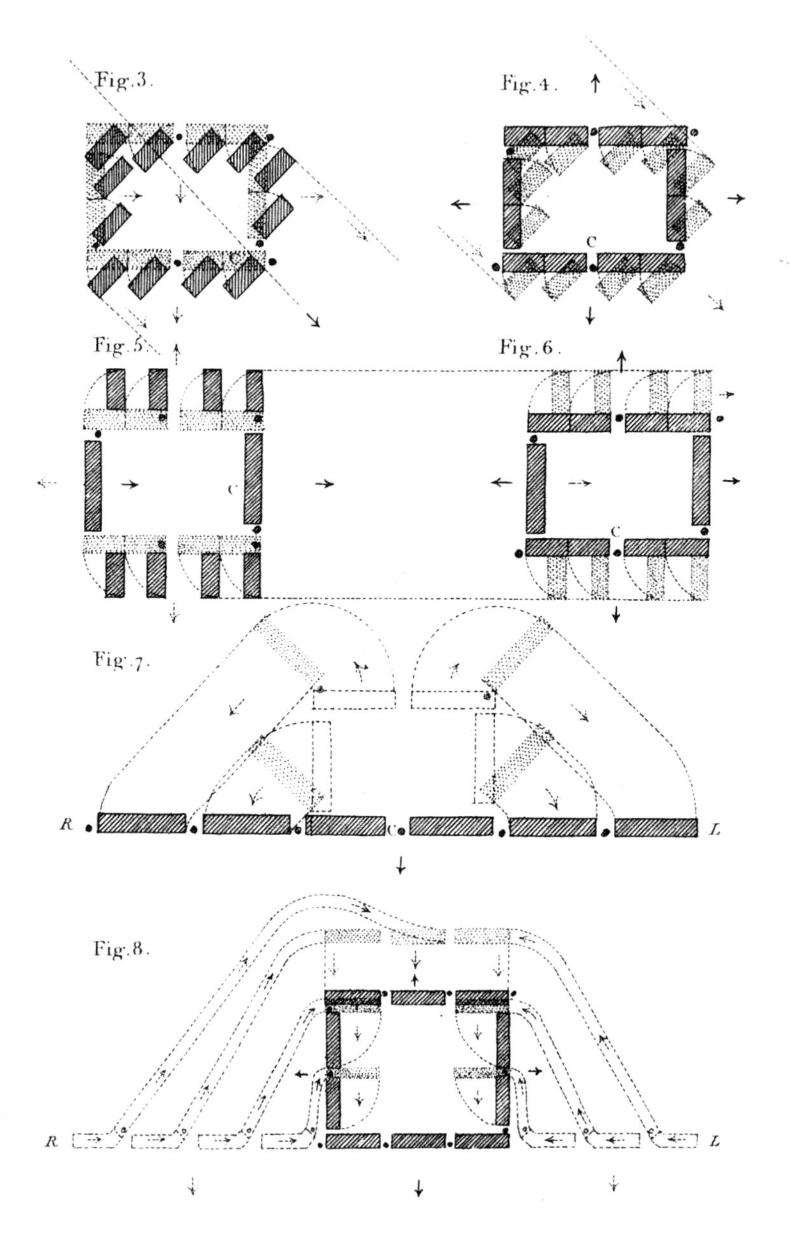

The hollow square (continued). Note the ways in which troops could march either directly forward or even obliquely after having formed a square. Formations of this kind must have been adopted by the Light Division, as it retired in square, surrounded by French cavalry, at Fuentes de Oñoro.

those famous bayonet charges, again described here in another absolutely typical example: 'Our troops fired a volley at a distance of a very few yards from the enemy, and instantly closed and pushed with the bayonet. Their adversaries rolled downhill in the greatest haste and consternation.' The key to the success of this doctrine partly lay in judging the optimum moment at which to launch the bayonet charge, but mainly in the thickness of the skirmish screen conducting the preliminary firefight. At its most basic level the screen comprised three principal elements. Firstly, a front line of riflemen, who engaged the enemy at comparatively long range and then, when pressed, retired into or even behind the main skirmish line. This in turn was made up of skirmishers armed with smooth-bored muskets. These could be loaded appreciably faster than rifles and whilst they were obviously not as accurate, in practice this made little or no difference given the much shorter ranges at

Phase four in the Battle of Albuera, 1811 (continued from pages 28–29): this map shows Cole's fight in greater detail. The skirmish line is notionally represented by dots, but otherwise all blocks represent infantry companies. All three battalions of Myers' Fusilier Brigade advanced in column of companies behind the right company (which in ordinary regiments of the line would have been designated the grenadier company) and therefore deployed into line to the left. The two Portuguese regiments probably marched in four battalion columns, the two right-hand battalions comprising five companies and the two left-hand battalions only four, their cazadores companies being in the skirmish line. Once the main battleline came within musket-shot of the enemy the skirmishers cleared away to the flanks rather than rejoining their parent units.

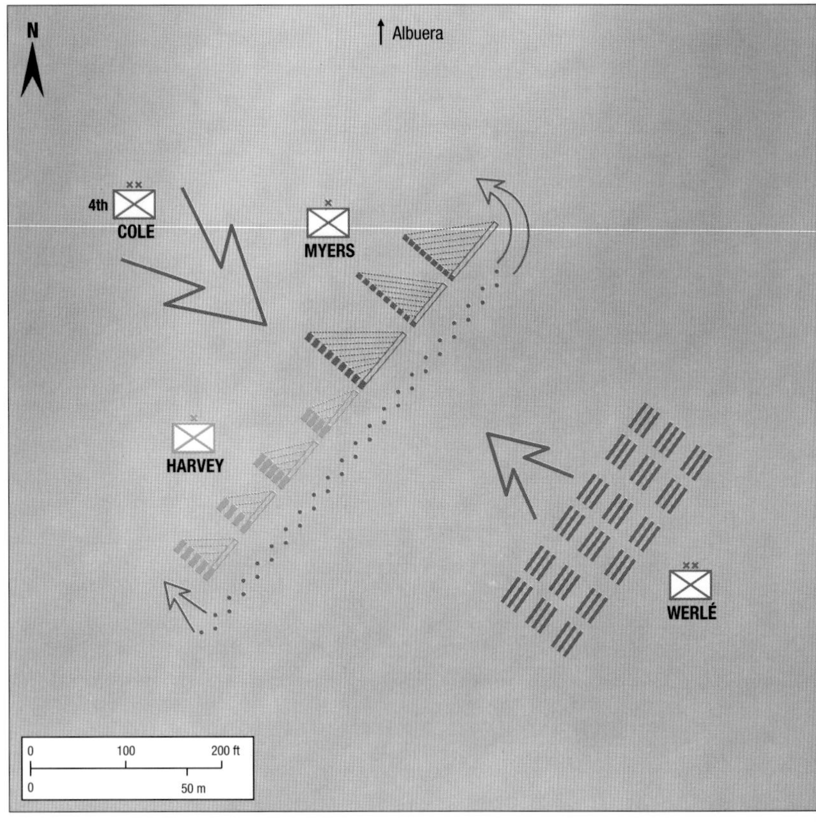

Phase five, showing Cole's Division deployed for the firefight. Note how the skirmishers have formed a column of companies on each flank rather than disrupting the battleline by falling back into it. Exactly the same procedure was followed at single battalion level. The Division's six British light companies (1/7th, 2/7th, 1/23rd, 2/27th, 140th and 97th) were on the right, while the five companies of the Loyal Lusitanian Legion and the cazadores companies of the 11th and 23rd Line were on the left.

which they engaged the enemy. The third line comprised formed bodies of supports, who could either feed additional men forward into the fighting line or form rallying points as they fell back.

So dense was this skirmishing line that not only did it disrupt and slow the French advance (even in the open it made it very difficult for French officers to judge when to deploy or charge) but also some French observers often had difficulty in distinguishing it from the notional main fighting line behind it. Consequently it was not uncommon for them to speak of having actually broken through the British front line before being counter-attacked and driven back by the second line.

Such a formidable skirmish line clearly required a very large number of men and its perceived importance may be gauged from the readiness with which the riflemen and regimental light companies who originally constituted it were progressively reinforced first with 'skirmishers', 'flankers' or 'marksmen' sent forward from the ordinary battalion companies, then by whole companies (initially perhaps as 'supports') and finally by complete battalions, as rather startlingly described by William Brown of the 45th Foot at Orthez on 27 February 1814:

> Our brigade had to pass along a narrow path directly in front of the enemy's centre, from which they kept up a heavy cannonade, by which we were sorely annoyed, and had many killed and wounded. We dashed on, however, at double quick time, and soon got under cover of the height on which the enemy was placed. Being then secure from the destructive fire of their cannon, our general halted, and, after drawing us up in close column by regiments, he seemed to get into a kind of quandary, and not to know what to do. Meantime the enemy's skirmishers advanced to the brow of the hill, and began to fire into us, until the Adjutant General, a most gallant officer, came galloping from the left exclaiming, "Good God! General Brisbane, why stand here while the brigade gets cut up? Form line, and send out the 45th skirmishing." Two companies being left with the colours, the rest of us ascended the hill, to be received in such a manner as I had never before experienced. We were but a skirmishing line opposed to a dense column supported by artillery and cavalry. The bullets flew thick as hail, thirteen men of my company alone fell within a few yards of me on the brow of the hill. Notwithstanding we pressed on, and the enemy after dreadful carnage gave way, and left us in possession of a ditch, which we held till the brigade came up in line. We then gave three cheers, charged the enemy's light troops, and drove them from another ditch parallel with the one we had just taken. Having repeatedly charged, and been charged in turn, we got on the height, from which we had a complete view of the dark masses of the enemy in column, one of which was moving against us, the officers hat in hand waving on the men in advance. By this time we were greatly diminished – nearly half down or disabled – and might have given way, if a staff-officer had not come up at the critical moment and encouraged us to hold our ground, as we should be relieved in a minute.

Highlanders of the 73rd Foot on the march by Atkinson, c.1805. Although the 73rd did not serve under Wellington, they were originally the 2nd Battalion of the 42nd Highlanders and their uniform was identical save for the dark green facings.

Perhaps the most telling feature of this remarkable account is the way in which Sir Edward Pakenham assumed without any preliminary enquiry that the 45th, an ordinary regiment of the line, was quite capable of acting as skirmishers and that its officers and men neither hesitated, questioned that order – nor disappointed him.

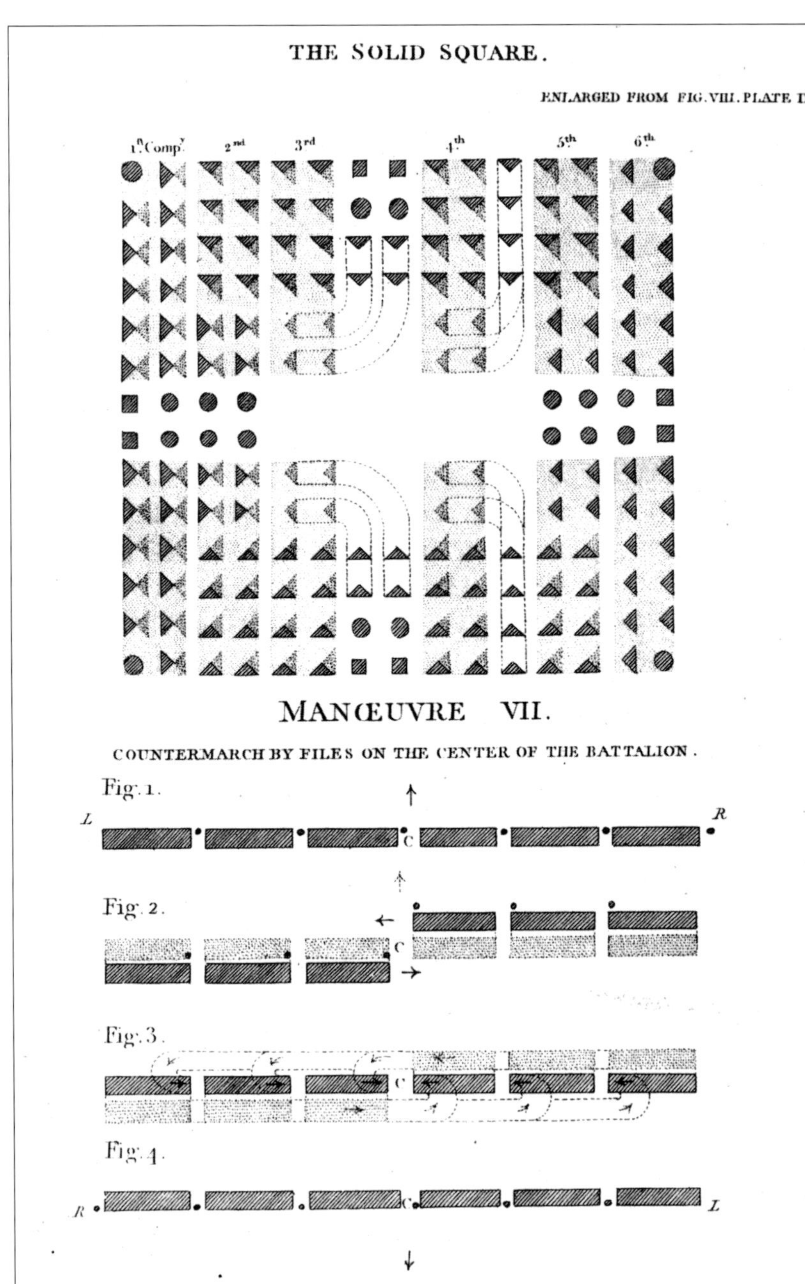

The solid square, more robust than the hollow square and consequently preferred if the enemy had no artillery close by. This very useful diagram from Smirke's crammer illustrates the position of each man: officers are indicated by squares and sergeants by discs. Private soldiers are indicated by triangles with the flat face to their front. Note how this formation is actually a double column of companies, and that when ordered to halt, most soldiers simply face to their outward flank, while the intervals between the companies are filled by the men from the inner files. Also shown is Manoeuvre VII, countermarch on the centre of a battalion.

British infantry units

1st Division – 'The Gentlemen's Sons'

The division was formed on 18 June 1809 under Sherbrooke, and, as it included a brigade of Footguards, it was nicknamed 'The Gentlemens' Sons'. Nevertheless, although invariably comprising 'good' regiments, including the King's German Legion, it was regarded as a social rather than a military elite and there is no evidence of it being deliberately employed on particularly important operations in preference to any other.

Served: Talavera, Busaco, Fuentes de Oñoro, Salamanca, Burgos, Vittoria, San Sebastian, Bidassoa, Nivelle, Nive and Bayonne.

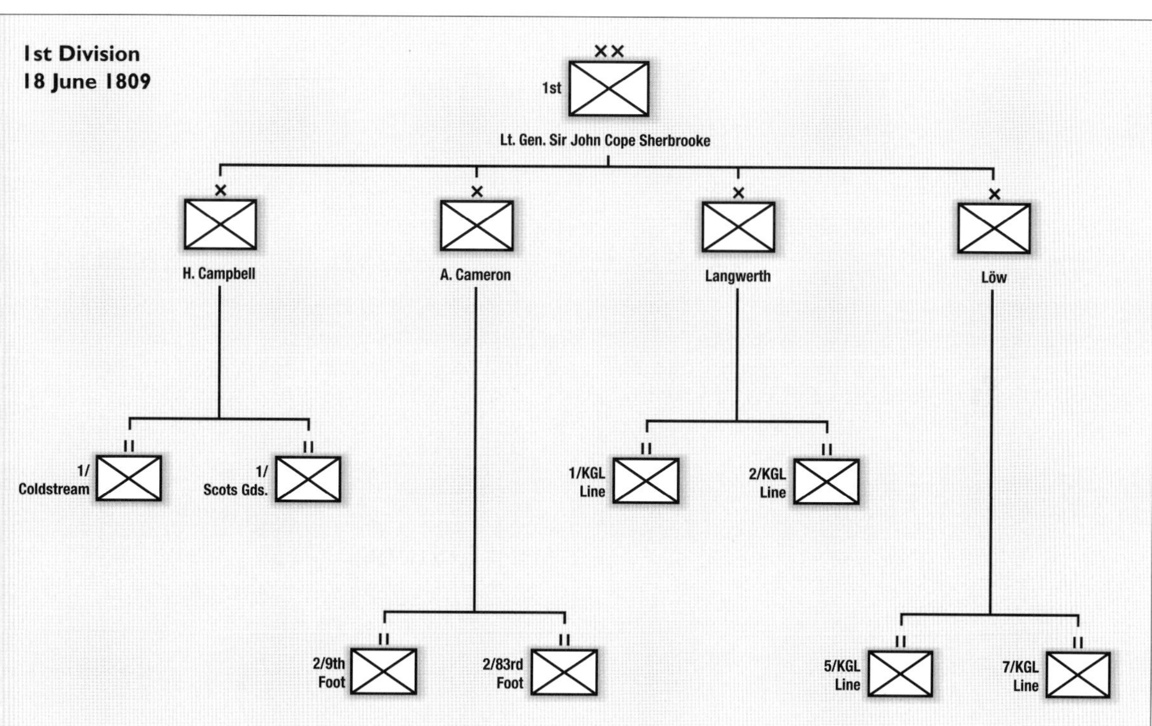

Subsequent alterations:

Campbell's Brigade:	Campbell was wounded at Talavera and replaced by Stopford, except for the period between 8 November and 15 December when Richard Hulse had the brigade.
Cameron's Brigade:	1/40th Foot came up from Cadiz to temporarily replace 2/9th Foot sometime before 21 June. 2/9th Foot then relieved 1/61st at Gibraltar, which joined shortly before Talavera and in turn replaced 1/40th, which transferred to 4th Division. After Talavera 2/24th and 2/42nd Foot replaced 2/83rd, who were sent down to Lisbon.
Langwerth's Brigade:	Langwerth was killed at Talavera and succeeded by Beck of 1/KGL, but all four KGL battalions were subsequently amalgamated into a single brigade under Löw on 1 November.

Sir John Cope Sherbrooke (1764–1830)

Served Peninsula 1809 – original commander of 1st Division – and then Lieutenant-Governor of Nova Scotia from shortly after Talavera until August 1818.

Commissions: ensign 4th Foot 7 December 1780; lieutenant 22 December 1781; captain 85th Foot 6 March 1783; captain 33rd Foot 23 June 1784; major 30 September 1793; lieutenant-colonel 1 March 1794; colonel (brevet) 1 January 1798; half-pay 5th Foot 29 October 1802; major-general 1 January 1805; lieutenant-general 4 June 1811.

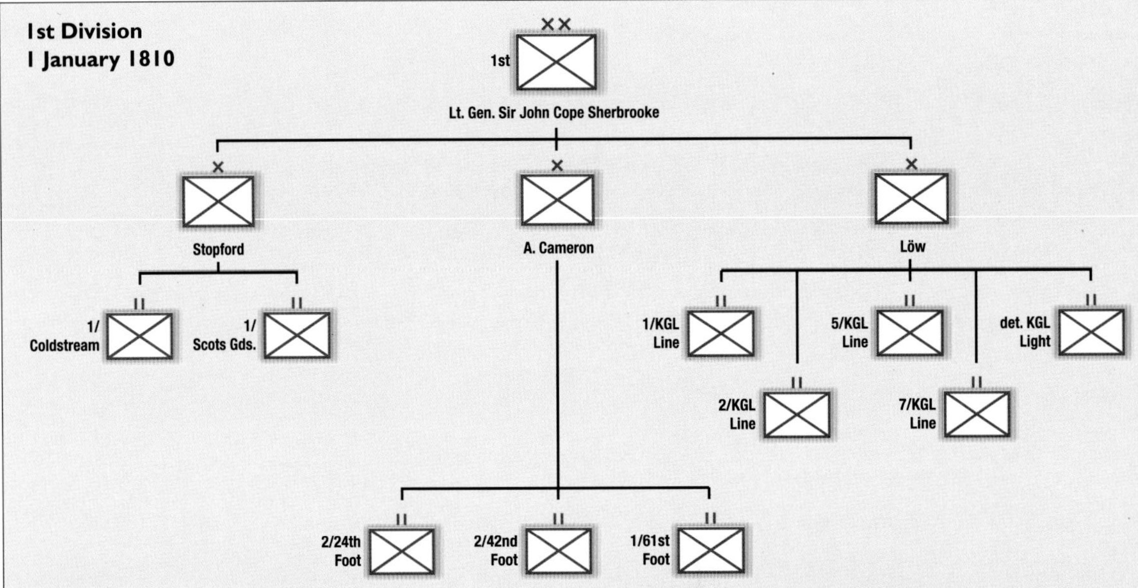

Subsequent alterations:

On 26 April 1810 Sir Stapleton Cotton was given command of the division after Sherbrooke went home sick, but then he in turn was transferred to the command of the newly organised cavalry division on 3 June, and replaced by Maj. Gen. Sir Brent Spencer.

Cameron's Brigade:	Cameron appears to have been sick from March onwards, although he was not officially replaced by Lt. Col. Lord Blantyre of 2/42nd Foot until 4 August. Cameron then briefly resumed command on 1 October but was invalided home on 26 November. In the meantime, on 12 September 1/79th Foot (which had been originally raised by Cameron in 1793) came up from Cadiz to replace 1/61st Foot, which was in turn intended to form the nucleus of a fourth brigade. However, the exchange was delayed until after Busaco.
Pakenham's Brigade:	A temporary formation under Edward Pakenham comprising 1/7th Fusiliers and 1/79th Foot which served with 1st Division at Busaco. Afterwards the delayed exchange between 1/79th and 1/61st Foot was carried out, and Pakenham's brigade transferred to 4th Division on 6 October.
Erskine's Brigade:	A new formation assembled between 24 September and 6 October and comprising 1/50th Foot, 1/71st Foot, 1/92nd Foot and one company 3/95th Rifles.

Sir Brent Spencer (1760–1828)
Son of Conway Spencer of Trumery, Co. Antrim. Served West Indies including capture of St Lucia; p.o.w. St Kitts February 1782; served Jamaica garrison 1790–94, then on St Domingo 1794 in command of flank battalion; badly defeated at Bombarde 1 May 1794; served St Vincent, Jamaica (Maroon revolt) and St Domingo again 1795–98, latterly commanding all troops in La Grand Anse until evacuation of St Domingo; served Helder Expedition 1799 and Egypt 1801; Eastern District staff 1803–07; colonel 9th Garrison Battalion 25 November 1806; commanded brigade at Copenhagen 1807; assigned to abortive Swedish expedition 1808 and afterwards in Peninsula 1808–09; fought at Roleia and Vimeiro and afterwards supported Wellington at the Cintra Inquiry; Colonel Commandant 2/95th Rifles 31 August 1809; again served in Peninsula May 1810 to July 1811 in command of 1st Division and acting as second in command to Wellington, but effectively retired after superseded by Thomas Graham. Throughout his career he was consistently noted to be exceptionally brave and determined but not particularly bright. Died at Great Missenden, Buckinghamshire, 29 December 1828.

Commissions: ensign 15th Foot 18 January 1778; lieutenant 12 November 1779; captain 99th (Jamaica) Foot 29 July 1783, exchanged to 15th Foot 4 September 1783; major 13th Foot 6 March 1791; local lieutenant-colonel in command of Dillon's Regiment (St Domingo); lieutenant-colonel 115th (Prince William's) Foot 2 May 1794, exchanged to 40th Foot 22 July 1795; brigadier (St Domingo) 9 July 1797; colonel (brevet) 1 January 1798; major-general 1 January 1805; lieutenant-general 4 June 1811; general 27 May 1828.

1st Division
1 January 1811

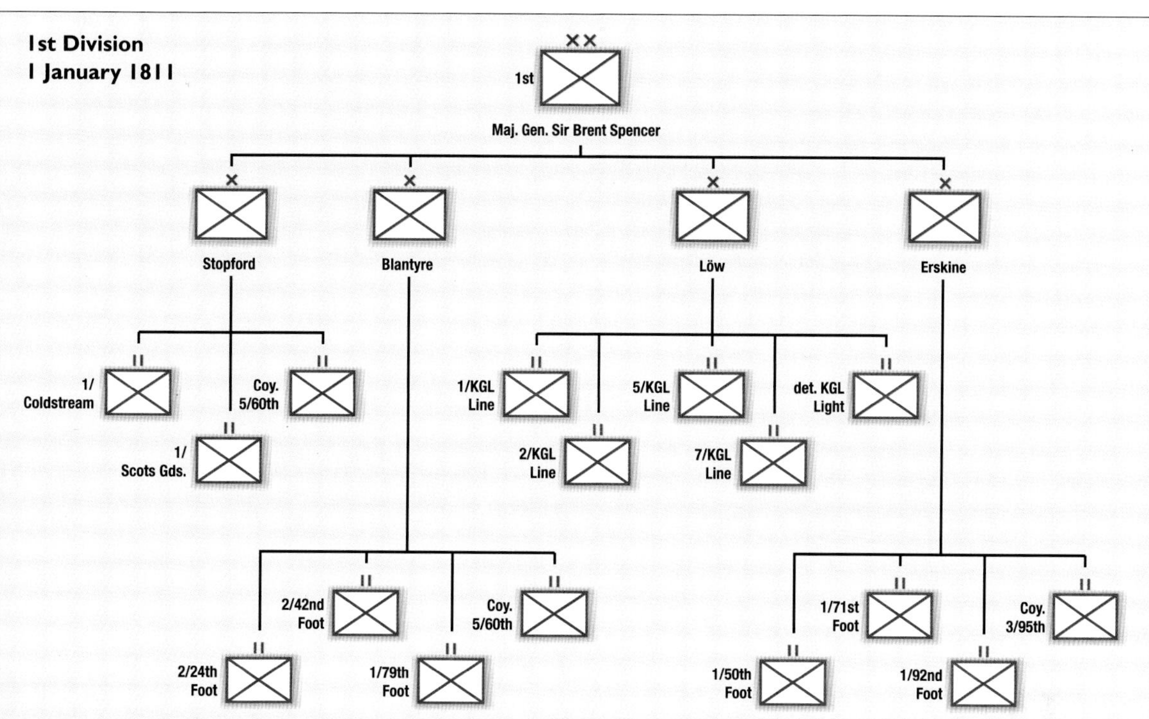

Subsequent alterations:

Spencer was promoted to lieutenant-general on 4 June but Wellington had long made clear his dissatisfaction with his performance as second in command of the army and he received leave to go home on 25 July. Command of the division then passed to Lt. Gen. Sir Thomas Graham on 9 August.

Stopford's Brigade:	Maj. Gen. Henry Campbell returned to command the brigade on 8 June, while Stopford went off to command a brigade in 4th Division on 18 June.
Blantyre's Brigade:	Lord Blantyre's temporary command came to an end with the appointment of Maj. Gen. Miles Nightingall on 23 January. However, Nightingall then left for Bengal on 25 June and Stopford returned from 4th Division to take over the brigade on 28 July. 1/26th Foot was added to the brigade on 21 July.
Löw's Brigade:	The detachments from the KGL Light Battalions rejoined their parent units on 6 June. 7/KGL was ordered to be drafted and returned to England on 26 June.
Erskine's Brigade:	On 6 February Sir William Erskine was promoted to the command of 5th Division and replaced by Kenneth Howard. The brigade was subsequently transferred to 2nd Division in the re-organisation that followed Albuera.

Sir Thomas Graham (1748–1843)
Third son of Thomas Graham of Balgowan, born 19 October 1748. No military experience prior to July 1793 when served as ADC to Lord Mulgrave at Toulon; served at Quiberon Bay, then British Military Commissioner to Austrian Army in Italy 1796–98; served Mediterranean 1798–1802; Minorca 1798; appointed to command land forces for Malta expedition; blockaded Valetta until surrender September 1800; served in abortive Swedish expedition 1808 and afterwards in Spain; temporary commissions confirmed after Corunna; commanded Brigade at Walcheren 1809 but invalided home; sent to command garrison of Cadiz, and won Battle of Barossa February 1811; appointed to command 1st Division June 1811, with 6th and 7th divisions also under his control; went home shortly before Salamanca suffering from eye infection, but returned to Peninsula in 1813 in time for Vittoria; again entrusted with semi-independent corps; besieged and successfully stormed San Sebastian, but again forced to retire due to ill-health; served Holland November 1813 until end of war; helped capture Antwerp and won Battle of Merexem but failed to take Bergen-op-Zoom 3 February 1814.

Commissions: lieutenant-colonel (temporary) 10 February 1794; colonel (temporary) 90th Foot 22 July 1795; brigadier-general November 1799; major-general 25 September 1803; lieutenant-general 25 July 1810; general 19 July 1821. Died 18 December 1843.

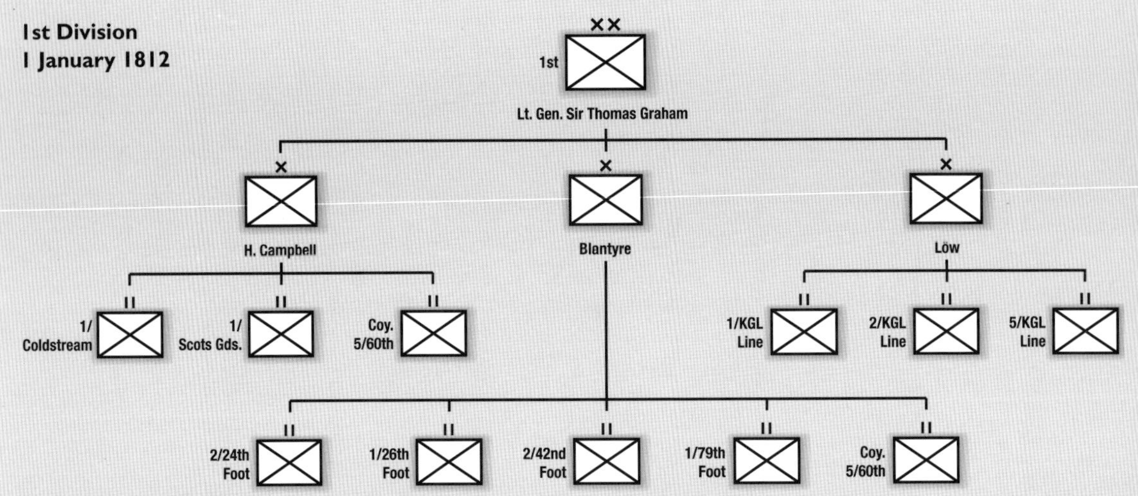

Subsequent alterations:

Graham went home ill on 6 July and Henry Campbell succeeded him in command of the division until 11 October, when Lord Edward Paget took over. Paget, however, was captured soon afterwards during the retreat from Burgos on 17 November and replaced by Sir William Stewart.

Campbell's Brigade: When Campbell was appointed to command the division on 6 July, the brigade passed to the Hon. T.W. Fermor of 3rd Footguards.

Blantyre's Brigade: Stopford had briefly resumed command before 1 February, but was absent again by 8 April. On 7 May Maj. Gen. William Wheatley was appointed in his place but died of typhus at Escorial on 1 September and was himself replaced by Stirling of 1/42nd Foot on 11 September.

1/26th Foot were considered too sickly for field service and by 8 March had been sent down to Gibraltar to relieve 1/82nd. They were replaced by 1/58th Foot who arrived on 2 April, and although orders were given to transfer this battalion to 5th Division on 1 June, it remained with the brigade until the re-organisation which followed the Burgos operation. This was probably because although 1/42nd Foot joined the brigade on 23 April, 2/42nd then went home on 19 May.

After Burgos a major re-organisation of the division took place. A new brigade comprising 1/1st and 3/1st Footguards under Howard (brought back from 2nd Division) was added on 10 November, while Stirling's Brigade (less its 5/60th company which went to Howard's Brigade) was transferred to 6th Division. On 6 December 1/KGL Light Battalion and 2/KGL Light Battalion both came from 7th Division but it is unclear whether they were added to Löw's Brigade, or formed a separate one under Colin Halkett – the latter seems more likely.

Henry Frederick Campbell

Served Flanders 1793 and again on the staff in 1794; in Peninsula with 2nd Brigade of Guards; briefly commanded 1st Division; badly wounded in face at Salamanca.

Commissions: ensign 1st Footguards 20 September 1786; lieutenant and captain 25 April 1793; captain and lieutenant-colonel 6 April 1796; colonel (brevet) 25 September 1803; major-general 25 July 1810; third major 1st Footguards 2 October 1813; lieutenant-general 4 June 1814; general 10 January 1837.

Kenneth Alexander Howard (1767–1845)

Served at Helder 1799 as Major of Brigade; served Peninsula at Vittoria and Nive as commander 1st Division. Married Lady Charlotte Primrose, with issue.

Commissions: ensign 2nd Footguards 21 April 1786; lieutenant and captain 2nd Footguards 25 April 1793; captain and lieutenant-colonel 30 December 1797; colonel (brevet) 1 January 1805; major-general 25 July 1810; lieutenant-general 12 August 1819; general 10 January 1837.

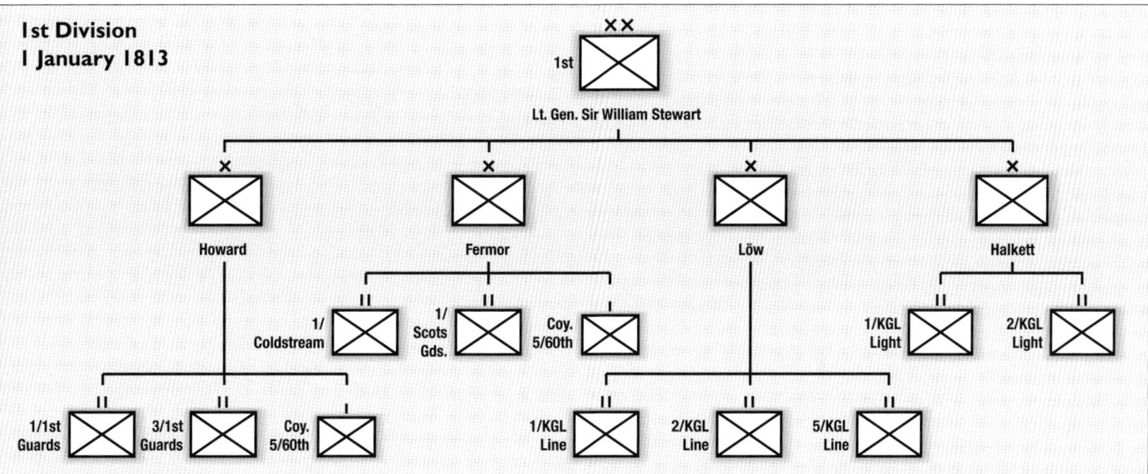

Subsequent alterations:

On 25 March Howard succeeded Stewart in command of the division. On 19 May Graham was officially re-appointed to the command, but in fact Howard remained in day-to-day charge of it since Graham was also acting as commander of the entire left wing of the army. When Graham again went home sick on 8 October, the division passed to Lt. Gen. Sir John Hope.

Howard's Brigade: During Howard's absence in command of the division his brigade was looked after by Col. Sir John Lambert of 1st Footguards. However, Lambert was promoted to major-general on 4 June 1813 and transferred to 6th Division on 2 July. Command of the brigade then passed to Col. Peregrine Maitland of 1st Footguards.

Löw's Brigade: Löw went home on 6 May and all the KGL battalions were then consolidated into a single brigade under Halkett, who was himself succeeded by Maj. Gen. Heinrich von Hinüber on 20 October.

Aylmer's Brigade: A new brigade under Lord Aylmer came out in July and joined the division sometime in August. Initially it comprised 76th Foot, 2/84th Foot and 85th Foot, but on 17 October 2/84th Foot was transferred to 5th Division and replaced by 2/62nd and on 24 November 77th Foot came up from Lisbon and was added to the brigade.

The 71st Highlanders at Vimiero, by Atkinson. Note how the Highlanders are advancing in ne at open order, with the ranks widely separated to avoid falling into confusion when he order to charge is given.

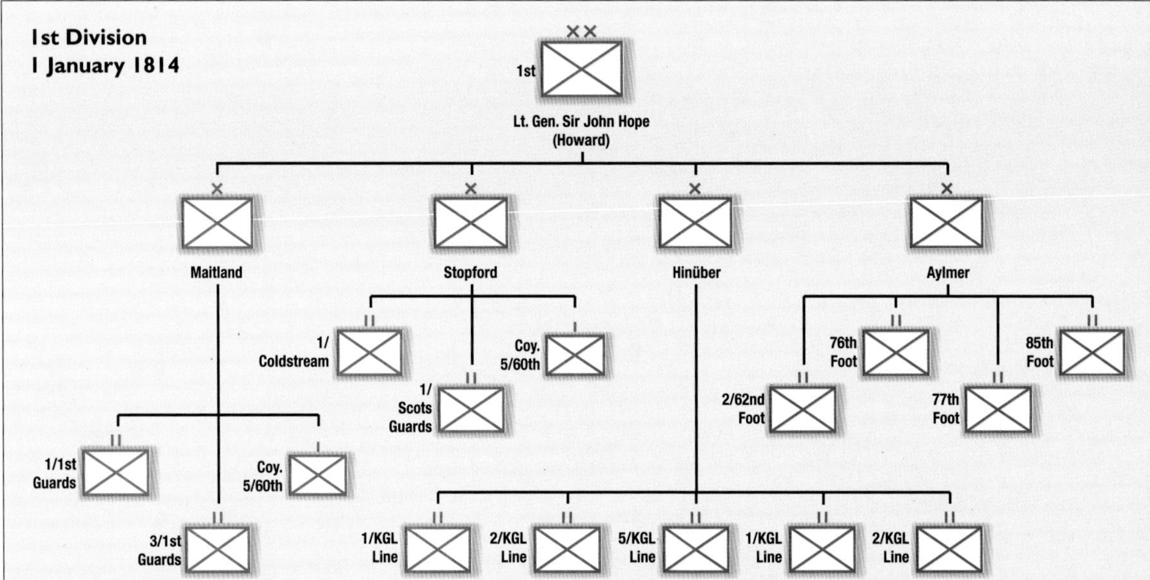

Subsequent alterations:

As Hope also commanded the left wing of the army, Howard remained in charge of the division as he had done under Graham.

Stopford's Brigade:	Stopford was wounded at Bayonne on 14 April and command of the brigade passed to Col. John Guise of 1/Scots Guards.
Aylmer's Brigade:	1/37th Foot joined the brigade before 25 March.

Hon. Edward Paget (1775–1849)
Second son of Earl of Uxbridge, born 3 November 1775. Served Flanders/Holland 1794–95 and as marine at Battle of Cape St Vincent 1797; served Egypt 1801, wounded at Alexandria; served in Mediterranean 1806 and assigned to abortive Swedish Expedition as commander of reserve and afterwards served on Corunna campaign; led attack across Douro at Oporto 12 May 1809 but lost left arm; returned to Peninsula late-1812 as commander of 1st Division and second in command to Wellington but made a p.o.w. 17 November during retreat from Burgos; not at Waterloo. C-in-C India 1822–25; then Governor of Chelsea Hospital. Died 13 May 1849.

Commissions: cornet and sub-lieutenant Lifeguards 23 March 1792; captain 54th Foot 7 December 1792; major 14 November 1793; lieutenant-colonel 28th Foot 30 April 1794; colonel (brevet) 1 January 1798; brigadier-general October 1803; major-general 1 January 1805; lieutenant-general (Portugal and Spain) 1809; lieutenant-general 4 June 1811; general 27 May 1825.

The above print by Dubourg (after Atkinson) shows Paget's capture during the retreat from Burgos.

2nd Division – 'The Observing Division'

The division was formed on 18 June 1809 under Sir Rowland Hill and latterly nicknamed 'The Observing Division', since most of its early service was spent as part of a corps of observation marking the French forces in Estramadura and Andalusia.

Served: Talavera, Busaco, Albuera, Burgos, Vittoria, Maya, Sorauren I and II, Nivelle, Nive, St Pierre, Orthez and Toulouse.

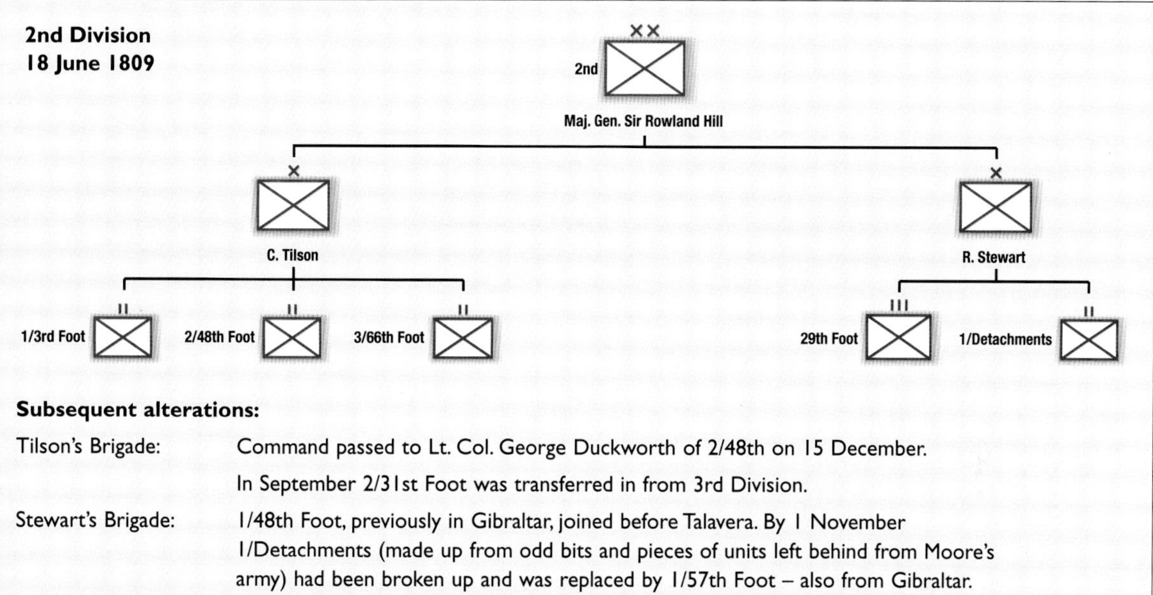

Subsequent alterations:

Tilson's Brigade:	Command passed to Lt. Col. George Duckworth of 2/48th on 15 December. In September 2/31st Foot was transferred in from 3rd Division.
Stewart's Brigade:	1/48th Foot, previously in Gibraltar, joined before Talavera. By 1 November 1/Detachments (made up from odd bits and pieces of units left behind from Moore's army) had been broken up and was replaced by 1/57th Foot – also from Gibraltar.
Craufurd's Brigade:	A new brigade under Brig. Gen. Catlin Craufurd was added in September, comprising 2/28th Foot, 2/34th Foot and 2/39th Foot.

Rowland (Lord) Hill (1772–1842)

Second son of Sir John Hill, born at Prees, Shropshire, 11 August 1772: studied at Strasbourg military academy. Served as ADC to General O'Hara at Toulon; Egypt in 1801; commanded brigade on Hanover Expedition; served throughout Peninsular War becoming Wellington's most trusted subordinate; slightly wounded at Talavera; commanded I Corps during Waterloo campaign (had horse shot from under him) and served as second in command Army of Occupation 1815–18. In retirement for next ten years, but made general 27 May 1825 and C-in-C Army 1828–42. Colonel Royal Horse Guards 19 November 1830. Created Baron Hill of Almaraz and Hardwicke 1814, Viscount 1842. Died 10 December 1842 at Hardwick Grange.

Commissions: ensign 38th Foot 31 July 1790; lieutenant 53rd Foot 24 January 1791; captain (brevet) 23 March 1793; captain 86th Foot 30 October 1793; major 90th Foot 10 February 1794; lieutenant-colonel 13 May 1794; colonel 1 January 1800; major-general 30 October 1805; lieutenant-general 1 January 1812; general 27 May 1825.

Hill was the most trusted of Wellington's subordinates, and was one of the few officers allowed an independent command.

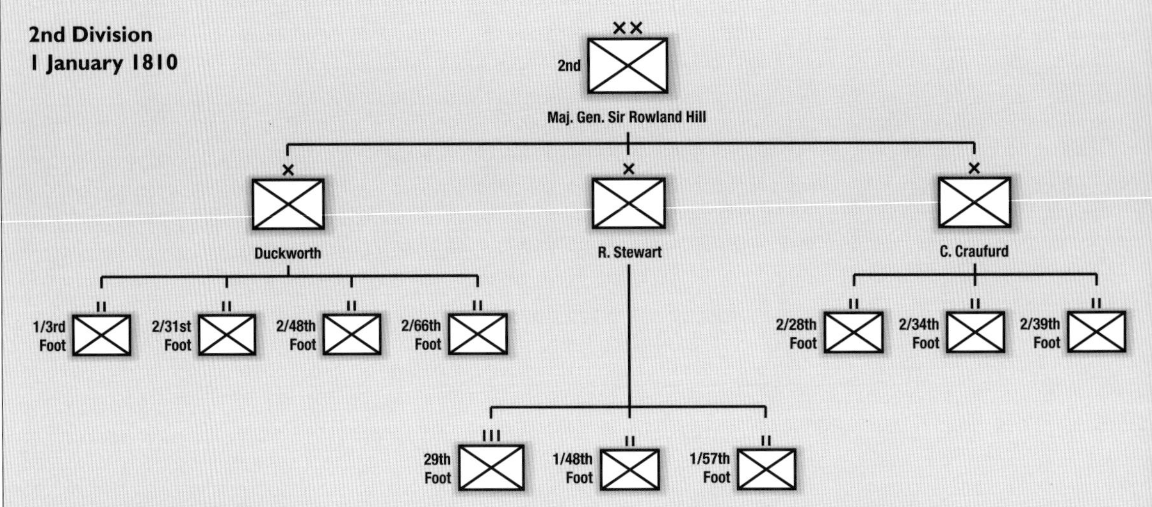

Subsequent alterations:

On 20 June Maj. Gen. Sir James Leith was nominated to command both the division 'under Hill' and Duckworth's Brigade, but instead on 8 July Leith was given command of a newly arrived brigade which became the nucleus of 5th Division in the following month. Consequently Sir William Stewart became Hill's deputy with effect from 8 August and formally took over the division when Hill went home sick in November.

Duckworth's Brigade: Officially taken over by Leith on 20 June and then by Stewart on 27 July. In practice, when Stewart was commanding the division the brigade was looked after for him by Lt. Col. Sir John Colborne of 2/66th Foot.

Stewart's Brigade: Robert Stewart went home sick before 1 September, leaving Col. William Inglis of 1/57th Foot to command the brigade, although he in turn was superseded by Maj. Gen. Daniel Hoghton on 8 October.

Craufurd's Brigade: Catlin Craufurd died of natural causes at Abrantes on 25 September and the brigade was temporarily commanded at Busaco by Lt. Col. George Wilson of 2/39th Foot. On 30 September Sir William Lumley took over.

Christopher Tilson (dates unknown)
Served in Peninsula 1809 and commanded a brigade in 2nd Division at Talavera; went home in December but then returned to Peninsula in 1812 (having changed his name to Chowne) and temporarily commanded 2nd Division as Hill's deputy.

Commissions: lieutenant-colonel 99th Foot 15 November 1794, half-pay; lieutenant-colonel 44th Foot 24 January 1799; colonel (brevet) 1 January 1800; brigadier-general (Mediterranean) 25 March 1805; major-general 25 April 1808; lieutenant-general 4 June 1813.

Sir William Stewart (1774–1827)
Fourth son of John, 7th Earl of Galloway. Popularly known as 'Auld Grog Wullie'. Instrumental in forming Experimental Rifle Corps/95th Rifles; commanded same at Ferrol and Copenhagen; Colonel Commandant 95th Rifles 31 August 1809; served in Peninsula, slightly wounded at Albuera, and badly wounded at Maya 25 July 1813, but remained strapped to saddle and in command of 2nd Division.

Commissions: ensign 42nd Highlanders March 1786; lieutenant 1787; captain Independent Company 24 June 1791; captain 22nd Foot 31 October 1792; major 31st Foot December 1794; lieutenant-colonel (unattached) 14 January 1795; lieutenant-colonel 67th Foot 1 September 1795; colonel (brevet) 1 January 1800; lieutenant-colonel 95th Rifles 28 August 1800; major-general 25 April 1808; lieutenant-general 4 June 1813.

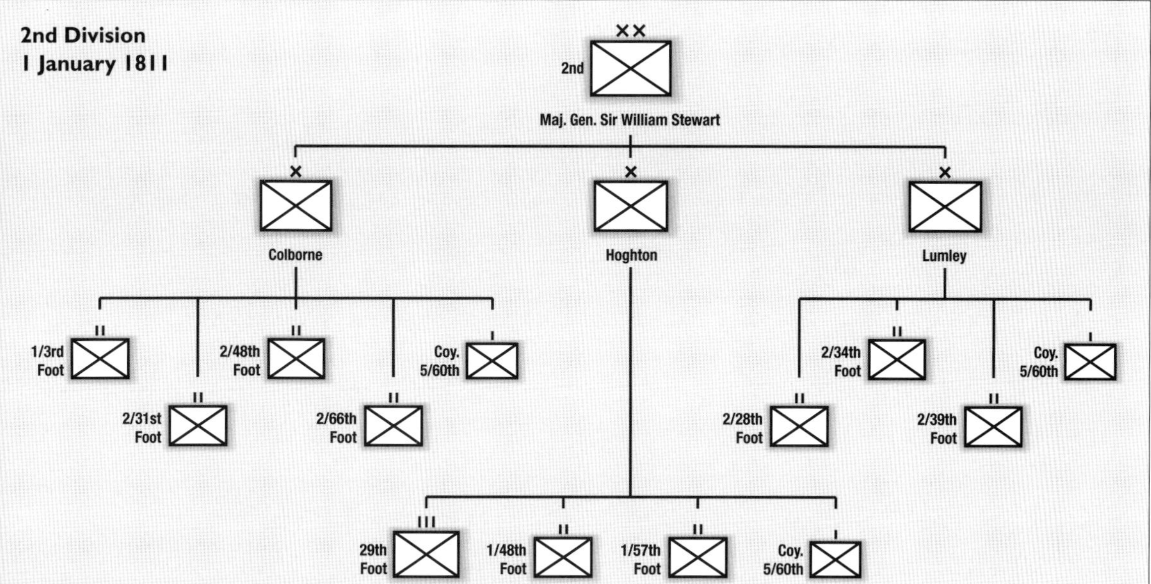

Subsequent alterations:

Hill returned from sick leave before the end of May and resumed command of both the division and the corps of observation. In the meantime the very heavy losses at Albuera necessitated a radical re-organisation of the division with effect from 6 June.

With the exception of 1/48th and 2/48th Foot the survivors of Colborne's and Hoghton's brigades were consolidated into a single provisional battalion and posted to Lumley's Brigade, which had actually been commanded by Lt. Col. Alexander Abercromby of 2/28th Foot at Albuera. Most of 2/48th Foot were drafted into 1/48th which was then posted to 4th Division while the remaining cadre of 2/48th went home to recruit. Two new brigades were therefore posted in; Howard's from 1st Division and Charles Ashworth's Portuguese. There were still three companies of 5/60th with the division at this time, probably all attached to Lumley's Brigade.

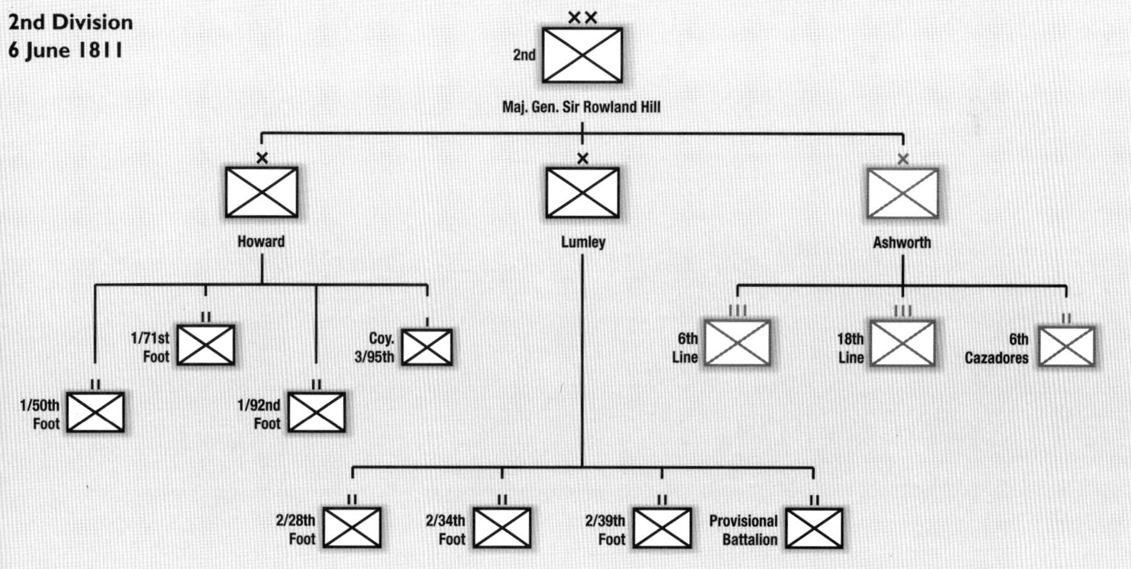

On 22 July, 1/28th Foot came up from Gibraltar and was also attached to Lumley's Brigade. At the same time, however, sufficient reinforcement drafts arrived to bring both 1/3rd and 1/57th Foot back up to strength and a further re-organisation therefore took place on 7 August (see diagram on page 44).

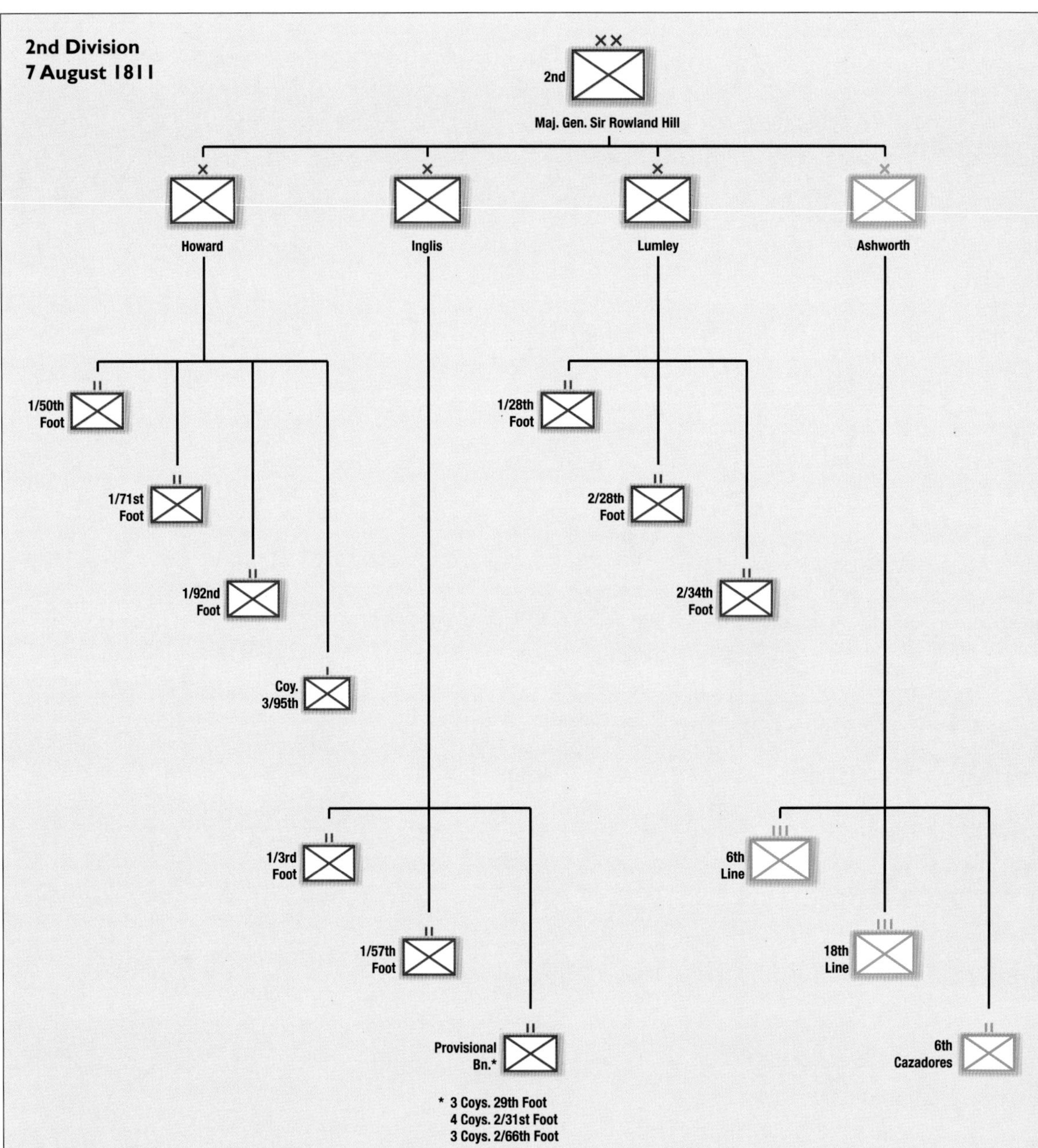

Subsequent alterations:

Howard's Brigade: On 21 August the 3/95th company was transferred to the Light Division and replaced by one of the three 5/60th companies.

Inglis's Brigade: Taken over by Sir John Byng on 21 September.

The remains of 29th Foot were ordered home to recruit on 3 October.

Lumley's Brigade: Lumley went home sick in early August but was not officially replaced until Lt. Col. George Wilson of 1/39th Foot took over the brigade on 9 October.

2/28th Foot were drafted into 1/28th on 21 August and sent home to recruit. 1/39th Foot arrived from Sicily on 20 October and were posted to the brigade. On 17 December the effectives of 2/39th Foot were drafted into the 1st Battalion and the remainder sent home.

2nd Division
1 January 1812

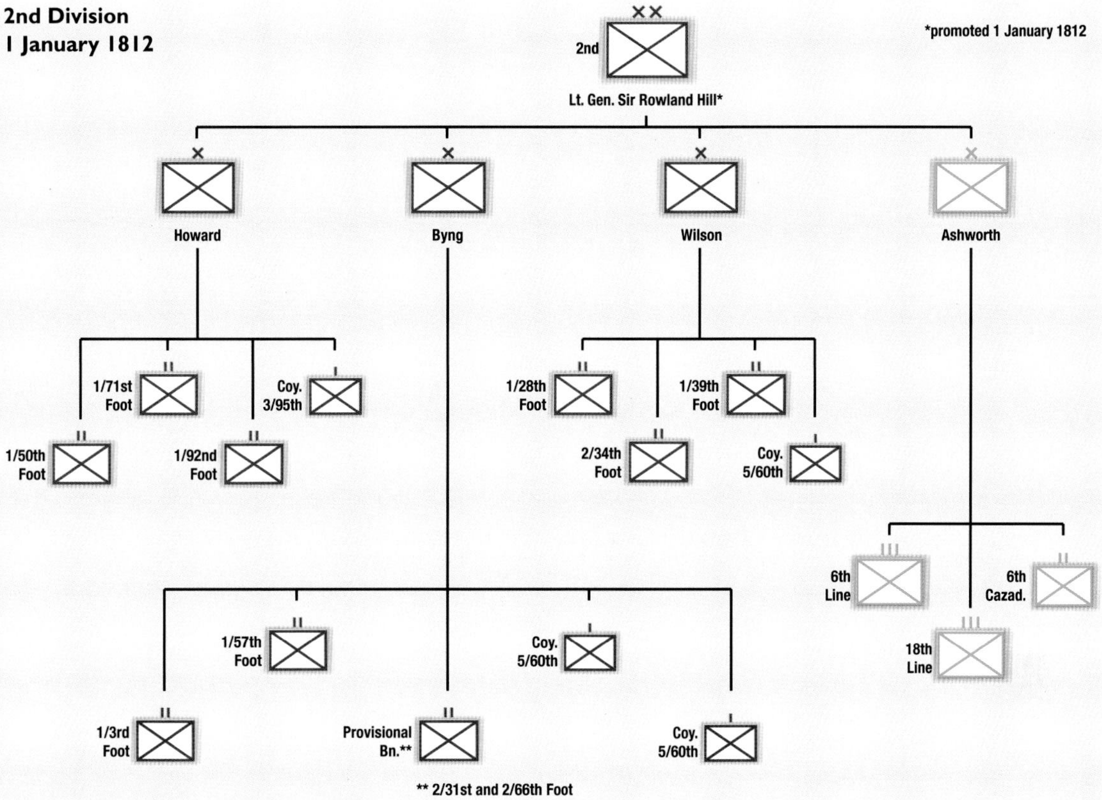

*promoted 1 January 1812

2nd — Lt. Gen. Sir Rowland Hill*

- Howard
  - 1/71st Foot
  - Coy. 3/95th
  - 1/50th Foot
  - 1/92nd Foot
- Byng
  - 1/57th Foot
  - Coy. 5/60th
  - 1/3rd Foot
  - Provisional Bn.**
  - Coy. 5/60th
- Wilson
  - 1/28th Foot
  - 1/39th Foot
  - 2/34th Foot
  - Coy. 5/60th
- Ashworth
  - 6th Line
  - 6th Cazad.
  - 18th Line

** 2/31st and 2/66th Foot

Subsequent alterations:

On 14 April Christopher Chowne (formerly known as Christopher Tilson until changing his name as a condition of a fortunate legacy) returned to the army and was officially appointed to command the division 'under Hill'. He was certainly present at Almaraz in May, but otherwise appears to have been elsewhere.

Howard's Brigade: On 10 November Howard was transferred to command a brigade in 1st Division – perhaps temporarily – and this brigade was taken over by Lt. Col. Henry Cadogan of 1/71st Foot.

British officers in the Peninsula, by Luard. The staff officer in the cocked hat on the right is easily identified by the characteristic long (dark blue) greatcoat. The surgeon on the far left appears to be wearing civilian clothes.

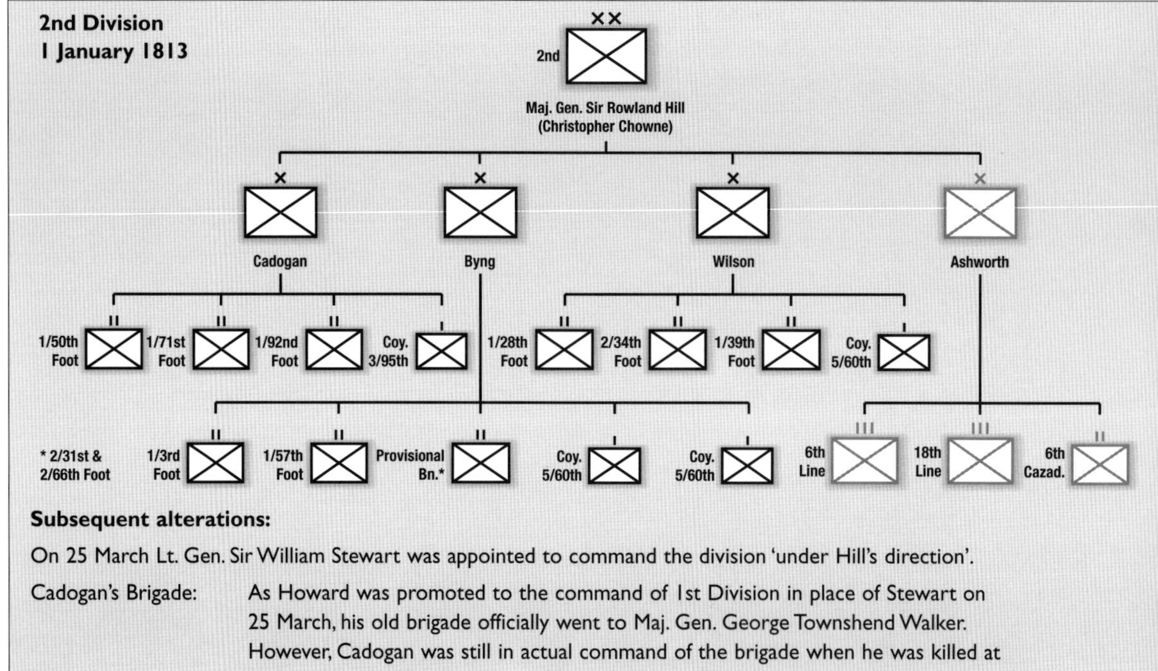

Subsequent alterations:

On 25 March Lt. Gen. Sir William Stewart was appointed to command the division 'under Hill's direction'.

Cadogan's Brigade: As Howard was promoted to the command of 1st Division in place of Stewart on 25 March, his old brigade officially went to Maj. Gen. George Townshend Walker. However, Cadogan was still in actual command of the brigade when he was killed at Vittoria; Lt. Col. John Cameron of Fassiefern (of 1/92nd Foot) then took over until he in turn was wounded at Maya; Lt. Col. Sir John Forster Fitzgerald of 5/60th next commanded the brigade until Walker finally arrived in August. However, on 18 November Walker was promoted on to the command of 7th Division and Maj. Gen. Sir Edward Barnes took over the brigade on 20 November.

Wilson's Brigade: Wilson died of fever at Moralejo 5 January 1813 and Col. Robert O'Callaghan of 1/39th Foot took over until 23 July when he was succeeded by Maj. Gen. William Pringle.

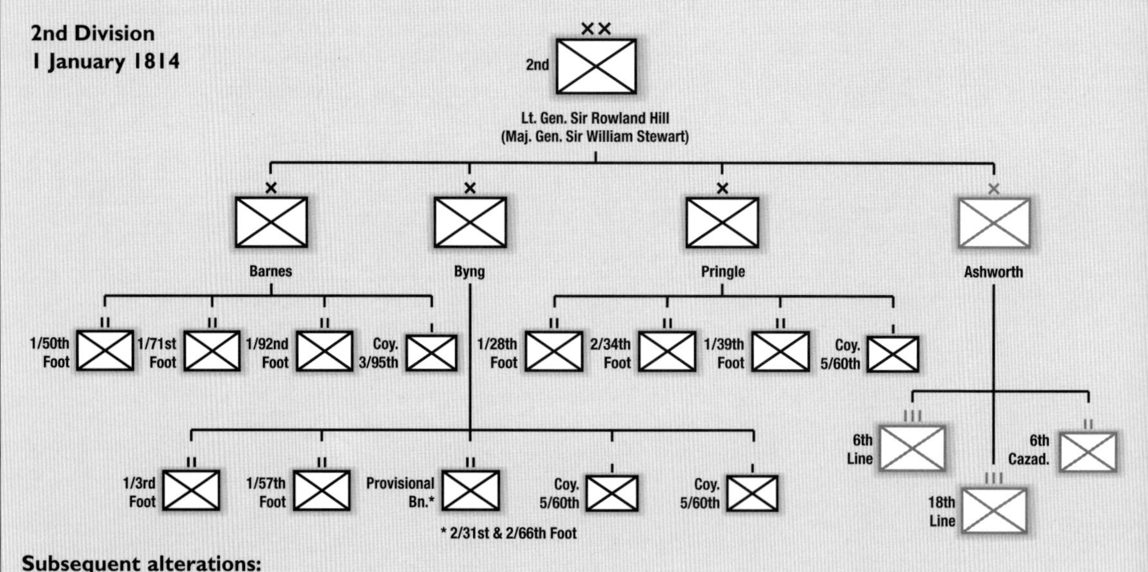

Subsequent alterations:

Pringle's Brigade: Pringle was badly wounded at St Palais 15 February 1814 and O'Callaghan again took over the brigade.

Ashworth's Brigade: Lt. Col. Henry Hardinge succeeded Ashworth on 13 December 1813.

3rd Division – 'The Fighting Division'

The division was formed on 18 June 1809 under Mackenzie. The nickname was a reflection of the fact that it was widely regarded as the most dependable of the divisions.

Served: Talavera, Busaco, Fuentes de Oñoro, Ciudad Rodrigo, Badajoz, Salamanca, Burgos, Vittoria, Sorauren I and II, Nivelle, Orthez and Toulouse.

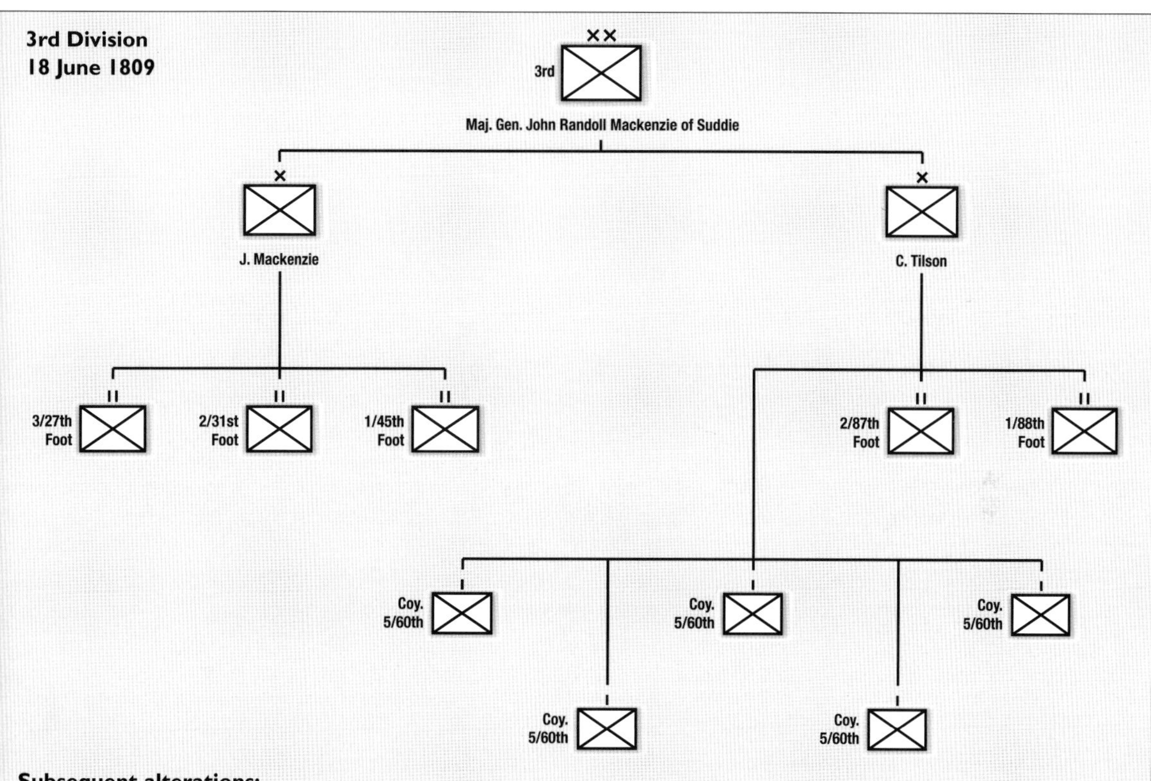

Subsequent alterations:

Mackenzie was killed in action at Talavera 28 July 1809 and replaced by Robert Craufurd.

Mackenzie's Brigade:	3/27th Foot was sent down to Lisbon and replaced by 2/24th just before Talavera. Following the battle the brigade was amalgamated with Donkin's (previously Tilson's) brigade.
Tilson's Brigade:	Tilson was transferred to 2nd Division on 21 June 1809 and replaced by Sir Rufane Shaw Donkin. In October Donkin gave up command and was replaced by Col. Henry Mackinnon. After Talavera the brigade was amalgamated with Mackenzie's old brigade. On 15 September 2/87th Foot was ordered down to Lisbon and at about the same time 2/24th and 2/31st Foot were transferred to 2nd Division.
Robert Craufurd's Brigade:	The Light Brigade was assigned, with its commander, to 3rd Division after Talavera in place of Mackenzie's Brigade. See the diagram on page 48 for its composition.

John Randoll Mackenzie (of Suddie) (d.1809)

Commanded 2/78th at Maida; served in Peninsula, commanded brigade in Portugal 1808, then 3rd Division on formation 18 June 1809. Killed in action at Talavera 28 July 1809.

Commissions: adjutant Marines 28 May 1780; first lieutenant Marines 3 November 1780; captain 78th Highlanders 13 March 1793; lieutenant-colonel 78th Highlanders 27 February 1796; colonel (brevet) 1 January 1801; major-general 25 April 1808.

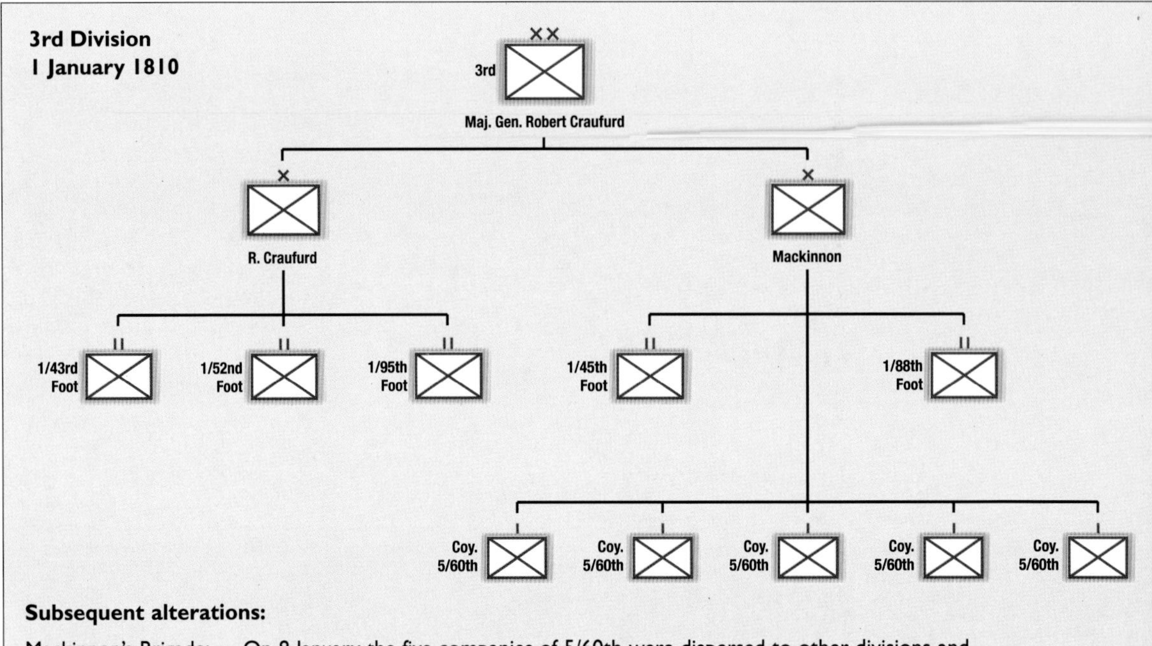

Subsequent alterations:

Mackinnon's Brigade: On 8 January the five companies of 5/60th were dispersed to other divisions and replaced on 22 February by 1/74th Foot.

On 22 February the division was completely re-organised under Sir Thomas Picton with Craufurd's Brigade becoming the nucleus of the new Light Division. In its place Lightburne's Brigade was transferred in from 4th Division and José Champelimaud's Portuguese Brigade was added.

3rd Division
22 February 1810

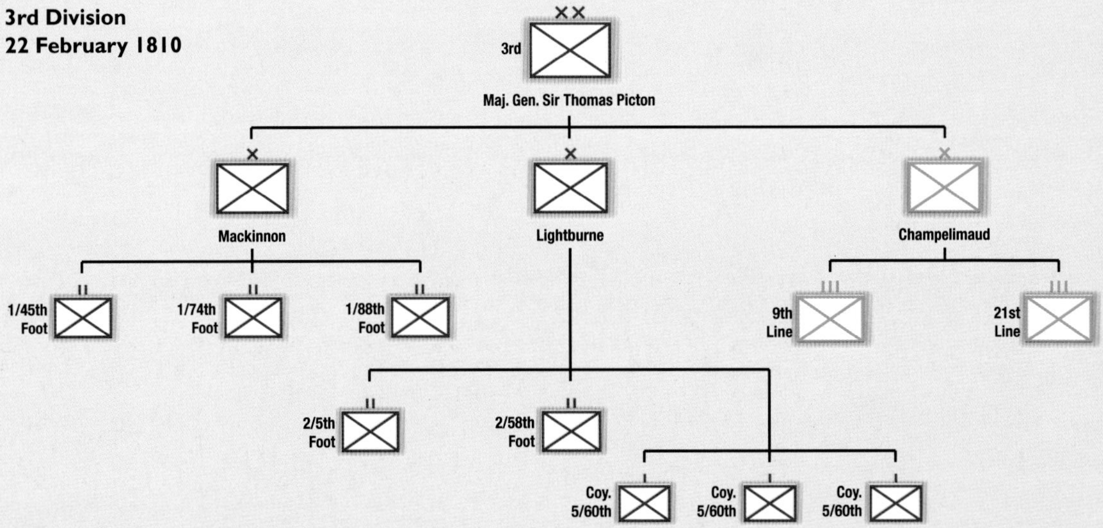

3rd
Maj. Gen. Sir Thomas Picton
Mackinnon
Lightburne
Champelimaud
1/45th Foot
1/74th Foot
1/88th Foot
9th Line
21st Line
2/5th Foot
2/58th Foot
Coy. 5/60th
Coy. 5/60th
Coy. 5/60th

Subsequent alterations:

Lightburne's Brigade: Sir Charles Colville was given command of the brigade on 10 October when Lightburne went home. 2/83rd Foot were posted to the brigade on 12 September but did not join until after Busaco, at which point 2/58th Foot was detached for garrison duty at Lisbon. They were in turn replaced by 94th Foot on 6 October.

Champelimaud's Brigade: Champelimaud was wounded at Busaco and replaced by Charles Sutton on 29 October.

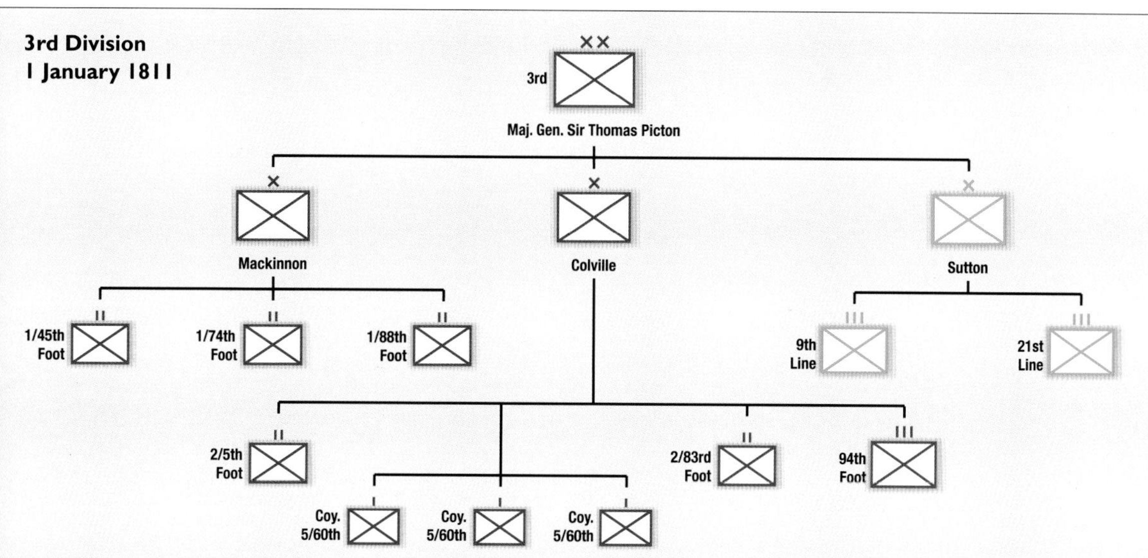

Subsequent alterations:

Mackinnon's Brigade: MacKinnon was absent sick between 1 July and 31 October and the brigade was commanded in his absence by Lt. Col. John Wallace of 1/88th Foot.

Colville's Brigade: Colville was temporarily transferred to the command of 2nd Division on 22 December and the brigade was commanded in his absence by Lt. Col. James Campbell of 94th Foot.

On 5 March the 5/60th companies were transferred to MacKinnon's Brigade and replaced by 2/88th Foot, but on 10 July 2/88th was drafted into 1/88th Foot and replaced on 22 July by 77th Foot.

Sutton's Brigade: Led by Manly Power at Fuentes de Oñoro, but Luis Palmeirim took command shortly afterwards.

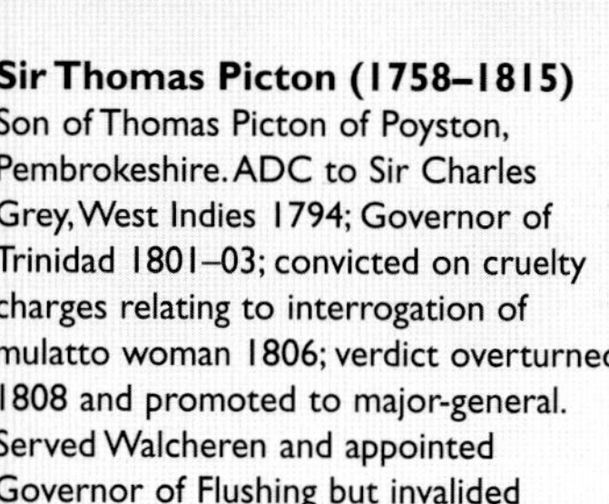

Sir Thomas Picton (1758–1815)
Son of Thomas Picton of Poyston, Pembrokeshire. ADC to Sir Charles Grey, West Indies 1794; Governor of Trinidad 1801–03; convicted on cruelty charges relating to interrogation of mulatto woman 1806; verdict overturned 1808 and promoted to major-general. Served Walcheren and appointed Governor of Flushing but invalided home; commander 3rd Division 1810 to end of Peninsular War, except for year after being wounded at Badajoz, 1812; K.B. 1813, G.C.B. 1814; commanded 5th Division 1815; badly wounded (some accounts suggest fatally) at Quatre Bras; killed at Waterloo.

Commissions: ensign 12th Foot 14 November 1771; captain 1778; half-pay 12th Foot 24 December 1787; lieutenant-colonel (brevet) 19 November 1794; lieutenant-colonel 56th Foot 1 May 1796; major-general 1808; lieutenant-general (Peninsula) September 1811; lieutenant-general June 1813.

The above right illustration shows Sir Thomas Picton's death at Waterloo, falling into the arms of an ADC. Curiously, the latter appears to be wearing the regulation uniform.

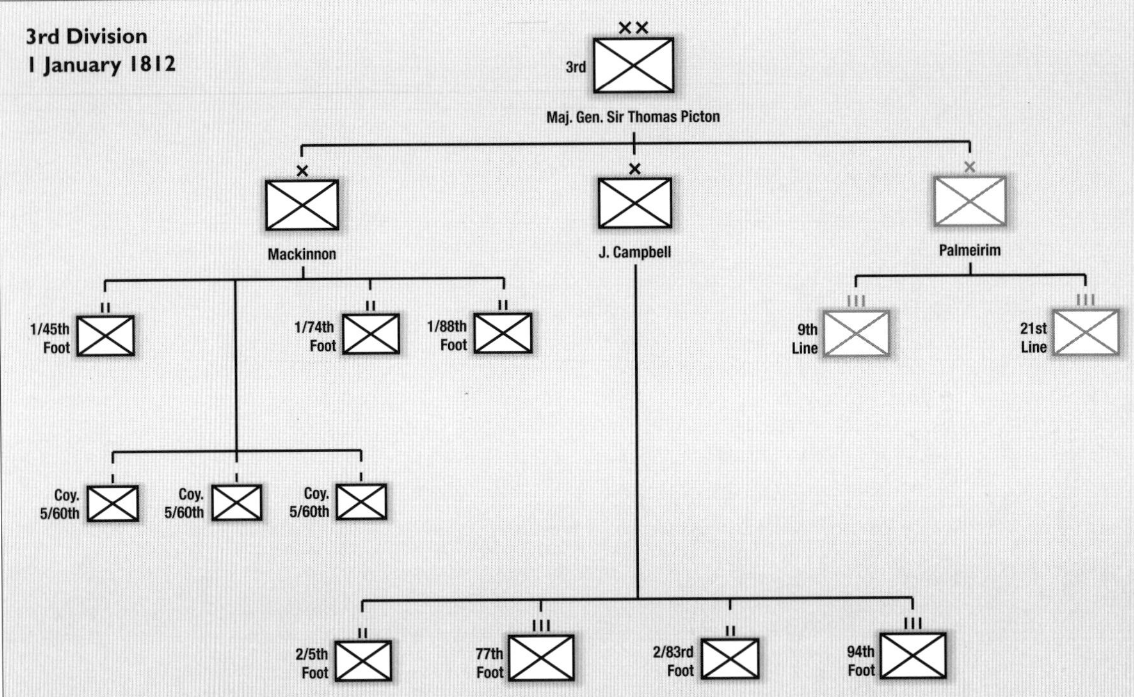

Subsequent alterations:

Picton was wounded at Badajoz and the division then temporarily commanded by Lt. Col. Wallace of 1/88th Foot. Picton went home on sick leave shortly before Salamanca and the division then went to Maj. Gen. Edward Pakenham, who commanded it for the rest of the year.

Mackinnon's Brigade: Mackinnon was killed at Ciudad Rodrigo on 19 January and on 8 February command passed to Maj. Gen. Sir James Kempt. He in turn was wounded at Badajoz and while Wallace of 1/88th Foot took charge of the division, Maj. Thomas Forbes of 1/45th Foot had the brigade. On Picton's return Wallace reverted to command of the brigade until invalided home after the retreat from Burgos.

77th Foot was withdrawn and sent down to Lisbon after Badajoz, being severely depleted in numbers.

Campbell's Brigade: Colville still being absent, Maj. Gen. Edward Pakenham was appointed to command the brigade on 28 June, but as he commanded the division at Salamanca, James Campbell of 94th Foot remained in actual command.

1/5th Foot was posted to the brigade on 1 June and both battalions served together at Salamanca, but on 27 July 2/5th was drafted into 1/5th Foot. On 17 October 2/87th Foot was posted to the brigade.

Palmeirim's Brigade: Champelimaud took over command before 17 March but was wounded at Badajoz and replaced in turn by Manly Power on 8 April.

12th Cazadores were posted to the brigade on 8 April.

John Alexander Wallace (1775–1857)

Served Seringapatam 1791–92; Minorca 1798; Egypt 1801; commanded 88th Foot throughout Peninsular War and after Badajoz briefly commanded 3rd Division.

Commissions: ensign 75th Highlanders 28 December 1798; lieutenant 6 April 1790; captain 58th Foot 8 June 1796; major 9 July 1803; lieutenant-colonel 28 August 1804; lieutenant-colonel 88th Foot; colonel (brevet) 4 June 1813; major-general 12 August 1819; lieutenant-general 10 August 1837.

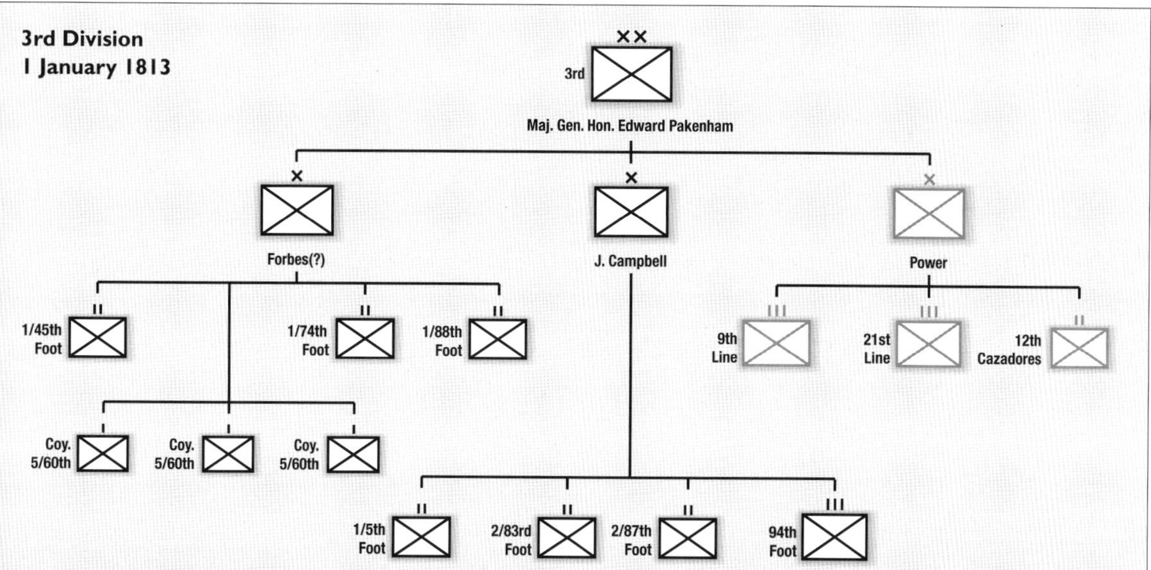

Subsequent alterations:

Pakenham was transferred to 6th Division on 26 January, Colville having returned sometime before that date. Picton also returned in May, whereupon Colville reverted to command of his brigade until 8 September when Picton went off sick again. On Picton returning in December, shortly after the crossing of the Nivelle, Colville was transferred to command the 5th Division.

Forbes's (?) Brigade:	No official brigade commander was designated until 25 March when Col. Thomas Brisbane was appointed *vice* the long-absent Kempt.
Campbell's Brigade:	Colville reverted to command of the brigade in May after Picton returned. However, he was temporarily posted to command 6th Division on 8 August and replaced by Sir John Keane, who officially took over the brigade after Colville was promoted to the command of 3rd Division on 8 September.
Power's Brigade:	Power was succeeded by Charles Sutton in July. 12th Cazadores left the brigade before 26 April and were replaced by 11th Cazadores.

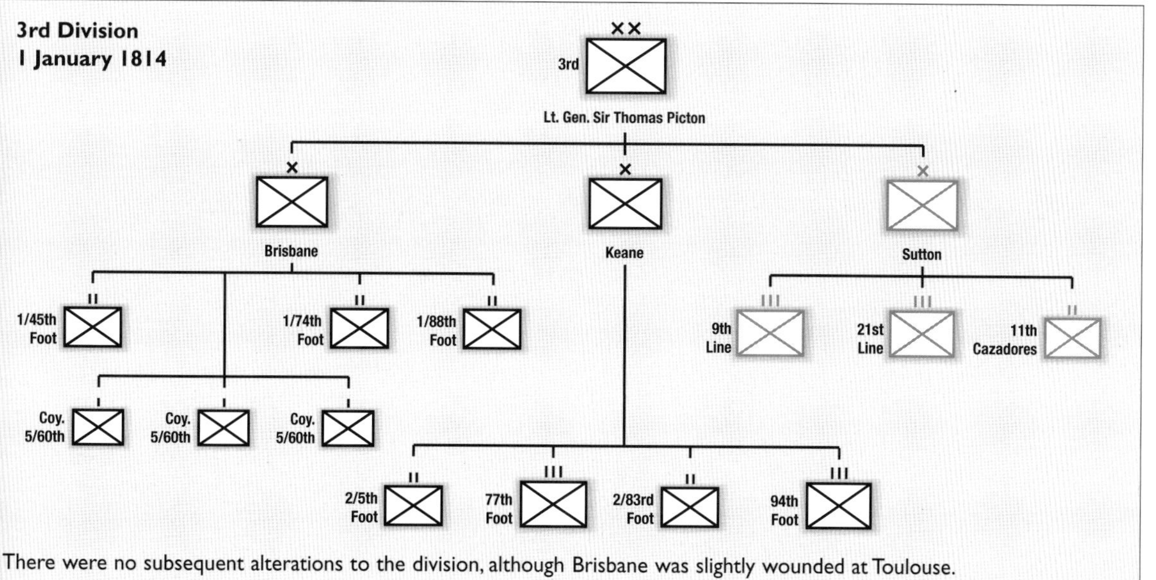

There were no subsequent alterations to the division, although Brisbane was slightly wounded at Toulouse.

4th Division – 'The Supporting Division/The Enthusiastics'

The division was formed on 18 June 1809 under Campbell. The reason for its early nickname is unclear, but it won its later one at Albuera.

Served: Talavera, Busaco, Albuera, Badajoz, Salamanca, Burgos, Vittoria, Sorauren I and II, Salain, Nivelle, Orthez and Toulouse.

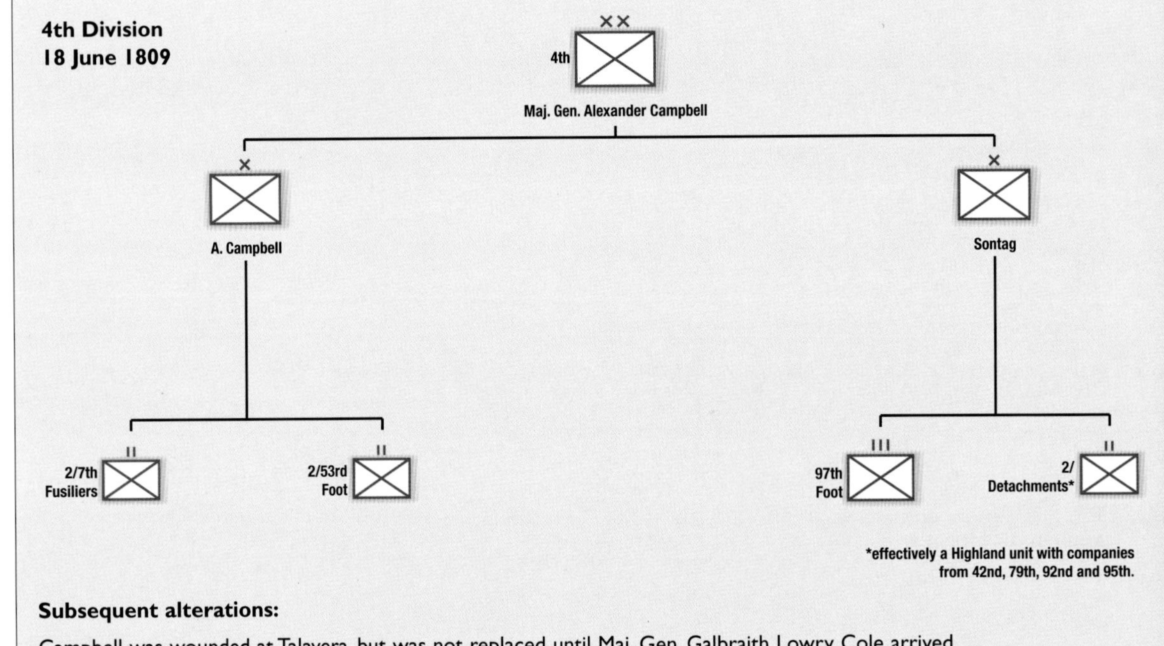

Subsequent alterations:

Campbell was wounded at Talavera, but was not replaced until Maj. Gen. Galbraith Lowry Cole arrived in October.

Campbell's Brigade: Actually commanded by Lt. Col. Sir William Myers of 7th Fusiliers while Campbell was leading the division, and after his wounding at Talavera. 1/11th Foot joined brigade in September.

Sontag's Brigade: Taken over before Talavera by Col. James Kemmis when his 1/40th Foot joined the brigade.

The 2nd Battalion of Detachments (another battalion cobbled together from Moore's strays) was sent home in October and replaced by 3/27th Foot.

Sir Alexander Campbell (1759–1824)

A 'near relation of Melfort'; married, firstly, Olympia Elizabeth Morshead, with issue – Lieutenant Morshead Campbell 74th Highlanders (k.i.a. Assaye) and Lieutenant-Colonel Allan William Campbell (qv) – and, secondly, Elizabeth Ann (maiden name unknown). Knighted when standing proxy for Wellington at his installation as a Knight of the Bath 1812. Created baronet 1814. Served as marine with Channel Fleet September 1780–May 1781, and again at Dogger Bank 5 August 1781; then Gibraltar garrison March 1782 to July 1783; in India with the 74th; commanded regiment at storming of Seringapatam 1799; served in Peninsula; commanded 4th Division 1809–10, then 6th Division 1811; slightly wounded by grapeshot in thigh at Talavera 28 July 1809. C-in-C Mauritius and Bourbon 1813–16. Died as C-in-C Madras 11 December 1824.

Commissions: ensign 1/1st (Royal) 1 November 1776; lieutenant 25 December 1778; captain 97th Foot 13 April 1780, half-pay 23 September 1783; captain 74th Highlanders 25 December 1787; lieutenant-colonel 74th Highlanders 4 December 1795; colonel (brevet) 25 December 1803; major-general 25 July 1810, lieutenant-general (East Indies) 9 March 1812; lieutenant-general 4 June 1814.

4th Division
1 January 1810

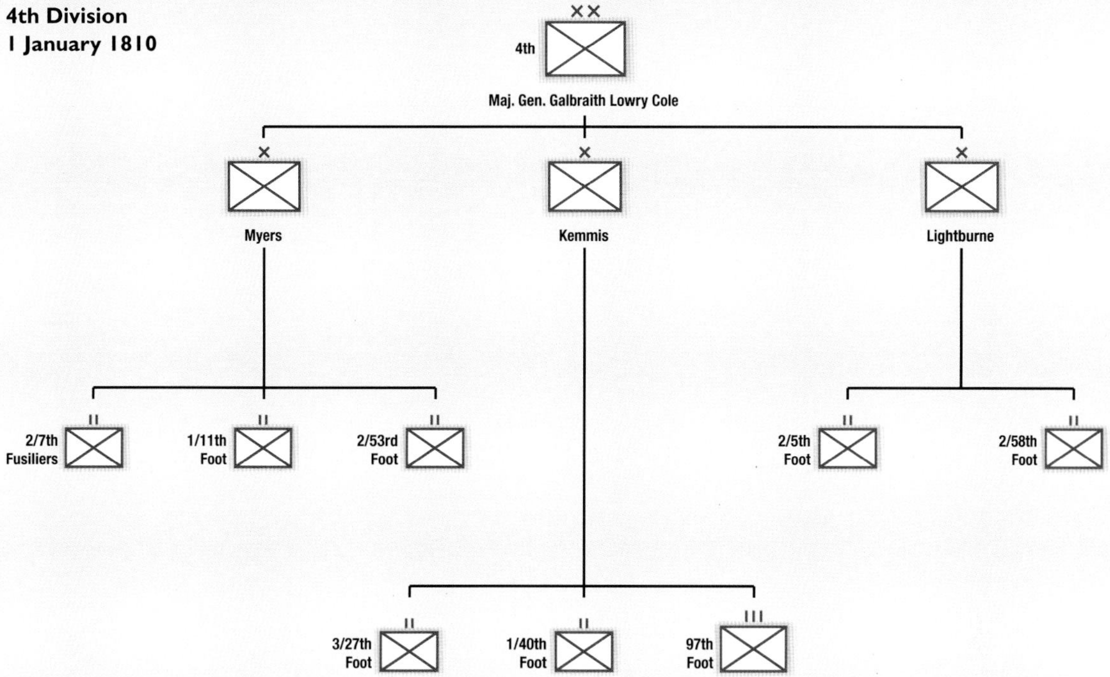

- 4th (XX) – Maj. Gen. Galbraith Lowry Cole
  - Myers (X)
    - 2/7th Fusiliers (II)
    - 1/11th Foot (II)
    - 2/53rd Foot (II)
  - Kemmis (X)
    - 3/27th Foot (II)
    - 1/40th Foot (II)
    - 97th Foot (III)
  - Lightburne (X)
    - 2/5th Foot (II)
    - 2/58th Foot (II)

Subsequent alterations:

Kemmis' Brigade:	Re-designated as senior brigade in the division on 22 February.
Myers' Brigade:	Campbell resumed command of his old brigade, but not the division, on or before 22 February. On 6 October the brigade went to form the nucleus of the new 6th Division, and was replaced by Pakenham's Brigade.
Pakenham's Brigade:	Transferred from 1st Division on 6 October to replace Campbell's brigade. It comprised 1/7th Fusiliers, 1/61st Foot and Brunswick Oels Jäger. On 12 November most of the Jäger were transferred to the Light Division, although one company remained with the brigade as riflemen. They were replaced by 1/23rd Fusiliers and on 17 November 1/61st Foot exchanged with 2/7th Fusiliers who came back from 6th Division to form what then became the Fusilier Brigade.
Lightburne's Brigade:	Joined the division on 2 January but then transferred to 3rd Division on 22 February, being replaced in turn by Thomas McMahon's Brigade.
T. McMahon's Brigade:	Portuguese brigade comprising 3rd and 15th Line added on 22 February to replace Lightburne's brigade. On 17 May the brigade was transferred to the 5th Division and replaced by Richard Collins's Brigade, comprising 11th and 23rd Line.

Galbraith Lowry Cole (1772–1842)
Born Dublin 1 May 1772, second son of Earl of Enniskillen. Served West Indies as ADC to Sir Charles Grey 1794; Egypt as Military Secretary to Sir John Hely Hutchinson; took command of 27th Foot 1805; served Italy 1806 in command of brigade and serving as second in command to Sir John Stuart at Maida; served throughout Peninsula as commander of 4th Division; wounded at Albuera and again severely at Salamanca; served in Army of Occupation 1815–18. Governor of Cape Colony 1828–33. Died 4 October 1842.

Commissions: cornet 12th Light Dragoons 31 March 1787; lieutenant 31 May 1791; captain 70th Foot 30 November 1792; major 31 October 1793; lieutenant-colonel Ward's Regiment 26 November 1794; colonel 1 January 1801; major-general 25 April 1808; lieutenant-general 4 June 1813; general 22 July 1830.

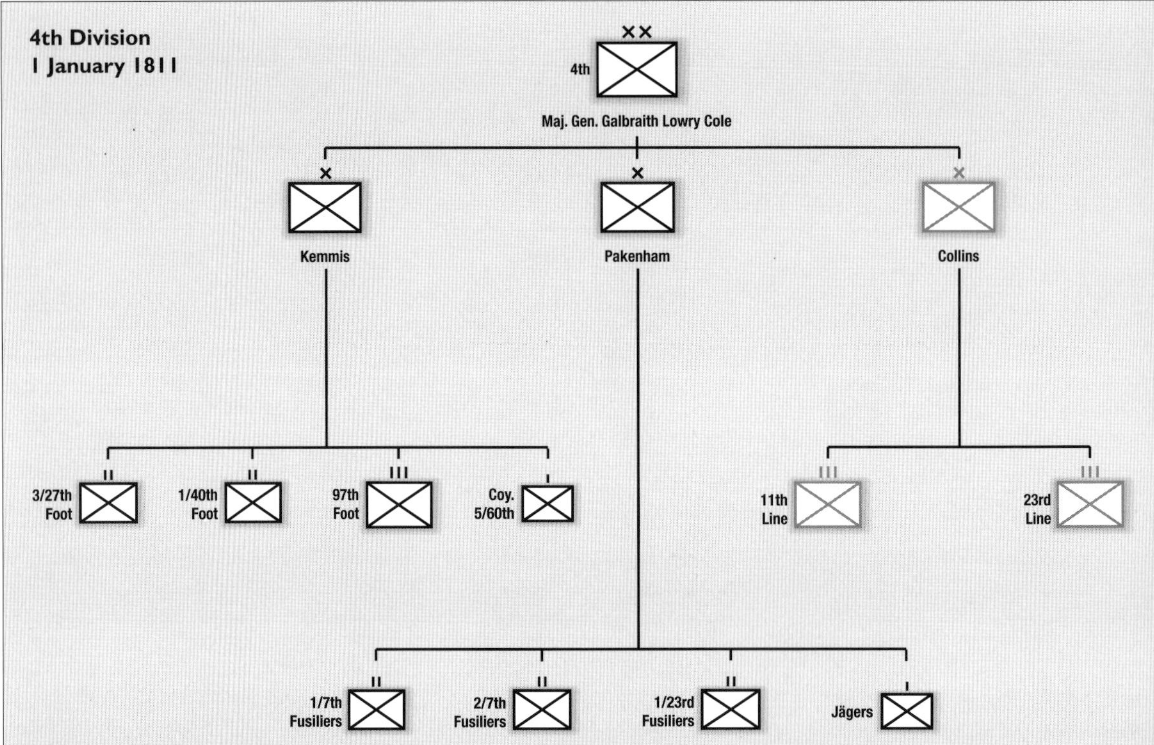

Subsequent alterations:

The division was taken over by Maj. Gen. Sir Charles Colville on 22 December, Cole having gone home sick.

Kemmis's Brigade:	Brunswick Oels Jägers joined the brigade after being thrown out of the Light Division before 1 February, but were then transferred on to the newly formed 7th Division on 5 March. 97th Foot was ordered home to recruit on 3 October.
Pakenham's Brigade	(Fusilier Brigade) Taken over by Maj. Gen. William Houston on 23 January, and then by Myers of 2/7th Fusiliers when he left to command the new 7th Division on 5 March. Myers was killed at Albuera and replaced by Maj. Gen. Edward Stopford on 18 June. He in turn was transferred to 1st Division on 28 July and Pakenham then had the brigade again. After Albuera 2/7th Fusiliers were drafted into 1/7th Fusiliers and the cadre ordered home on 26 June, being replaced by 1/48th Foot.
Collins's Brigade:	Temporarily commanded by William Harvey at Albuera, while Collins had a provisional brigade drawn out of the Elvas Garrison, comprising 5th Line and 5th Cazadores. 1/Loyal Lusitanian Legion joined the brigade on 14 March and by September had been renamed 7th Cazadores.

Sir Charles Colville (1770–1843)

Second son of John, 9th Baron Colville. Served St Domingo 1793–95; wounded in landing at Tiburon; commanded 13th Foot in Egypt 1801; served Martinique; served Peninsula at Fuentes de Oñoro; wounded while leading assault at Badajoz 6 April 1812 (shot through left thigh and lost finger of right hand); wounded again at Vittoria; commanded reserve at Hal 18 June 1815 and consequently not present at Waterloo. Married Jane Mure of Caldwell, Ayrshire, 1818, with issue. Died Hampstead 27 May 1843.

Commissions: ensign 6 December 1781; lieutenant 28th Foot 30 September 1787; captain Independent Company 24 January 1791, exchanged to 13th Foot 18 May 1791; major 13th Foot 2 September 1795; lieutenant-colonel 26 August 1796; colonel (brevet) 1 January 1805; major-general 25 July 1810; lieutenant-general 12 August 1819; general 10 January 1837.

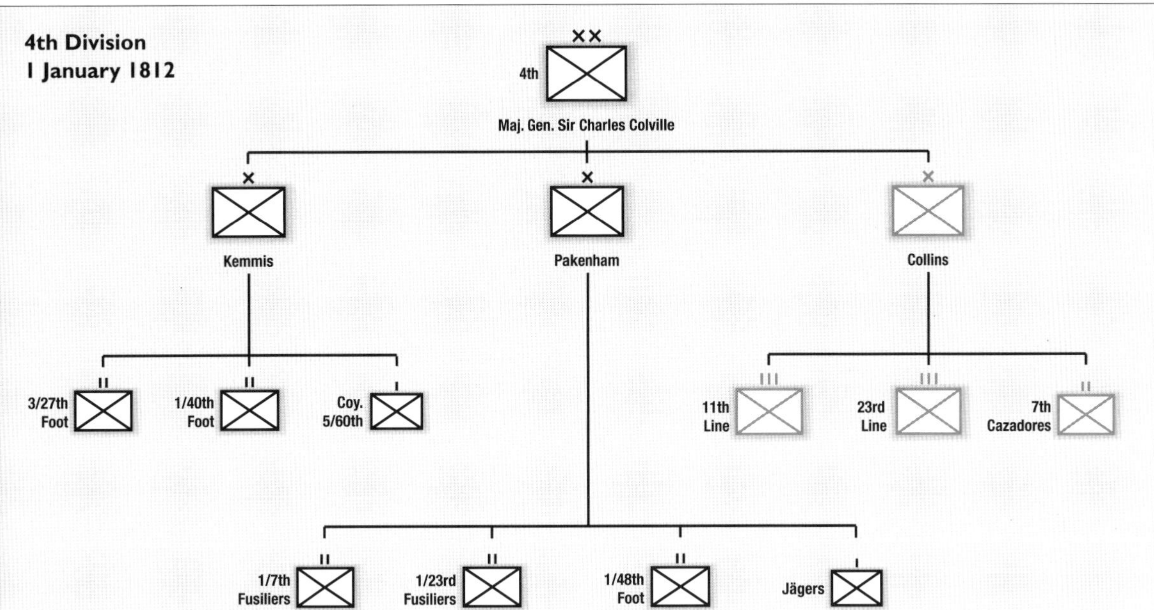

Subsequent alterations:

Colville was wounded at Badajoz in April, but the division was kept vacant until Cole returned in June. However, he in turn was wounded at Salamanca on 22 July and it appears to have been commanded by Maj. Gen. Sir William Anson until Cole again returned on 15 October.

Kemmis's Brigade:	Kemmis departed before 1 April and the brigade was commanded at Badajoz by Lt. Col. Charles Harcourt of 1/40th. It was taken over by Anson on 9 April. 1/48th Foot was transferred from Skerrett's Brigade after 17 October and 2/Provisional Battalion (2nd Foot & 1/53rd Foot) was added on 6 December.
Pakenham's Brigade:	Taken over by Maj. Gen. Barnard Bowes on 9 February. He was then transferred to 6th Division on 2 May and the brigade was commanded by Lt. Col. Henry Ellis of 1/23rd Fusiliers until Skerrett took over sometime towards the end of the year. 1/82nd Foot was posted to the brigade on 17 October, and 1/48th Foot was then transferred to Anson's Brigade. However, 1/82nd Foot was then transferred to 7th Division on 28 November and replaced by 20th Foot.
Skerrett's Brigade:	Skerrett was actually appointed to command Pakenham's Brigade on 17 October but appears to have remained in command of a brigade which he brought up from Cadiz which served with 4th Division from 26 October until it went into winter quarters at the end of the year. It was then broken up. It comprised 3/1st Guards, 2/47th Foot, 2/87th Foot and two companies of 2/95th Rifles.
Collins's Brigade:	Taken over by William Harvey before 17 March, and then by Thomas Stubbs at Salamanca.

Sir William Anson (b.1772)

Served on Continent 25 February to 25 April 1793, ordered home on promotion; again served on Continent 1 April 1794 to 9 May 1795 'when the army returned'; embarked for Sicily 25 July 1806 and returned to England 4 January 1808; embarked for Spain 9 September 1808, fought at Corunna and returned 30 January 1809; embarked for Zeeland (Walcheren) 16 July 1809 and back by 14 September 1809; served in Peninsula again, saw action at Salamanca, Vittoria, Pyrenees, Nivelle, Orthez and Toulouse.

Commissions: ensign 1st Footguards 13 June 1789; lieutenant and captain 25 April 1793; captain and lieutenant-colonel 28 September 1797; colonel (brevet) 30 October 1805; major-general 4 June 1811; lieutenant-general 12 August 1819; general 10 January 1837.

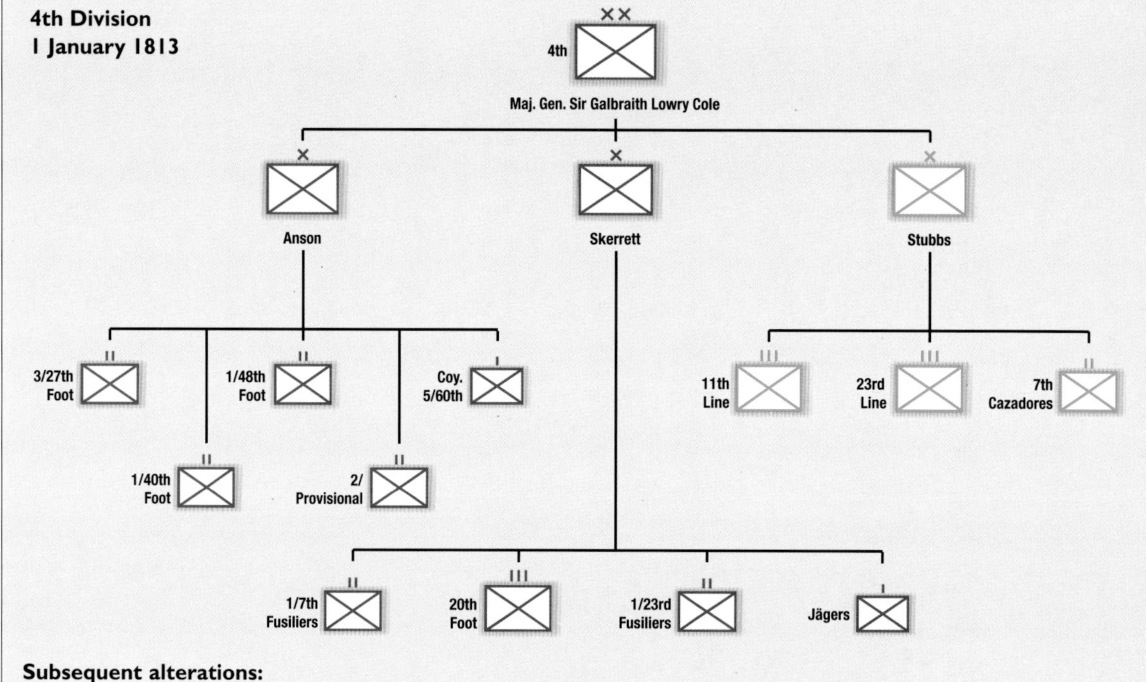

Subsequent alterations:

Skerrett's Brigade:	Skerrett was transferred to The Light Division on 2 July and the brigade taken over by Maj. Gen. Robert Ross.
Stubbs's Brigade:	Taken over by James Miller before 1 September and commanded at Nivelle by Jose de Vasconcelos.

The command structure and composition of the division was unchanged in 1814. Although Ross was wounded at Orthez on 27 February no replacement was appointed.

ABOVE The fight for the canal crossings at Toulouse, 1814. This may show a light company in action, but by this stage in the war the loose formations depicted here could have just as easily been adopted by any infantry unit.

5th Division – 'The Pioneers'

This division had a rather slow and uncertain gestation, which may be the origin of its curious nickname. The nucleus of the division was a brigade commanded by Maj. Gen. Sir James Leith comprising three battalions which had served at Walcheren – 3/1st Foot, 1/9th Foot and 2/38th. Although arriving at Lisbon in April 1810 they were very sickly with 'Walcheren Fever' and do not appear in army returns until 8 July. On 4 August the brigade was temporarily placed under the command of Lt. Col. James Stevenson Barnes of 3/1st Foot while Leith began preparations to form his division. On 30 September Barnes was superseded by Brig. Gen. Andrew Hay (also of 3/1st Foot) and on 6 October Leith was formally appointed to command the division. At the same time a Portuguese brigade under W.F. Spry was ordered to be added, together with a second British one although the latter does not appear to have been completed until over a month later – its commander, Maj. Gen. James Dunlop, was only appointed on 5 November and 1/4th Foot do not appear in returns until 15 November. In the meantime on 12 November a rifle company of the Brunswick Oels Jäger was added to each British brigade.

Served: Busaco, Fuentes de Oñoro, Badajoz, Salamanca, Burgos, Vittoria, San Sebastian, Bidassoa, Nivelle, Nive and Bayonne.

Sir James Leith (1763–1816)
Colonel 4th West India Regiment 1 January 1801; served Peninsula latterly in command of 5th Division, where badly, but not dangerously, wounded at Salamanca 22 July 1812; badly wounded at storming of San Sebastian 31 August 1813. Was Governor of Barbados when he died aged 53 on 16 October 1816.

Commissions: captain 23 November 1782; captain 50th Foot 25 June 1784; lieutenant-colonel Aberdeen (Princess of Wales) Fencibles 25 October 1794; colonel (brevet) 25 October 1794; major-general 25 April 1808; lieutenant-general (Spain and Portugal) 6 September 1811.

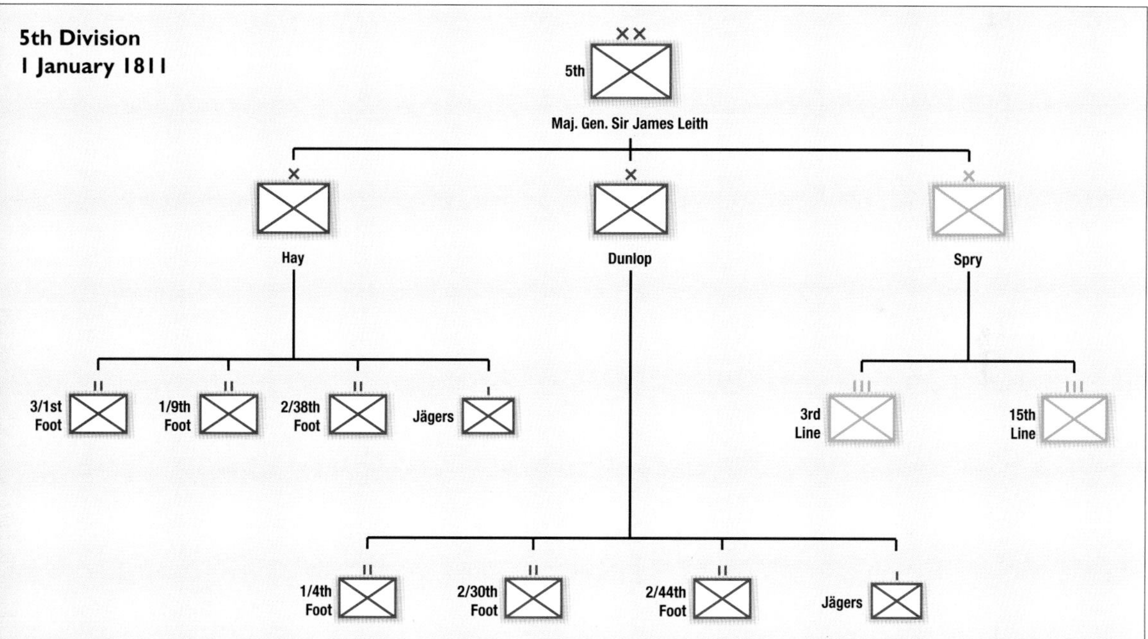

Subsequent alterations:

Leith was absent from 1 February, being temporarily replaced by Dunlop, until Sir William Erskine was appointed to command the division on 6 February. Erskine in turn was absent in command of the 'Advance Guard' between 7 March and 22 April and so Dunlop again acted up during this period and yet again after Erskine's permanent departure on 11 May, until finally superseded as both brigadier and acting divisional commander by Maj. Gen. George Townshend Walker on 2 October. Leith then returned to command the division on 1 December, having been appointed lieutenant-general 'in Spain and Portugal' on 6 September.

Dunlop's Brigade:	While Dunlop (and later Walker) was acting divisional commander the brigade was looked after by Lt. Col. Charles Bulkeley Egerton of 2/44th Foot.
Spry's Brigade:	2/Loyal Lusitanian Legion was added as the light infantry element on 14 March – and renamed 8th Cazadores by September.

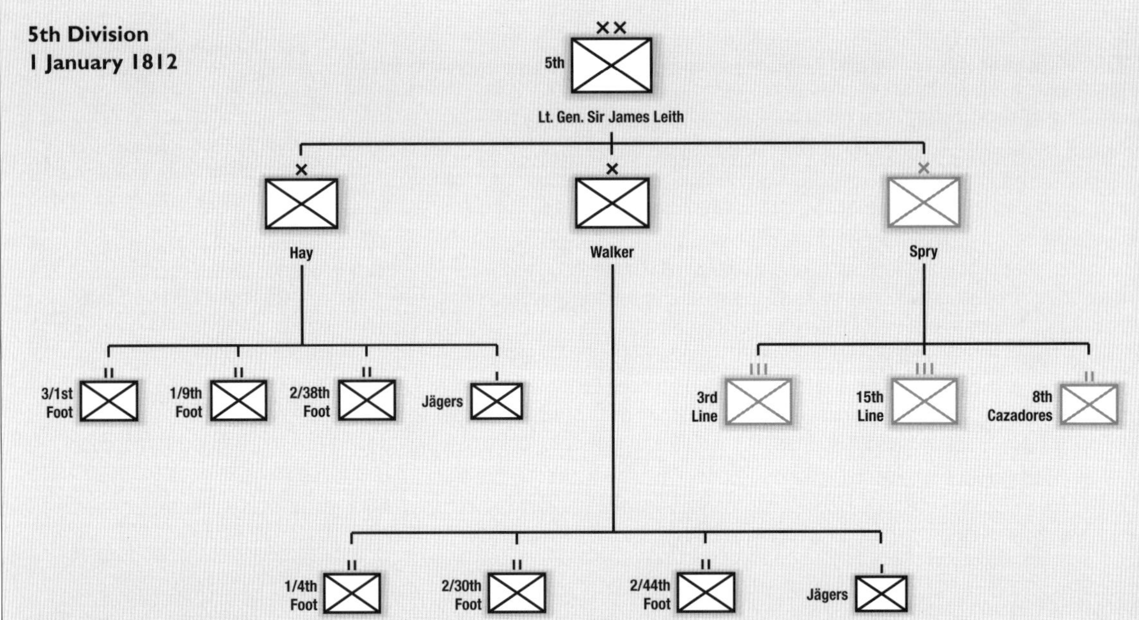

Subsequent alterations:

Leith was wounded at Salamanca and invalided home, being succeeded by Richard Hulse. However, Hulse died of natural causes on 7 September and was in turn succeeded temporarily by Pringle until Maj. Gen. John Oswald was appointed to command the division on 25 October.

Hay's Brigade: Hay went absent on 8 June and the brigade was temporarily commanded by Greville of 1/38th Foot until Richard Hulse was appointed on 31 July. However, since Hulse had to look after the division in Leith's absence after Salamanca, Greville probably remained in day-to-day command throughout. Col. Sir Edward Barnes was officially given command of the brigade on 28 October – although he seems to have been in actual command a few days earlier. On 6 December Barnes was transferred to 7th Division but Hay had returned by the end of the year.

1/38th Foot came out to the Peninsula in June and fought at Salamanca with the brigade although it was not officially posted in until 8 August. 2/38th Foot was ordered drafted into 1/38th on 6 December and then sent home.

Walker's Brigade: Walker was wounded at Badajoz and the brigade then had no designated commander until Maj. Gen. William Pringle was appointed on 28 June. While Pringle was in temporary command of the division after Hulse's death, the brigade was looked after by Lt. Col. Francis Brooke of 1/4th Foot.

2/4th Foot was posted to the brigade on 10 May but drafted into 1/4th Foot on 6 December and sent home. On the same date 2/30th Foot and 2/44th Foot were temporarily amalgamated as 4/Provisional Battalion. In the meantime 2/47th Foot was posted to the brigade on 17 October.

John Oswald (1771–1840)

Born at Dunnikier, Fife 2 October 1771. Served Martinique, St. Lucia, Guadaloupe. Badly wounded at Helder 19 September 1799. Served in Mediterranean; Malta, Maida and the capture of Scylla, then Peninsula; commanded 5th Division in absence of Sir James Leith. Slightly wounded at storming of San Sebastian 31 August 1813. Married (1) Charlotte Murray-Aynsley 1812, (2) Emily Jane Murray 1829. Died at Dunnikier 8 June 1840. Described as a handsome six-footer who was very formidable in hand to hand combat as at the capture of Scylla in 1806.

Commissions: second lieutenant 7th Fusiliers 1 February 1788; lieutenant 29 January 1789; captain Independent Company 24 January 1791; captain 35th Foot 23 March 1791; major 1 September 1795; lieutenant-colonel 35th Foot 30 March 1797; colonel (brevet) 30 October 1805; major-general 4 June 1811; lieutenant-general 12 August 1819; general 10 January 1837.

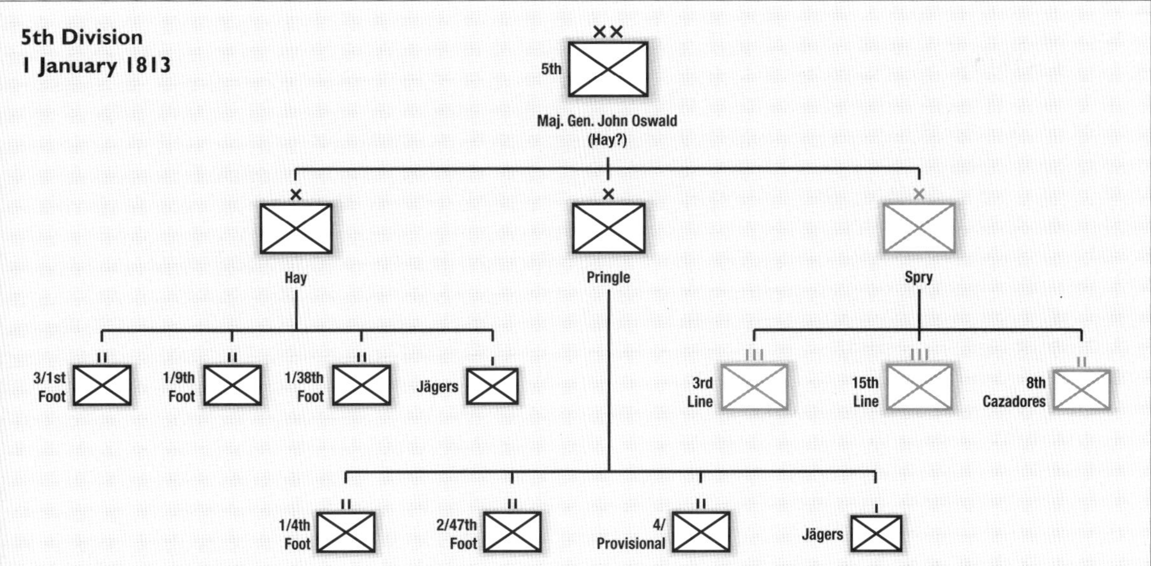

Subsequent alterations:

Oswald was absent at the beginning of the year and Hay appears to have commanded the division until he returned sometime in April. Leith then resumed command on 30 August but was wounded at San Sebastian on 1 September. Oswald happened to be still on hand and briefly took over the division again, but by 9 October command had temporarily reverted to Hay, pending Sir Charles Colville's appointment sometime in December.

Hay's Brigade: On both occasions while Hay was commanding the division Greville of 1/38th Foot again looked after the brigade.

2/47th Foot was transferred in from Robinson's Brigade (see below).

Pringle's Brigade: Col. Frederick Phillipse Robinson was appointed to command the brigade on 9 March. On his being wounded outside Bayonne on 10 December command passed to Piper of 1/4th Foot, but he in turn was wounded next day and so was succeeded in turn by Tonson of 2/84th Foot.

2/59th Foot was posted to the brigade on 12 April and 4/Provisional Battalion ordered home on 10 May. On 17 October 2/84th Foot was posted in from Aylmer's Brigade of 1st Division, and 2/47th Foot transferred to Hay's Brigade.

Spry's Brigade: Luiz de Rego Barreto was in command of the brigade at the Bidassoa on 9 October and thereafter until the end of the war.

William Henry Pringle (dates unknown)
Served Peninsula, at Salamanca; temporarily commanded 5th Division; commanded brigade at Maya 1813, Nive, Nivelle, badly wounded at St Palais 15 February 1814.

Commissions: cornet 16th Light Dragoons 6 July 1792; lieutenant 24 February 1793; captain 15 October 1794; major 111th Foot 19 September 1794, reduced 1795; lieutenant-colonel 5 December 1799; colonel (brevet) 25 October 1809; major-general 1 January 1812; lieutenant-general 27 May 1825.

Andrew Hay (1762–1814)
Served in Peninsula, wounded during Corunna campaign; commanded brigade in 5th Division – temporarily commanded division – and was killed in action during sortie from Bayonne 14 April 1814.

Commissions: captain (late) 72nd Foot, half-pay by reduction 1783; major 1 September 1794; major 93rd Foot 9 December 1795 – reduced; lieutenant colonel 1 January 1798; lieutenant-colonel 3/1st (Royal) Regt 19 March 1807; major-general 4 June 1811.

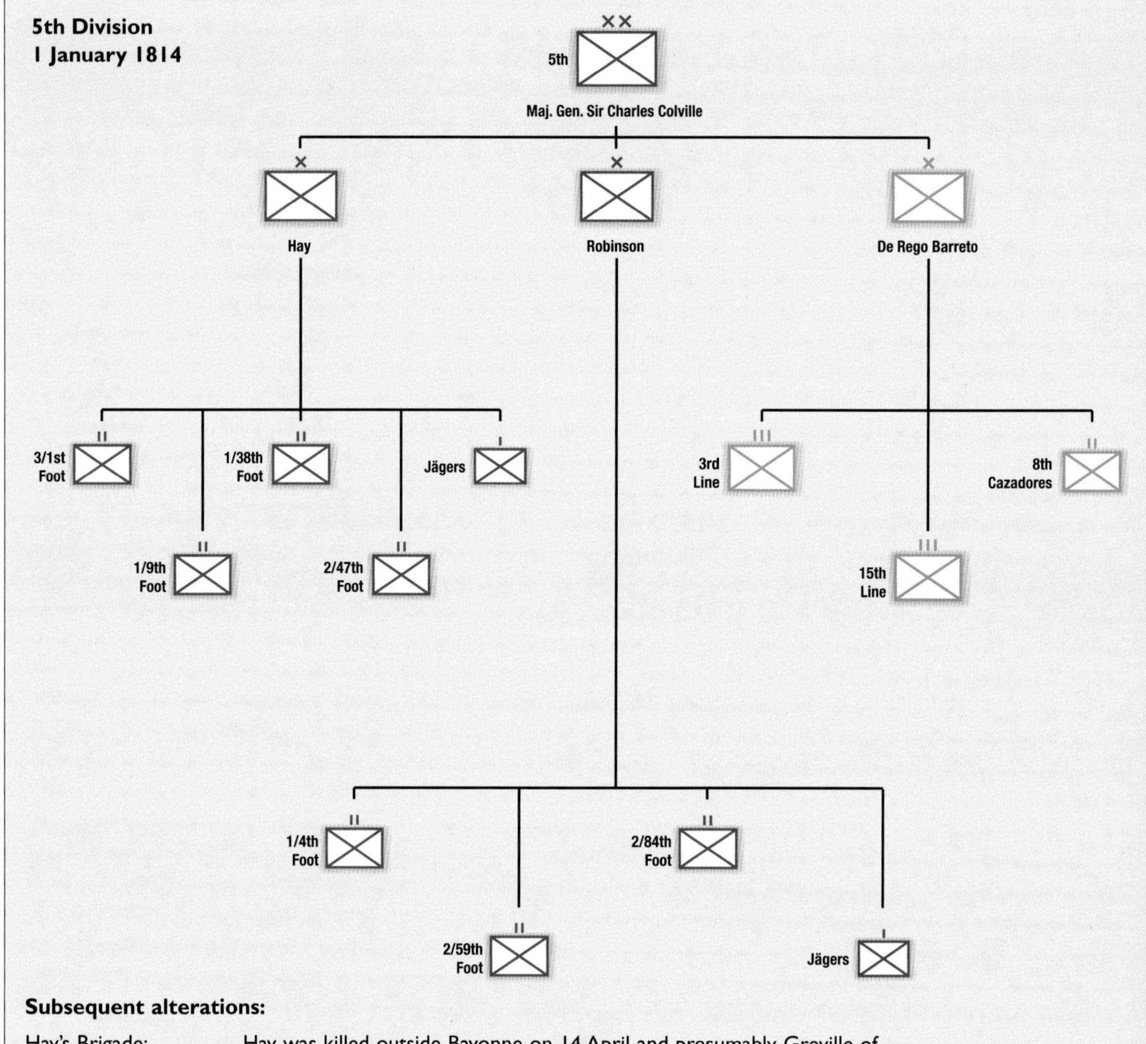

Subsequent alterations:

Hay's Brigade:	Hay was killed outside Bayonne on 14 April and presumably Greville of 1/38th Foot took over the brigade again as usual.
Robinson's Brigade:	Although returning to duty shortly after being wounded, Robinson was compelled to return home on 1 February and Tonson again took over.

James Dunlop (1758?–1832)
Served in North America during Revolutionary War. Served India 1789–1800; Cannanore, Seringapatam 1791–92 and afterwards on Bombay staff as military secretary to Governor until returning to regiment in 1796; served at Seedaseer and Seringapatam 1799 where wounded in command of one of the assault columns; returned to England 1800; appointed to Western District Staff 1804, then Eastern District in command of Highland Brigade at Colchester until taken off Staff in June 1806; served on staff in Peninsula October 1810 and commanded brigade in 5th Division, taking over the division in December and leading it throughout 1811 campaign.

Commissions: lieutenant 82nd Foot January 1778; captain May 1782, half-pay 1784; captain 77th Foot 1787; major (brevet) May 1794; major 77th Foot September 1795; lieutenant-colonel 12 November 1795; colonel (brevet) 25 September 1803; exchanged into 59th Regiment 1803; brigadier-general 25 July 1804; major-general 25 July 1810; lieutenant-general 4 June 1814.

6th Division – 'The Marching Division'

The division was ordered to be formed on 6 October 1810 by taking Alexander Campbell's Brigade from 4th Division and adding Baron Eben's Independent Portuguese Brigade. Since Campbell was to be G.O.C. of the division, Richard Hulse was appointed to command his brigade on 14 November and on 17 November 1/61st Foot replaced 2/7th Fusiliers who went back to 4th Division on the formation of the Fusilier Brigade.

Served: Fuentes de Oñoro, Salamanca, Burgos, Vittoria, Sorauren I and II, Nivelle, Nive, Orthez and Toulouse.

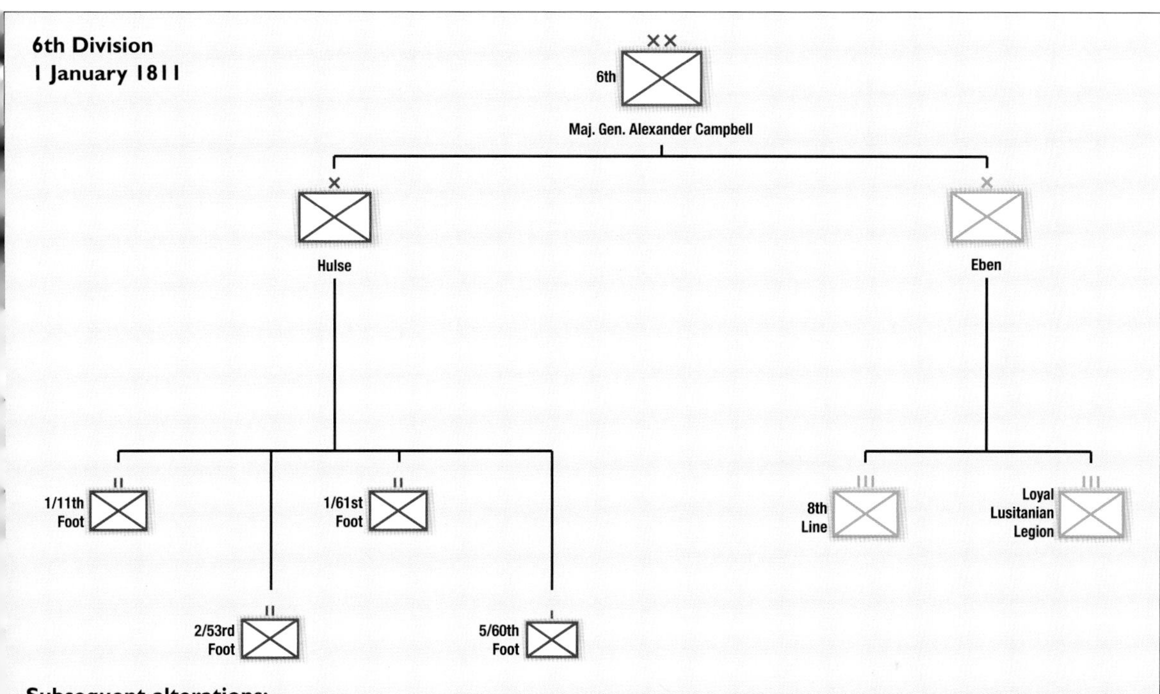

Subsequent alterations:

Campbell was ordered out to India in November, and temporarily replaced by Maj. Gen. Robert Burne.

Burne's Brigade:	A new brigade formed and added to the division on 5 March. Initially comprising 2nd Foot and 1/36th Foot, it was joined by 1/32nd Foot on 21 July.
Eben's Brigade:	On 14 May the two battalions of the Loyal Lusitanian Legion were transferred as cazadores to the 4th and 5th divisions, and were replaced by the 12th Line. At about the same time Eben himself was temporarily replaced as brigade commander by George Madden.

Robert Burne (1755–1825)

Served Peninsula in command of 6th Division. Governor of Carlisle 8 September 1818.

Commissions: ensign 36th Foot 28 September 1773; lieutenant 13 January 1777; captain 7 May 1784; major (brevet) 1 March 1794; major 36th Foot 15 April 1794; lieutenant-colonel (brevet) 1 January 1798; lieutenant-colonel 36th Foot 13 November 1799; colonel (brevet) 25 April 1808; major-general 4 June 1811.

Sir Henry Clinton (1771–1829)

Second son of Sir Henry Clinton KCB. ADC to Duke of York 1795; commanded 6th Division in Peninsula and also had a division at Waterloo. Married 1799, died 11 December 1829.

Commissions: ensign 10 October 1787; ensign 1st Footguards 12 March 1789; lieutenant and captain 30 November 1792; captain and lieutenant-colonel 20 October 1796; lieutenant-general.

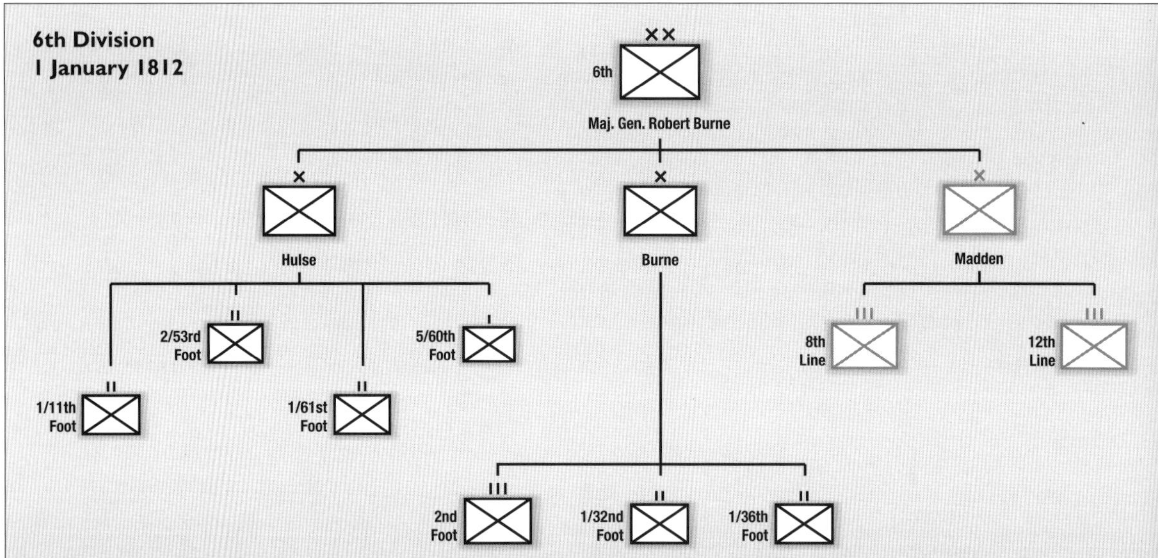

Subsequent alterations:

Lt. Gen. Sir Henry Clinton was appointed to command the division on 9 February.

Hulse's Brigade:	Hulse was transferred to command a brigade in 5th Division on 31 July and Lt. Col. George Bingham of 2/53rd Foot then took over until both brigades were amalgamated under Hinde on 11 November. This became necessary when 2/53rd and 2nd Foot were formed into 2/Provisional Battalion and transferred to 4th Division.
Burne's Brigade:	Burne had left by 1 April and was replaced by Maj. Gen. Barnard Bowes on 2 May; he in turn was killed in the attack on the San Cayetano fort at Salamaca on 24 June, and Hinde of 1/32nd Foot then took over. Amalgamated with Bingham's Brigade on 11 November.
Stirling's Brigade (Highland Brigade):	Transferred from 1st Division when both the original brigades were amalgamated on 11 November. At this time it comprised 1/42nd and 1/79th Foot, although 1/91st Foot joined it on 14 December.
Madden's Brigade:	Eben seems to have remained in nominal command until 30 April when the Conde de Rezende took command. He, however, was invalided on 4 October and George Madden again took over. 9th Cazadores were posted to the brigade on 10 April.

Hon. Edward Michael Pakenham (1778–1815)

Second son of Earl of Longford. Served Ireland 1798 then West Indies 1801–03; wounded St Lucia 1803; served Copenhagen 1807 and Martinique 1809; wounded in assault 1 February; served Peninsula, appointed A-AG 15 November 1809 and D-AG 3 March 1810; also acted as Adjutant General during Stewart's absences from December 1809 to January 1810 and again from December 1810 to May 1811, before finally resigning as D-AG 1 January 1812; in the meantime, appointed to a brigade in 1st Division August 1810 and took command of 3rd Division after Picton wounded at Badajoz, then transferred to 6th Division 1813; appointed Adjutant General 10 May 1813 but resumed command of 6th Division 30 July at Sorauren; again Adjutant General August 1813 to end of Peninsular War; appointed to command North America 24 October 1814 and killed at New Orleans 8 January 1815.

Commissions: ensign 92nd Foot 1794; major 33rd Light Dragoons 6 December 1794, exchanged to 23rd Light Dragoons 1798; lieutenant-colonel 64th Foot 1799, exchanged to 1/7th Fusiliers 1805; major-general (Portugal and Spain) 1811; major-general 1812.

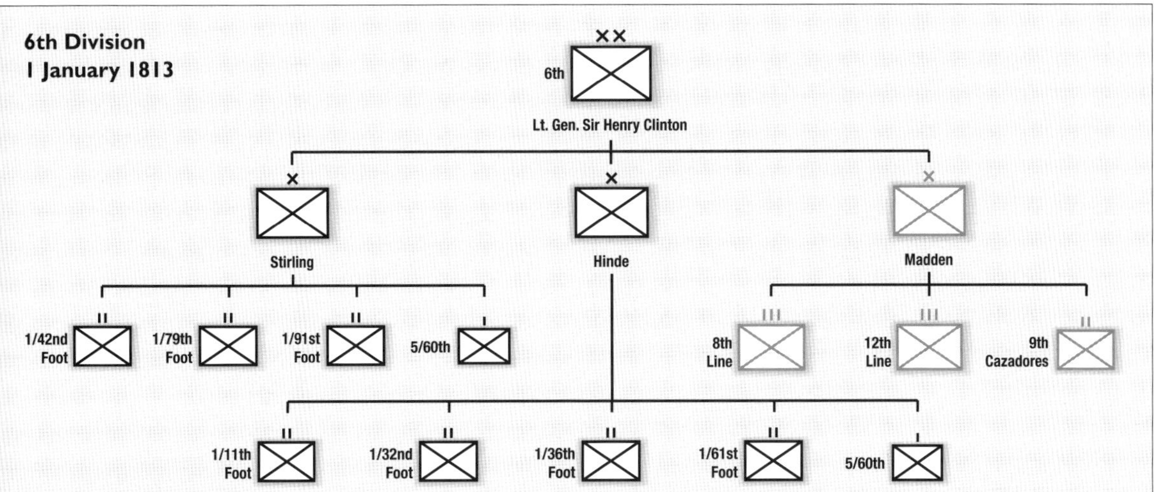

Subsequent alterations:

Clinton was temporarily replaced by Pakenham on 26 January, but upon the latter being appointed Adjutant General on 25 June, Clinton briefly returned. Denis Pack then got the division on 22 July only to be wounded at Sorauren on 28 July. This necessitated Pakenham taking over again before command passed to Colville by 8 August. Clinton then returned to the division shortly after 9 October.

Stirling's Brigade (Highland Brigade):	Maj. Gen. Sir Denis Pack was appointed to command the brigade on 2 July. Stirling then reverted to command of 1/42nd Foot but again commanded the brigade when Pack moved on up to command the division. However, when Clinton returned to duty in October Pack resumed command of the brigade and Stirling went home.
Hinde's Brigade:	Maj. Gen. Sir John Lambert was appointed to command *vice* Hinde on 2 July – both Lambert and Pack receiving their brigades as a direct result of having been promoted to major-general on 4 June.
Madden's Brigade:	Taken over by James Douglas of 8th Line in August.

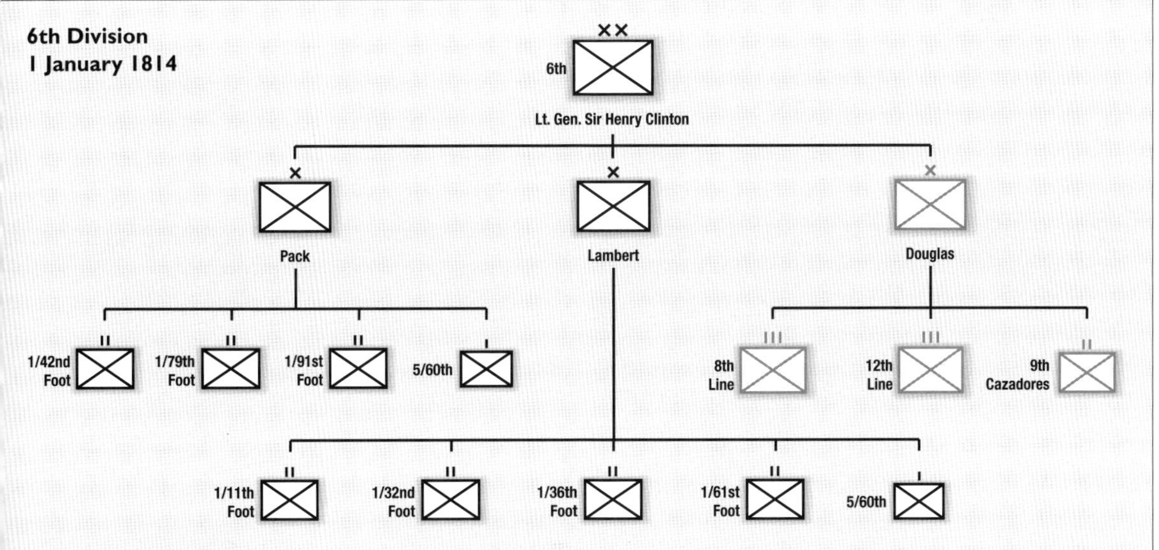

Subsequent alterations:

None of any consequence. Both Pack and Douglas were wounded at Toulouse. 1/32nd Foot missed the battle having been sent to St Jean de Luz for reclothing.

7th Division – 'The Mongrels'

First ordered to be formed on 5 March 1811 under Maj. Gen. William Houston, this was certainly the most cosmopolitan (and diversely uniformed) of Wellington's divisions. Consequently, although its officers tried hard to convince anyone who would listen to them that they were another Light Division, the rest of the army persisted in unkindly referring to them as 'The Mongrels'.

Served: Fuentes de Oñoro, Salamanca, Burgos, Vittoria, Maya, Sorouren II, Salain, Nivelle, and Orthez.

William Houston 1766–1842
Born 10 August 1766. Served at taking of Minorca; Egypt 1801; Walcheren 1809, and Peninsula; commanded 7th Division at Fuentes de Oñoro. Married Lady Jane Maoland 1808 with issue.

Commissions: ensign 18 July 1781; lieutenant 2 April 1782; captain 13 March 1783; captain 19th Foot 20 July 1785; major 1 March 1794; lieutenant-colonel 18 March 1795; lieutenant-colonel 58th Foot 10 June 1795; colonel (brevet) 29 April 1802; major-general 25 October 1809; lieutenant-general 4 June 1814; general 10 January 1837.

Died at Bromley Hill, Kent, 8 April 1842.

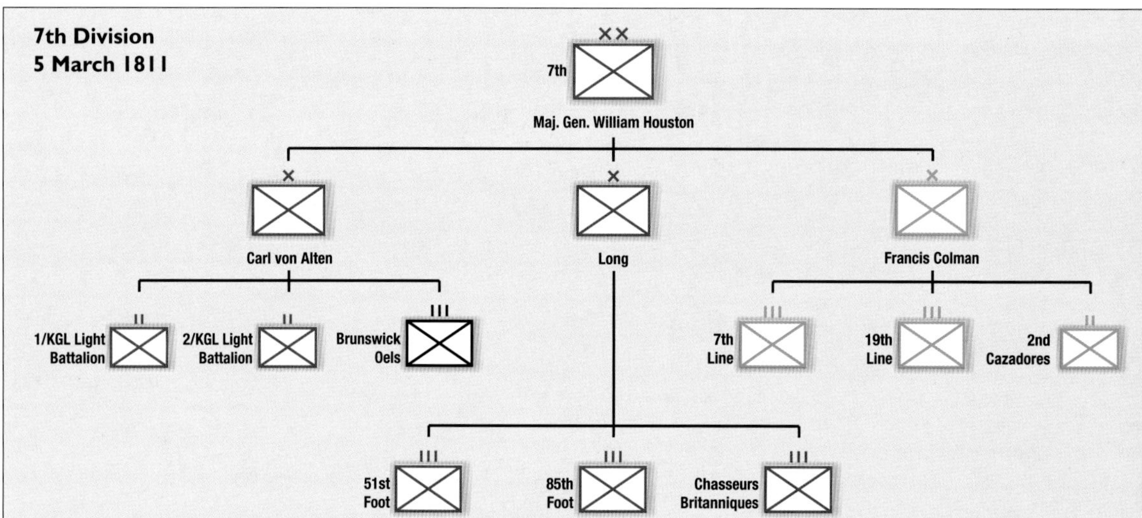

Both KGL light battalions were in Estramadura with Beresford at the time and did not join the division until after the siege of Badajoz. At this point it may be observed that the first brigade had two battalions dressed in green and one in black; the second brigade was dressed in red, and the third brigade was in blue and brown.

Subsequent alterations:

Houston was invalided home sometime before 1 August, when Sontag was appointed to command the division in his place. Sontag, however, was in turn invalided on 15 October and Carl von Alten therefore took over.

Alten's Brigade:	When Alten took command of the division, his brigade passed to Colin Halkett.
Long's Brigade:	On 19 March Long was transferred to command Beresford's cavalry and replaced on 31 March by Maj. Gen. John Sontag. Between 1 August and 15 October Sontag also commanded the division and the brigade was probably looked after by de Bernewitz of 68th Foot, although he was not confirmed in this role until 23 December.
	68th Foot was posted to the brigade on 19 July, and 85th Foot ordered home to recruit on 3 October.
Colman's Brigade:	Taken over first by Frederico Lecor shortly after joining the division, then by Luis Palmeirim between May and August. Colman resumed command on 12 August.

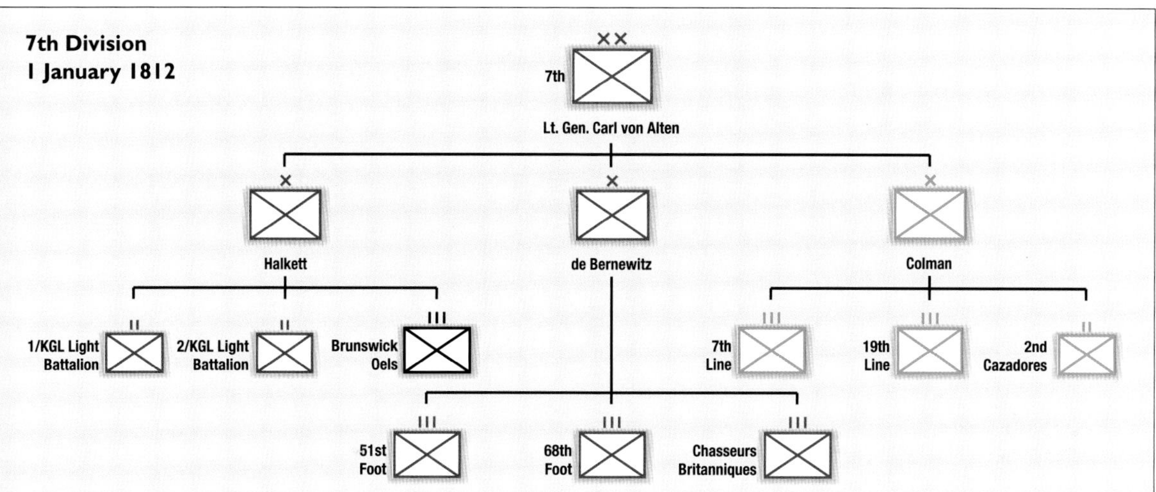

Subsequent alterations:

On 2 May Alten was transferred to command the Light Division and replaced by Lt. Gen. Sir John Hope. Unfortunately Hope went sick on 23 September and was not replaced by Maj. Gen. George, Earl of Dalhousie until 25 October.

Halkett's Brigade: Taken over by Col. Edward Barnes on 3 December. On 28 November 1/6th Foot was posted to the brigade, but on 6 December both KGL battalions were transferred to 2nd Division and replaced by 3/Provisional Battalion (2/24th and 2/58th Foot).

De Bernewitz's Brigade: 1/82nd Foot was posted to the brigade from 4th Division on 28 November.

Colman's Brigade: Colman died on 12 December 1811 'from fever and debility, brought on by exertions' in Portugal. However, Richard Collins did not take over the brigade until 27 February.

John Sontag (d.1816)
Served Helder 1799 as ADC to Sir Ralph Abercromby; Military Superintendent of Hospitals; served Peninsula, successively commanded brigade in 7th Division, then the division itself for a time before being invalided home in October 1811.

Commissions: lieutenant-colonel (Brevet) 5 October 1795; colonel (brevet) 25 September 1803; major-general 25 July 1810; lieutenant-general 4 June 1814.

Sir John Hope, Earl of Hopetoun (1765–1823)
Colonel 92nd Highlanders 3 January 1806; appointed to command 7th Division 2 May 1812, then 1st Division 1813; commanded left wing of army during invasion of France 1814, but wounded and made a p.o.w. during sortie from Bayonne 14 April 1814. Died in Paris 22 August 1823.

Commissions: captain 17th Light Dragoons 31 October 1789; lieutenant-colonel 25th Foot 26 April 1793; colonel (brevet) 3 May 1796; lieutenant-general 25 April 1808.

George Ramsay, Earl of Dalhousie (1770–1838)
Served Gibraltar; commanded 2nd Foot on Martinique – badly wounded there in 1795; served Ireland 1798, Helder 1799 and Egypt 1801, Walcheren and the Peninsula; appointed to command 7th Division 25 October 1812; captain-general and C-in-C of forces in North America 1819.

Commissions: cornet 3rd Dragoon Guards 2 July 1787; captain of Independent Company; captain 2/1st (Royal) Regt 4 January 1791; major 2nd Foot 27 June 1792; lieutenant-colonel 22 August 1794; colonel (brevet) 1 January 1800; major-general 25 April 1805; lieutenant-general 4 June 1813.

George Townshend Walker (1764–1842)
Served Flanders 1793; Tournai; Copenhagen 1807; Walcheren and Peninsula; badly wounded at Badajoz 6 April 1812, and less seriously wounded at Orthez 27 February 1814, while commanding 7th Division.

Commissions: second lieutenant 4 March 1782; lieutenant 13 March 1783; captain-lieutenant 14th Foot 13 March 1789; captain 60th Foot 4 May 1791; major 28 August 1794; lieutenant-colonel 50th Foot 6 September 1798; colonel (brevet) 25 April 1808; major-general 4 June 1811; lieutenant-general 19 July 1821; general 28 June 1838.

7th Division
1 January 1813

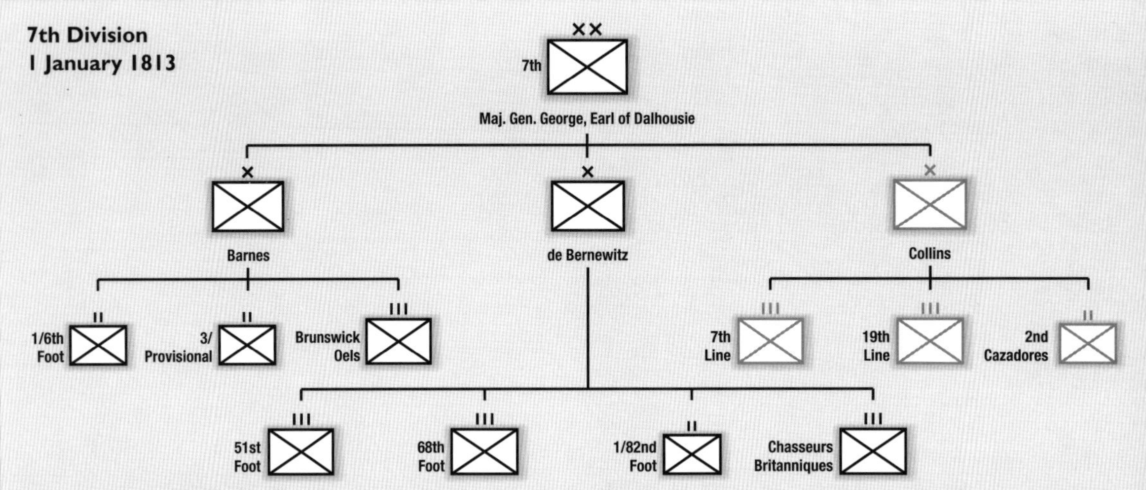

Subsequent alterations:

Dalhousie went home after the crossing of the Bidassoa on 9 October and was temporarily replaced by the Portuguese general Carlos Le Cor. However, Le Cor was transferred to take command of Hamilton's Portuguese Division on 18 November and Maj. Gen. George Townshend Walker was appointed to command the 7th Division 'in Dalhousie's absence'.

Barnes's Brigade:	Barnes went to 2nd Division on 20 November and his brigade was taken over by Gardiner.
de Bernewitz's Brigade:	Brig. Gen. William Inglis was appointed to command the brigade on 21 May (and made major-general on 4 June) but did not actually take over until the campaign in the Pyrenees. Lt. Col. William Grant of 1/82nd Foot was badly wounded while commanding the brigade at Vittoria.
Collins's Brigade:	Collins was killed on 17 February and between March and October the brigade was commanded by Frederico Le Cor, and thereafter by John Doyle.

7th Division
1 January 1814

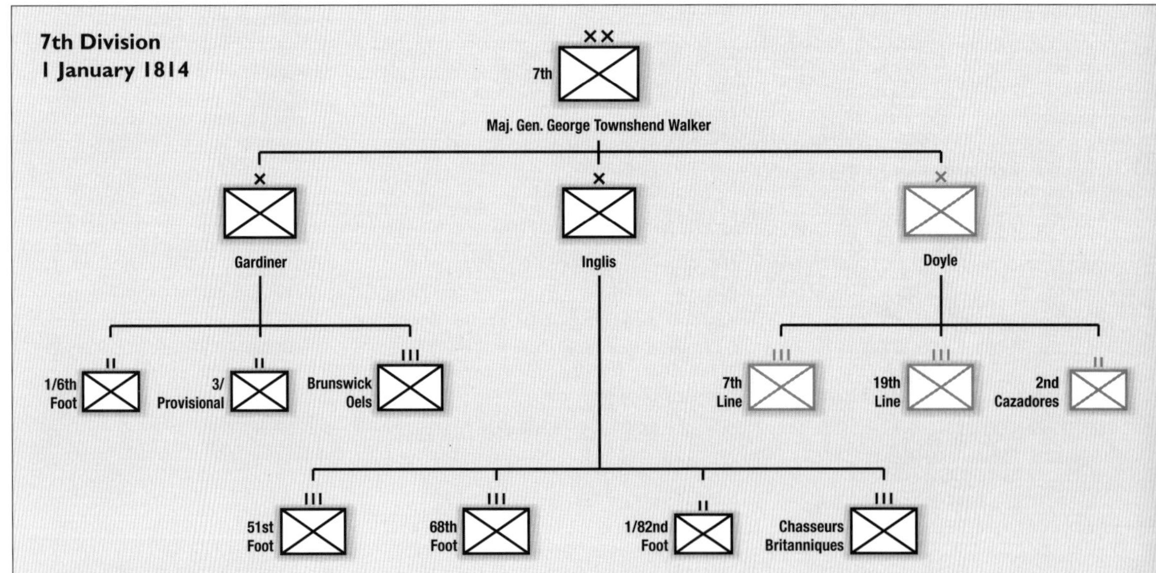

Subsequent alterations:

Walker was wounded at Orthez, and Dalhousie returned to resume command of the division almost immediately afterwards.

The Light Division – 'The Division'

Formed on 22 February 1810 under Brig. Gen. Robert 'Bob' Craufurd, it was initially no more than a reinforced brigade comprising 1/43rd Foot, 1/52nd Foot and 1/95th taken from 3rd Division and two Portuguese battalions (1st and 3rd Cazadores). However, on 4 August it was reorganised into two equal-sized brigades under Col. Thomas Beckwith of 1/95th and Lt. Col. Robert Barclay of 1/52nd Foot. Its numerical weakness was to some extent offset by the near permanent attachment of the 1st Hussars KGL, and later the Cavalry Staff Corps.

Served: Busaco, Fuentes de Oñoro, Ciudad Rodrigo, Badajoz, Salamanca, Burgos, Vittoria, Vera, Bidassoa, Nivelle, Nive, Orthez and Toulouse.

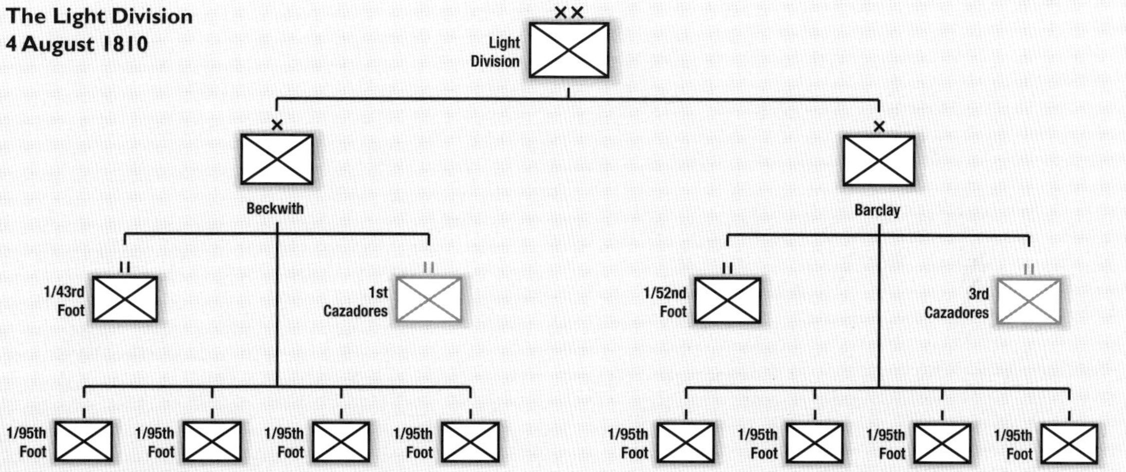

The Light Division 4 August 1810

- XX Light Division
  - X Beckwith
    - II 1/43rd Foot
    - II 1st Cazadores
    - I 1/95th Foot
    - I 1/95th Foot
    - I 1/95th Foot
    - I 1/95th Foot
  - X Barclay
    - II 1/52nd Foot
    - II 3rd Cazadores
    - I 1/95th Foot
    - I 1/95th Foot
    - I 1/95th Foot
    - I 1/95th Foot

Subsequent alterations:

Beckwith's Brigade:	One company of 2/95th Foot joined the brigade at some time before 1 October.
Barclay's Brigade:	Barclay was wounded at Busaco and consequently replaced as brigade commander by Lt. Col. James Wynch of 1/4th Foot.
	On 12 November nine companies of the Brunswick Oels Jäger were posted to the brigade.

Robert Craufurd (1764–1812)

Born Newark, Ayrshire, 5 May 1764. Served India 1790–92; resigned 17 October 1793 but took up liaison positions with Austrian Staff 1793–97; served Waldstein's Chasseurs and Hompesch's Chasseurs; D-QMG Ireland 1798; served as liaison officer with Russo-Austrian forces Switzerland 1799 and on Helder Expedition same year; commanded brigade at Buenos Aires, then commanded Light Brigade in Peninsula 1808 – successfully evacuated it from Vigo; returned to Peninsula with brigade 1809, subsequently enlarged to division. Killed at storming of Ciudad Rodrigo 19 January 1812.

Commissions: ensign 25th Foot 1779; captain 11 December 1782, on half-pay 1783 but exchanged to 75th Foot 1 November 1787; colonel (brevet) 26 January 1797; lieutenant-colonel 60th Foot 1797; brigadier-general 1810; major-general 4 June 1811.

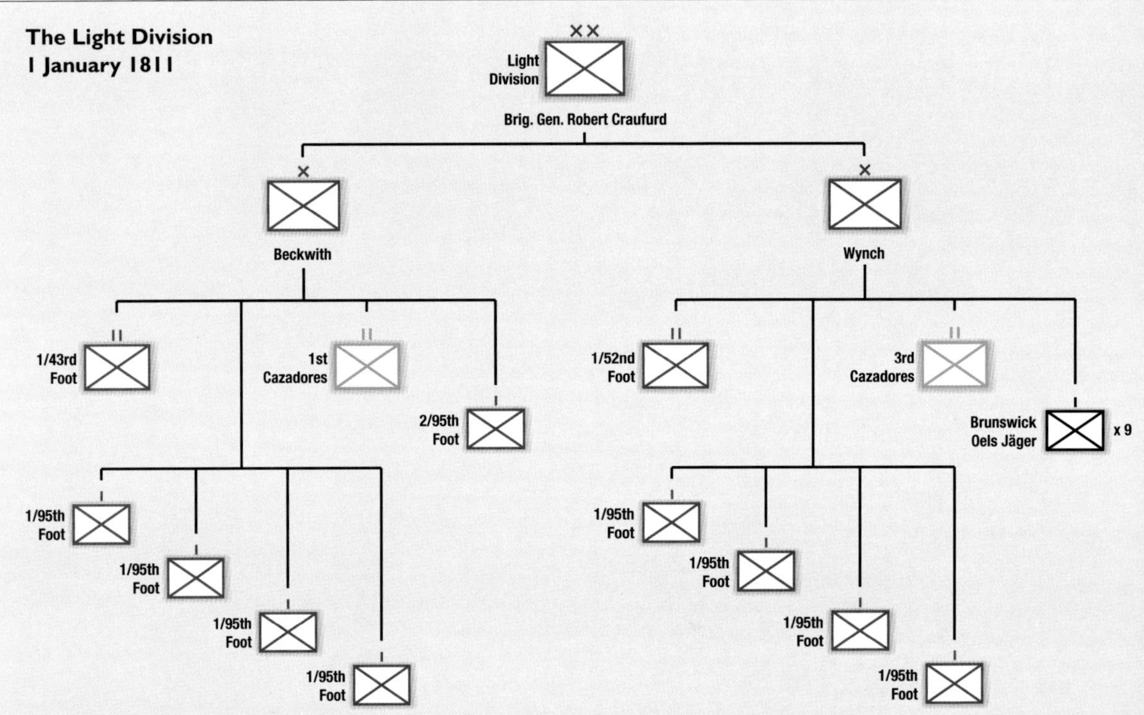

Subsequent alterations:

Craufurd went on leave shortly before 8 February, but the division was temporarily commanded by Maj. Gen. Erskine between 7 March and his return on 22 April. He was himself promoted to major-general on 4 June 1811.

Beckwith's Brigade: Beckwith was invalided home on 1 August and replaced by Lt. Col. Andrew Barnard of 1/43rd Foot. RHQ and five companies of 3/95th Foot were posted to the brigade on 21 August. A second company of 2/95th was also posted to the brigade by 1 October.

Wynch's Brigade: Wynch died of typhus at Lisbon on 6 January 1811 and was replaced on 7 February by Col. George Drummond of 1/52nd Foot. He in turn died of 'malignant fever' on 8 September 1811 and was succeeded by Maj. Gen. John Ormsby Vandeleur on 30 September.

The Brunswick Oels, having made themselves thoroughly detested by the rest of the division, were posted to the newly formed 7th Division on 5 March. They were replaced on the same day by the newly arrived 2/52nd Foot.

Sir Andrew Francis Barnard (1773–1855)

Born Fahan, Co. Donegal, son of Rev. Henry Barnard DD. Inspecting Field Officer of Militia in Canada and Nova Scotia 28 January 1808; served in Peninsula, badly wounded at Barossa 5 March 1811; served at Ciudad Rodrigo and Badajoz, briefly commanded Light Division; badly wounded at Nivelle; served at Waterloo; Lieutenant-Governor Chelsea Hospital 26 November 1849. Died at Chelsea Hospital 17 January 1855.

Commissions: ensign 90th Foot 26 August 1794; lieutenant 81st Foot 23 September 1794; captain-lieutenant 13 November 1794; captain 29 September 1795, exchanged 2 December 1795 to 55th Foot; captain and lieutenant-colonel 1st Footguards 19 December 1799; major 7th West India Regiment 2 January 1808; lieutenant-colonel (Staff) 28 January 1808; lieutenant-colonel 1st (Royal) 15 December 1808, exchanged 29 March 1810 to 43rd Foot, then 1/95th Rifles; colonel (brevet) 4 June 1813; major-general 12 August 1819; lieutenant-general 10 January 1837.

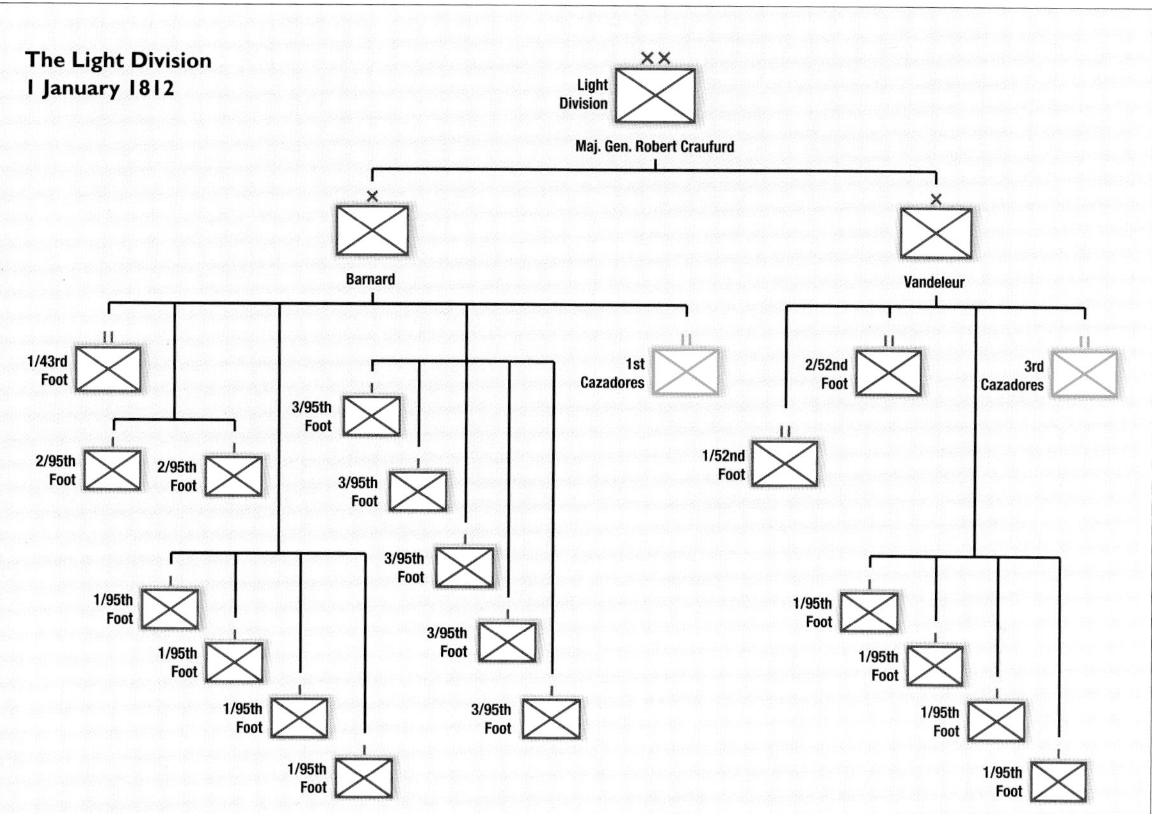

Subsequent alterations:

Craufurd was killed at Ciudad Rodrigo on 19 January and since Vandeleur was wounded at the same time, Lt. Col. Barnard took temporary command of the division. Vandeleur was fit enough for duty by 15 April, but Lt. Gen. Carl von Alten was appointed to command the division on 2 May.

Barnard's Brigade: When Alten took over the division the 1/95th companies were transferred to join the others in Vandeleur's Brigade. On 24 August they were again split up, but then re-united again at the end of the year – this time in what was still being referred to as 'Beckwith's Brigade'. The two companies of 2/95th were also transferred to Vandeleur's Brigade at the beginning of May.

Vandeleur's Brigade: When Vandeleur was wounded at Ciudad Rodrigo the brigade was taken over by Lt. Col. Edward Gibbs of 1/52nd Foot. He in turn was wounded, losing an eye at Badajoz, but Vandeleur resumed command on 15 April.

2/52nd Foot was drafted into 1/52nd on 23 February and the cadre sent home to recruit. By 8 May all the 1/95th companies were serving in the brigade, but half of them went back to the other brigade on 24 August and the remainder followed by the end of the year. At the beginning of May the two companies of 2/95th were transferred across from 'Beckwith's Brigade' and joined by four others.

Charles von Alten (1764–1840)
ADC Baron de Reden 1790; served Flanders 1793–95 as ADC to Freytag; served Germany 1805 under Cathcart; commanded brigade at Copenhagen 1807; subsequently served Walcheren and in Peninsula, successively commanding 7th and Light divisions. Badly wounded at Waterloo. Later became Inspector General and Minister of War.

Commissions: ensign Hanovarian Guards 24 July 1781; captain 1790; major 30 October 1795; lieutenant-colonel 1802; transferred to British service as lieutenant-colonel 1/KGL Light Battalion 16 November 1803; colonel commandant 1803; major-general July 1810; lieutenant-general (Europe) same date; *general der infanterie* (Hanovarian Army) September 1816.

The Light Division
1 January 1813

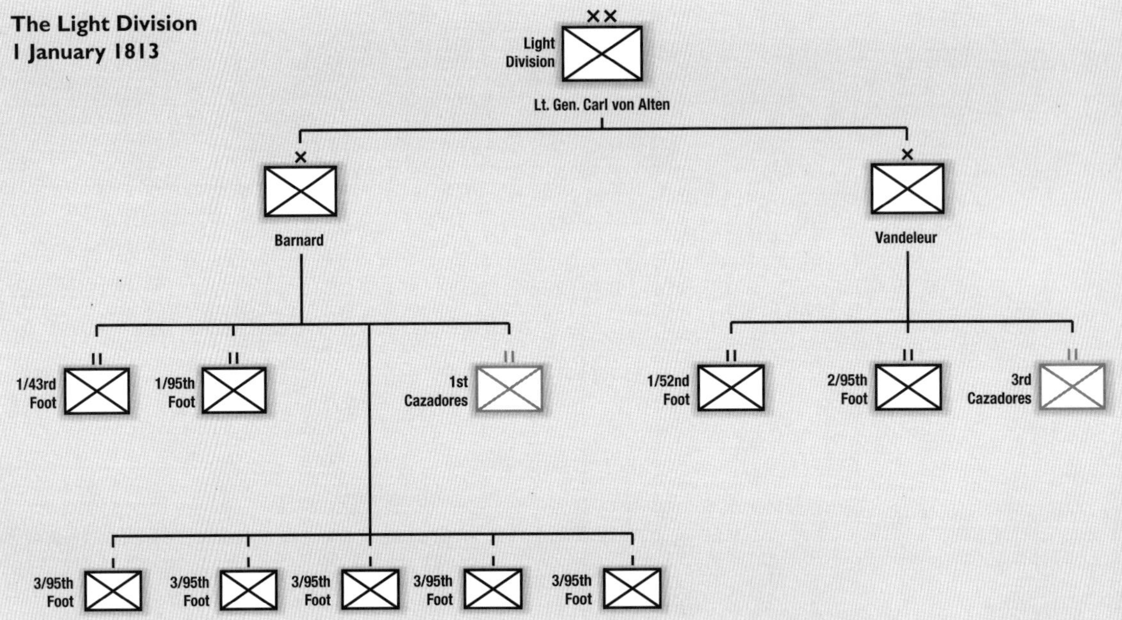

XX
Light Division
Lt. Gen. Carl von Alten
X
Barnard
X
Vandeleur
II
1/43rd Foot
II
1/95th Foot
II
1st Cazadores
II
1/52nd Foot
II
2/95th Foot
II
3rd Cazadores
I
3/95th Foot
I
3/95th Foot
I
3/95th Foot
I
3/95th Foot
I
3/95th Foot

Subsequent alterations:

Barnard's Brigade: Barnard remained in temporary command of what was still being referred to as 'Beckwith's Brigade' until 23 March when Maj. Gen. Sir James Kempt was appointed to it.

Vandeleur's Brigade: On 2 July Vandeleur was given a cavalry brigade and was succeeded by Maj. Gen. John B. Skerrett. However, he went home in September and was succeeded in turn by Lt. Col. John Colborne of 1/52nd Foot.

The Portuguese 20th Line was assigned to the brigade in October 1812 but never joined and instead the 17th Line was attached on 26 April.

The Light Division
1 January 1814

XX
Light Division
Lt. Gen. Carl von Alten
X
Kempt
X
Colborne
II
1/43rd Foot
II
1/95th Foot
II
1st Cazadores
III
17th Line
II
2/95th Foot
II
1/52nd Foot
II
3rd Cazadores
I
3/95th Foot
I
3/95th Foot
I
3/95th Foot
I
3/95th Foot
I
3/95th Foot

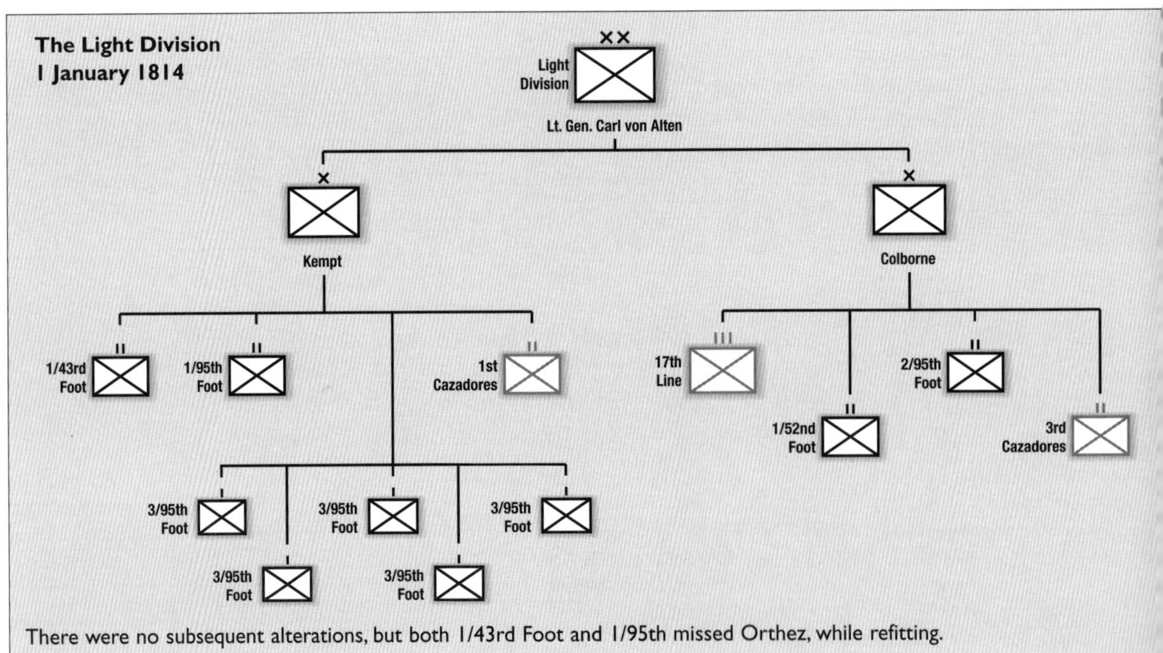

There were no subsequent alterations, but both 1/43rd Foot and 1/95th missed Orthez, while refitting.

Portuguese infantry units

From September 1809 Beresford organised the Portuguese infantry into a number of brigades, initially comprising just two line infantry regiments, though once the cazadores were fit for service a single-battalion regiment was added to each brigade. By the summer of 1811 there were 10 brigades, of which six were eventually attached to British infantry divisions, two operated independently, and two made up an all-Portuguese infantry division.

The division was formed under the command of Maj. Gen. John Hamilton (with the Portuguese rank of Marechal de Campo) on 16 December 1809 and served throughout the following year attached to 2nd Division. Wellington afterwards stated that it was originally intended to add British units to it as and when they became available in order to eventually form an 8th Infantry Division on the same pattern as the other seven. Unfortunately the unforeseen need to rebuild the British brigades of the shattered 2nd Division after Albuera meant that it had to remain an all-Portuguese formation, comprising just two brigades under Agostinho Luiz de Fonseca and Archibald Campbell.

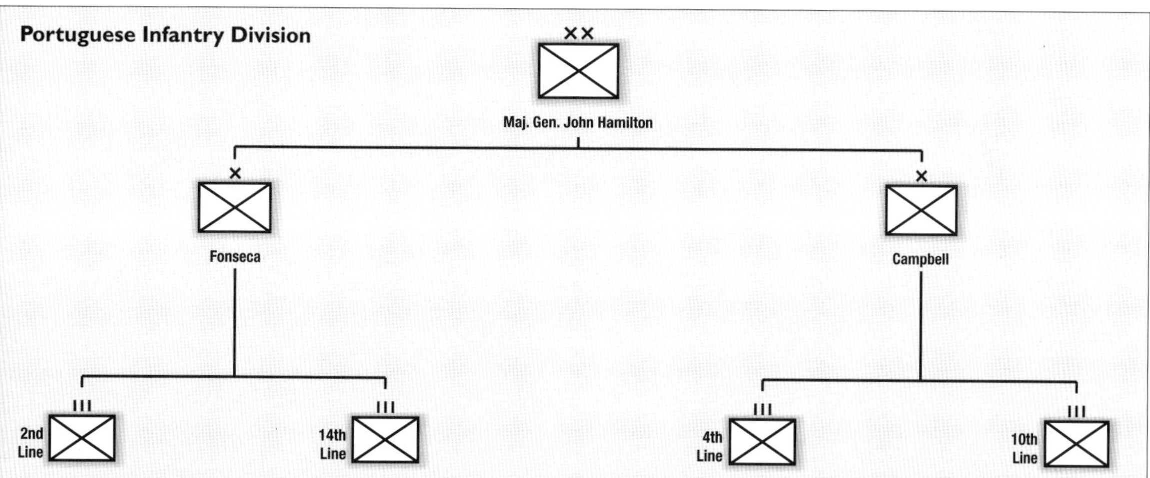

Subsequent alterations:

Owing to ill health, Hamilton had to temporarily give up command of the division in February 1813. Command passed to Silveira who led it until Hamilton's return at the beginning of November. However, Carlos Le Cor then took over the division on 18 November and thereafter led it until the end of the war.

Fonseca's Brigade: Fonseca was replaced by Antonio da Costa in June 1811.

Campbell's Brigade: Campbell was replaced by Power in April 1812, but he in turn went to 3rd Division in July and Campbell resumed command until succeeded by Buchan in November 1813.

10th Cazadores were posted to the brigade on 8 April 1812.

John Hamilton (1755–1835)
Of Woodbrook, Co. Tyrone. Served Bengal; Seringapatam 1792; then St Domingo 1796–97; Inspector General of Portuguese infantry October 1809; commanded Portuguese Division throughout most of Peninsular War; colonel 2/Ceylon Regiment 18 January 1813; Governor of Duncannon 10 May 1814 *vice* Benson. Married Emily Sohia Monck, with issue.

Commissions: ensign East India Company (EIC) service 1 March 1773; lieutenant EIC October 1776; captain EIC 1 March 1781; transferred to King's service as captain 76th Foot 1 November 1788; major (brevet) 1 March 1794; lieutenant-colonel 61st Foot 1 February 1795; colonel (brevet) 29 April 1802; major-general 25 October 1809; lieutenant-general 4 June 1814.

Independent Portuguese Brigades

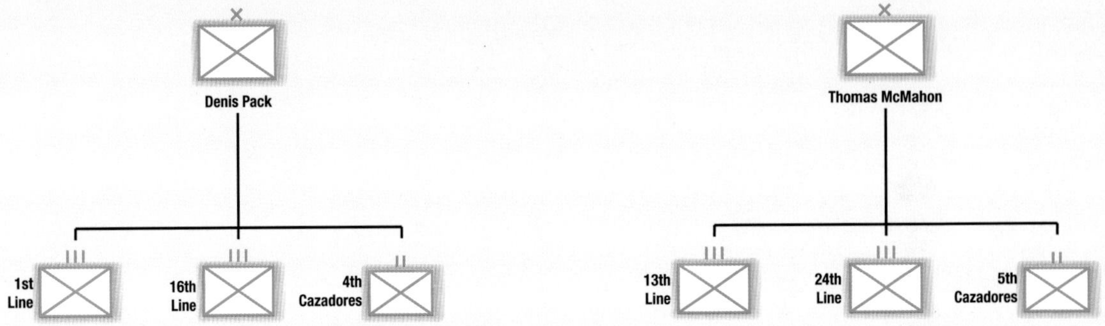

Denis Pack

1st Line | 16th Line | 4th Cazadores

Thomas McMahon

13th Line | 24th Line | 5th Cazadores

Subsequent alterations:

Pack's Brigade:	Taken over by John Wilson on 19 July 1813. However, he was wounded on 10 November and Archibald Campbell was appointed in his place on 23 November.
	4th Cazadores were posted to the brigade on 5 August 1810.
McMahon's Brigade:	Formed 20 July 1811. McMahon was replaced by Thomas Bradford on 20 January 1812.
	24th Line joined the brigade on 22 August 1811.

William Carr Beresford (1768–1854)
Beresford was nominated by Wellington to take charge of rebuilding the Portuguese Army, and proved himself a very capable military administrator. However, he was a far from successful field commander, who came very close to losing the Battle of Albuera.

Illegitimate son of Earl of Tyrone (later Marquess of Waterford) born 2 October 1768. Early entries in *Army List* name him as *Carr* Beresford. Lost eye in shooting accident in Nova Scotia 1786. Served Toulon 1794; took 88th Foot to India 1799 and served on Egyptian Expedition under Baird 1801; commanded brigade at capture of Cape Colony 1806 and Buenos Aires Expedition in same year; taken prisoner but escaped after six months; sent to occupy Madeira late-1807; served throughout Peninsular War; assigned to reorganisation of Portuguese army with local rank of lieutenant-general and Portuguese rank of marshal; remained in Portuguese service until 1819 revolution; Master-General of Ordnance 1828. Created viscount 1823, died Bedgebury, Kent, 8 January 1854.

Commissions: ensign 16th Foot 27 August 1785; lieutenant 25 June 1789; captain Independent Company 24 January 1791; exchanged to 69th Foot 31 May 1791; major 1 March 1794; lieutenant-colonel 124th Foot 11 August 1794; lieutenant-colonel 88th Foot 1 September 1795; colonel (brevet) 1 January 1800; brigadier-general 11 February 1804; major-general (Portugal) 4 September 1807; major-general 25 April 1808; lieutenant-general 1 January 1812; general 27 May 1825.

Denis Pack (1772–1823)
'Sweet Denis Pack' was the only son of Very Rev. Thomas Pack, Dean of Ossory. Commanded 71st Highlanders at Buenos Aires, severely wounded and made p.o.w. but escaped and commanded provisional battalion until evacuation; served Peninsula, in Portuguese service July 1810 to April 1813, subsequently commanded brigade in the 6th Division; slightly wounded in Pyrenees 30 July 1813 and badly wounded at Toulouse 10 April 1814; served at Waterloo, wounded. Married Lady Elizabeth Beresford 10 July 1816, with issue. Died 24 July 1823.

Commissions: cornet 14th Light Dragoons 30 November 1791; captain 5th Dragoon Guards 27 February 1796; lieutenant-colonel 71st Foot; colonel (brevet) 25 July 1810; major-general 4 June 1813.

Spanish infantry units

The Spanish Army does not, properly speaking, form a part of this study since, notwithstanding Wellington's grudging appointment as Generalissimo in 1812, it operated throughout the war as a very independent allied force. An exception, however, was the small Castilian division commanded by Mariscal de Campo (major-general) Don Carlos de Espãna which served during the 1812 campaign and most of the 1813 campaign as an integral part of Wellington's own army, before reverting to Spanish control as part of Freire's 4th Army.

Since 1810 Spanish infantry regiments had a theoretical establishment of three battalions but few ever achieved this, and even those that did rarely fielded all of them in the same place. To all intents and purposes therefore they were single-battalion formations and this was officially recognised in March 1812 when their new establishment was fixed at just one battalion comprising six companies of fusiliers, one of grenadiers and one of cazadores or light infantry totalling in excess of 720 officers and men, though as usual this

Landing troops in the face of the enemy, a print by Dubourg after Atkinson. The only real assault landing undertaken by substantial numbers of troops was at Alexandria in 1801. However, throughout the Peninsular War a number of relatively small raids were launched on the coast of Spain, either in support of local forces or as a diversion during Wellington's own operations.

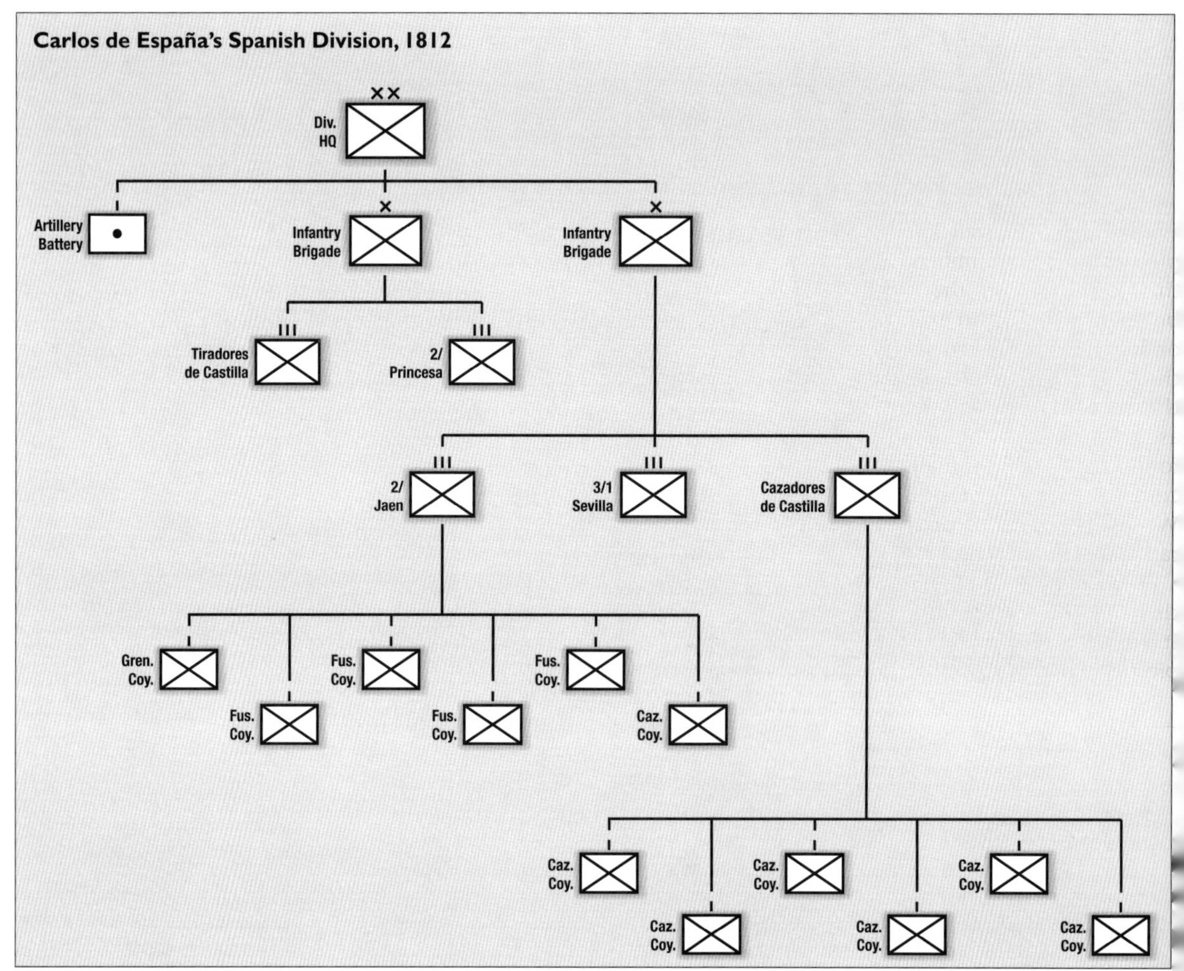

Carlos de España's Spanish Division, 1812. This organisational matrix has been drawn up on the assumption that the regiments making up the division still clung to the pre-1812 organisation. It is possible that the veteran 2/Princesa itself mustered two battalions so that there were two line battalions and one light battalion in each brigade. The whole division was in fact the equivalent of a large Portuguese brigade.

On the assumption that it was indeed organised according to the pre-1812 establishment and that 2/Princesa had only one battalion, it will have mustered 15 companies of grenadiers and fusiliers, and 15 companies of light infantry. On the other hand if the 1812 establishment was followed, it will have deployed 21 companies of grenadiers and fusiliers and 19 companies of light infantry. In either case it should be considered a light corps.

represented an aspiration rather than reality. A little confusingly, those second and third battalions cut adrift from the senior one retained their old titles rather than taking on new ones. Thus although the second battalion of the old Princesa regiment was now (on paper at least) an independent regiment in its own right, it continued to be designated 2/Princesa.

Spanish tactical doctrine is far from clear as their infantry tended to be rather poorly trained, but bitter experience had taught them the value of skirmishers, and the proportion of light infantry appears to have been at least comparable if not greater than that fielded by the Portuguese brigades in Wellington's service.

Carlos De España's division was certainly typical of the Spanish army in that it was made up of a mixture of 'old' regular regiments, including the hard-fighting Princesa, and some more recently raised volunteers. With a total strength of 3,360 officers and men at Salamanca it was approximately half the size of the Anglo-Portuguese divisions. Although some details are unclear it appears to have consisted of two brigades. The first comprised the veteran 2/Princesa, (which was a very strong unit and may actually have been organised in two battalions), and a light infantry unit, the *Tiradores* (sharpshooters) *de Castilla*. The second certainly comprised two line battalions and a light infantry unit.

Attached to the division, although not an integral part of it, was Don Julian Sanchez' *Lanceros de Castilla*, a one-time guerrilla unit which had matured into a very useful regular reconnaissance regiment.

Cavalry

Wellington, as is well known, had a very poor opinion of his cavalry. This proceeded from a number of causes, but the most important was the simple fact that the nature of the service precluded the tight autocratic control that he was accustomed to exercising over his infantry. Consequently, he was in the ordinary course of events reluctant to let it out of his sight or to allow its officers the latitude allowed in other armies. This in turn meant that while he formed them first into one and then two divisions, they were never employed tactically as such. Unlike the infantry divisions they were merely administrative formations and eventually both were abolished. Sir Stapleton Cotton, who commanded the 1st Cavalry Division for most of the war, acted throughout as Wellington's chief of cavalry – a staff role comparable to the CRA and CRE – rather than in a tactical role like his infantry counterparts.

The highest level of tactical control exercised on the battlefield was therefore the brigade, initially made up of two regiments but latterly of three. It was very rare for individual regiments to operate independently, except on picquet duties, and ordinarily infantry divisions were not allocated an organic

A British light dragoon. Most of Wellington's cavalry probably wore overalls and rode dock-tailed horses. Note that there was very little, if any, difference in the size of the horses for the heavy and light cavalry: both rode large, broad-chested mounts.

A light dragoon charging. The practice of levelling the sword at head height was widely adopted but required considerable strength, and notwithstanding the supposed superiority of the point some observers considered that the right elbow was highly vulnerable.

cavalry unit for scouting purposes. The exception was the frequent attachment of the 1st Hussars KGL to the Light Division, but even this was very much an ad hoc arrangement for specific operations.

At the outset of the war all cavalry regiments were organised in ten troops, each with an official establishment of 63 troopers besides the usual allowance of commissioned and non-commissioned officers. Once in the field attrition was just as much of a problem for the cavalry as the infantry. Generally speaking cavalrymen personally tended to be physically superior to the poor infantry, but horses were a different matter and regiments rarely mustered much more than about 400 sabres fit for duty.

Since cavalry regiments did not have the equivalent of a second battalion, two of the troops were designated as the regimental depot and permanently retained at home for recruiting and basic training. The service troops were paired off to form squadrons – ordinarily the smallest tactical unit capable of operating independently. Heavy cavalry regiments, variously designated as Dragoon Guards or Dragoons, had four service squadrons until 1811 when the establishment was reduced to three. Light cavalry on the other hand, variously designated as Light Dragoons or Light Dragoons (Hussars), not only retained their four squadrons but even had a fifth added in September 1813.

Otherwise the differences between heavy and light cavalry regiments – however titled – in the British Army were largely cosmetic. There were no regiments equipped as lancers until after the war and whilst all troopers had pistols and carbines, these were only used by sentries (and even then chiefly for sounding the alarm rather than actually shooting anyone) or for skirmishing ineffectually on the picquet line. In battle both heavy and light dragoons invariably used their swords. The 'heavies' were dressed in red jackets and carried straight-bladed swords, while the 'lights' were dressed in blue jackets or hussar costume, with curved sabres. Both, however, rode what were big horses by continental standards and followed the same 1796 *Instructions and Regulations for the Formations and Movements of the Cavalry*.

Portuguese cavalry

Beresford's success in reorganising and revitalising the Portuguese infantry was not mirrored by a similar reform of the cavalry. There were a number of reasons for this but essentially it boiled down to the simple facts that good infantry are much cheaper to equip and far easier to train than good cavalry, and that good horses are in even shorter supply. There was a certain element of a vicious circle in this, insomuch as without horses it was impossible to create an efficient cavalry, yet at the same time so long as the cavalry remained inefficient, there was obviously a certain reluctance to allocate them horses and forage, which were otherwise badly needed by the British Army. The result was that the Portuguese had to make do with an inadequate number of rather small horses, which in turn meant that only six of the 12 regiments were ever fully mounted.

The organisation of Portuguese cavalry regiments was broadly similar to British ones, with eight companies making up four squadrons; the only real difference being that the establishment called for just 56 troopers in a company rather than the 63 allowed for British ones. They were indeed intended to be 'in every respect, similar to British cavalry, and manoeuvre upon the same principles'. Therein perhaps lay the problem, for as will be discussed ahead British cavalry doctrine amounted to nothing more subtle than charging straight at the enemy whenever the opportunity occurred. British officers such as D'Urban expected the Portuguese regiments to which they were attached to

Sir William Payne
Served Peninsula in command of cavalry 1809 to June 1810.
Commissions: lieutenant 1st Dragoons 14 July 1777; captain 15 April 1782; major 1794; lieutenant-colonel 1 March 1794; lieutenant-colonel 3rd Dragoon Guards 5 October 1796; colonel (brevet) 1 January 1798; brigadier-general (Ireland) 1802–05; lieutenant-colonel 10th Light Dragoons 12 September 1805; major-general 1 January 1805; lieutenant-general 4 June 1811.

do the same and were constantly disappointed to find them an 'uncertain sort of people' with a distressing tendency to scatter and run – sometimes, rather excitingly, leaving them in the lurch. Such criticism undoubtedly lay at the root of the failure of the short-lived experiment of attaching two Portuguese brigades to the 1st Cavalry Division in 1811. Yet the criticism was manifestly unjust in that the Portuguese were simply light cavalry who were quite capable of acting as such, but too poorly mounted to act as battle cavalry. In fact had they been properly employed by officers who understood both their limitations and also their potential, they could have been very useful indeed as scouts and skirmishers on their own ground.

British cavalry tactics

Wellington's reluctance to let the cavalry out of his sight also proceeded from a widely shared perception that cavalry officers lacked the professionalism of their pedestrian colleagues in the infantry. That this was by no means an ill-founded prejudice is borne out not only by a rather patchy record on active service but also quite graphically by a horrifying remark carelessly expressed by Cornet the Marquis of Worcester of the 10th Light Dragoons (Hussars) on being placed under arrest by his commanding officer for neglecting drill parades. Col. Quentin angrily informed him that even if he was the King's son he would be put under arrest for neglecting his duty. Far from being cowed, Worcester loftily declared to his mistress with mingled astonishment and indignation that this was the most disgusting and vulgar thing he had ever heard, for, 'what has a King's son, or a duke's son, to do with the usual discipline observed to lieutenants in the army?'

Unfortunately this attitude was widely shared by a great many of his colleagues and led eventually to the infamous 'Quentin Affair' when most of the regiment's officers conspired to have their commanding officer court-martialled. A number of relatively trivial charges were brought against Quentin but it soon became clear that his real 'crime' was attempting to impose some discipline on the aristocratic rabble. In the end not only was he exonerated, but the Prince Regent himself also intervened to throw all the officers concerned out of the regiment. This in itself caused an uproar in some quarters, and one supporter rhetorically asked 'are six and twenty spirited offspring of the truly noble Devonshire, the patriotic

Stapleton Cotton, Lord Combermere (1773–1865)

Second son of Sir Robert Cotton, Baronet, born 14 November 1773. Served Flanders and Holland 1793–94; served at Cape and afterwards in India 1799; commanded brigade, 14th and 16th Dragoons in Peninsula 1808–09, then briefly commanded 1st Division; returned home on father's death 1810 but soon returned to Peninsula to command Wellington's cavalry with local rank of lieutenant-general; wounded after Salamanca but returned after Vittoria to command cavalry for remainder of war; not at Waterloo but commanded cavalry in Army of Occupation 1815–18. C-in-C India 1825–30. Died 21 February 1865.

Commissions: second lieutenant 23rd Fusiliers 26 February 1790; lieutenant 16 March 1791; captain 6th Dragoons 28 February 1793; major 28 April 1794 but promotion to lieutenant-colonel 25th Light Dragoons backdated to 9 March 1794; colonel 1 Jan 1800, exchanged to 16th Light Dragoons; major-general 2 November 1805; lieutenant-general 1 January 1812; general 27 May 1825; field marshal 1855.

A front rank of light dragoons charging with highly improbable precision, particularly with regard to their swords. Nevertheless, this was how it was supposed to work in theory, if not in practice.

Sir John Slade (1767–1859)
Son of John Slade of Maunsel Grange, Somerset. Served Peninsula, in command of Hussar Brigade under Sir John Moore 1808–09; again commanded cavalry brigade in Peninsula August 1809 to June 1813 including a brief period in command of 1st Cavalry Division; generally regarded as incompetent. Married (1) Anna Eliza Dawson 1792, (2) Matilda Ellen Dawson 1822. Fathered 11 sons and 4 daughters.

Commissions: cornet 10th Light Dragoons 10 May 1780; lieutenant 28 April 1783; captain 24 October 1787; major 1 March 1794; lieutenant-colonel 29 April 1795; lieutenant-colonel 1st Dragoons 18 October 1798; colonel (brevet) 29 April 1802; brigadier-general (Ireland) 28 May 1807; major-general 25 October 1809; lieutenant-general 4 June 1814; general 10 January 1837.

Leinster, the beneficient Beaufort, the virtuous Egremont, and other houses ... to be scattered through a select number of regiments, for pity, and for tuition and correction?' However, as the government rather tartly pointed out, the case 'would prove to the young officers of high birth, how little their (social) rank or connections would avail them, if they were not attentive to their duty.' *The Times* rather more pithily expressed the hope that the 10th would now become a proper regiment of English cavalry 'rather than a regiment of dancing masters or merry-andrews.'

Whilst this deplorable attitude to proper soldiering was most commonly found in the fashionable hussar regiments, it was, unfortunately, only the most extreme expression of a general malaise afflicting all of the cavalry.

Professional soldiers had always been well aware of the need to separate the functions of heavy 'battle' cavalry from that of light cavalry, whose field of operations properly lay in scouting and skirmishing. The effectiveness of the former was widely agreed to depend not on the trooper's weapons (or armour) but on being mounted on large and powerful horses. Such horses needed to be kept in good condition, and above all it was important to avoid working them too hard until they were actually needed. It followed therefore that instead of breaking down expensive troop horses on outpost work, smaller, hardier horses should be employed instead, ridden by men who understood their business.

Unfortunately these light cavalrymen, whether successively designated throughout history as light horse, harquebusiers, dragoons, light dragoons and most recently as hussars, all without exception displayed a depressing tendency to re-invent themselves as battle cavalry. Dragoons, for example, when first raised in the 17th century were merely mounted infantry who were primarily tasked with scouting and outpost duties, but as time went by they became increasingly reluctant to get off their horses. By the middle of the 18th century they had become so completely assimilated within the cavalry proper that the old regiments of heavy 'horse' were themselves re-designated as Dragoon Guards – the latter part of their title serving only to preserve their old social superiority. This in turn necessitated the raising in the 1750s of what were called 'light' dragoons specifically for outpost work. Predictably enough after a very promising start, they in turn, despite in some cases taking on the name and sartorial foibles of hussars, very soon forgot that their *raison d'être* was scouting and skirmishing. The Marquis of Worcester and his aristocratic friends affected considerable admiration for the dashing exploits of the Prussian hussar General Zeiten, but when given the opportunity to emulate him it was very much a case of all dash and no substance. To officers like Worcester, the unglamorous outpost work was probably far too much like hard work.

Indeed William Tomkinson of the 16th Light Dragoons famously noted: 'To attempt giving men or officers any idea in England of outpost duty was considered absurd, and when they came abroad, they had all this to learn. The fact was, there was no-one to teach them.' In all fairness it might also be remarked that there was also a shortage of sufficient open space on which to practise cavalry tactics.

The natural consequence was that while drill and discipline was tight enough at a troop or even squadron level, British cavalry were on the whole undertrained by continental standards. As Tomkinson once more lamented, 'In England I never saw nor heard of cavalry taught to charge, disperse and form, which if I taught a regiment one thing should be that'.

Notwithstanding the various 'formations and movements' prescribed in the 1796 regulations, British cavalry tactics in the end normally amounted to nothing more sophisticated than lining up two deep with squadrons abreast and charging straight at the enemy. This applied to complete regiments and brigades as well as to individual squadrons, and in his comprehensive instructions issued to the cavalry forming the Army of Occupation in 1815 Wellington stressed the overriding importance of maintaining a reserve.

Strangely enough, despite the rather obvious importance of this point, it was a lesson which British cavalry never quite grasped. In fact even as late as Waterloo, the destruction of the 'Union Brigade' was largely down to the fact that the pre-designated reserve unit – the 2nd Dragoons (Scots Greys) – enthusiastically moved up to join the main battle line at the outset of the charge. As usual therefore the initial contact was spectacularly successful, but once the French recovered sufficiently to mount a counter-attack with fresh troops, the absence of British reserves proved fatal.

In an 1826 critique Wellington provided a revealing insight into his Peninsular cavalry. The determined professionalism of the King's German Legion cavalry eventually imparted a certain degree of competence in outpost work to their British colleagues, and once they had mastered their proper role the Duke found them useful enough, 'first ... upon advanced guards, flanks &c. as the quickest movers and to enable me to know and see as much as possible in the shortest space of time; secondly to use them in small bodies to attack small bodies of the enemy's cavalry.' Unfortunately, he went on, because they 'would gallop (and) could not preserve their order ... although I consider one squadron a match for two French squadrons ... I should not have liked to see four British squadrons opposed to four French squadrons; and as numbers increased, and order became more necessary, I was more unwilling to risk our cavalry without having a greater superiority of numbers.'

Cavalry units

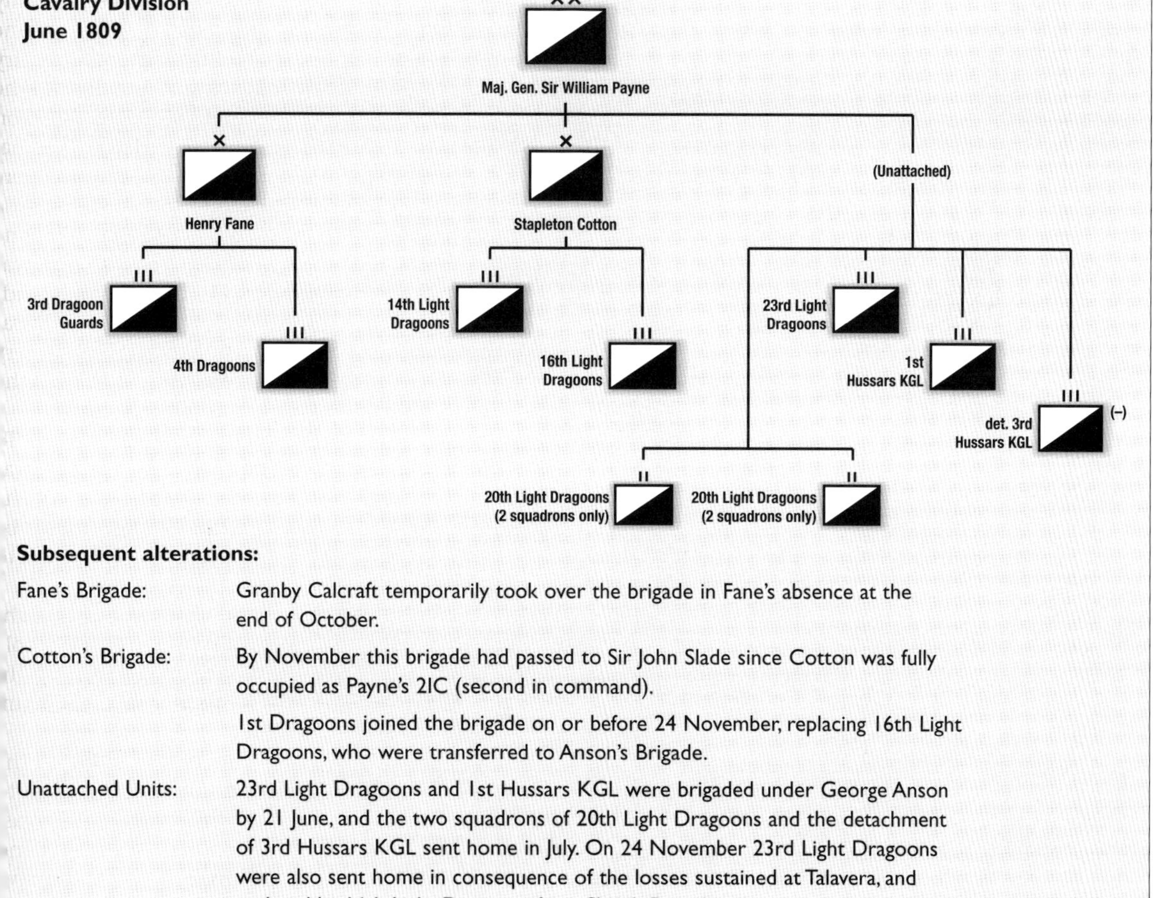

Subsequent alterations:

Fane's Brigade:	Granby Calcraft temporarily took over the brigade in Fane's absence at the end of October.
Cotton's Brigade:	By November this brigade had passed to Sir John Slade since Cotton was fully occupied as Payne's 2IC (second in command).
	1st Dragoons joined the brigade on or before 24 November, replacing 16th Light Dragoons, who were transferred to Anson's Brigade.
Unattached Units:	23rd Light Dragoons and 1st Hussars KGL were brigaded under George Anson by 21 June, and the two squadrons of 20th Light Dragoons and the detachment of 3rd Hussars KGL sent home in July. On 24 November 23rd Light Dragoons were also sent home in consequence of the losses sustained at Talavera, and replaced by 16th Light Dragoons from Slade's Brigade.

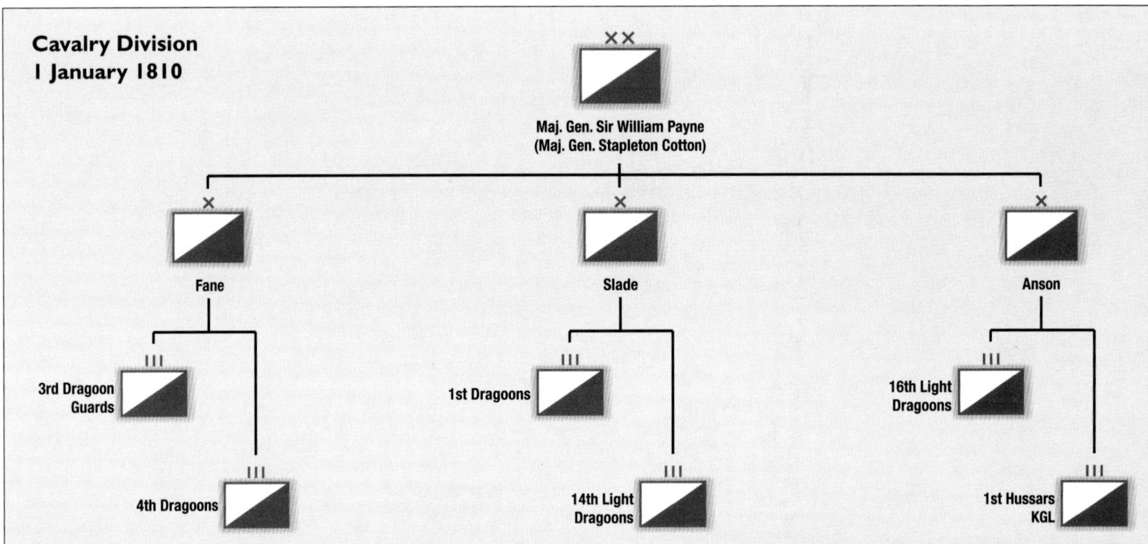

Subsequent alterations:

Payne went home sometime before 1 June and Cotton officially took over command on 3 June.

Fane's Brigade: Taken over by De Grey on 13 May. For his part Fane was attached to Hill's force in Estremadura in command of the newly arrived 13th Light Dragoons and two Portuguese brigades made up of the 1st and 7th Cavalry and the 5th and 8th Cavalry. He went home sick at the end of the year.

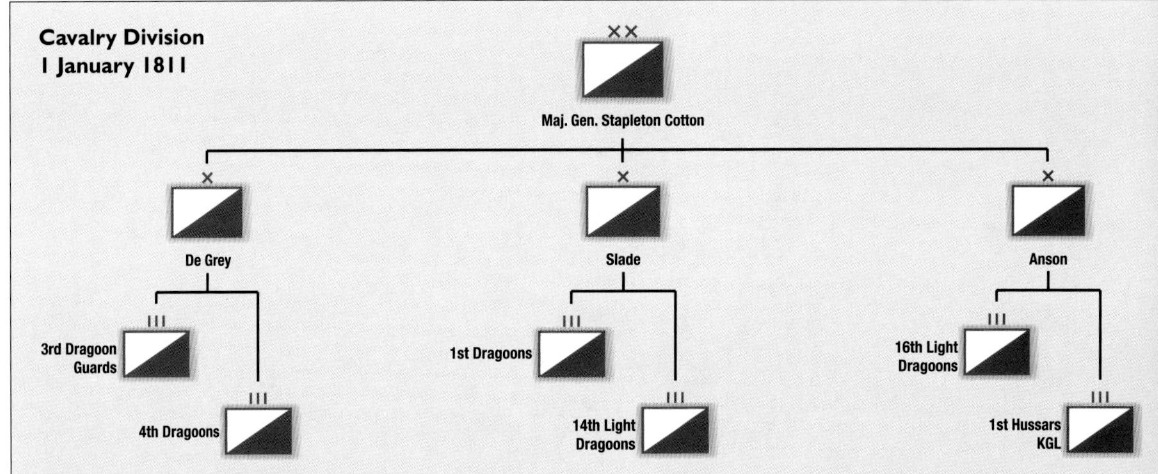

Subsequent alterations:

Cotton went home on 15 January and in his absence the division was commanded first by Slade until 7 March, then by Sir William Erskine (who also had the Light Division at the time), until Cotton returned on 22 April.

Slade's Brigade: While Slade was looking after the division his brigade was commanded by Col. Samuel Hawker of 14th Light Dragoons.

13th Light Dragoons were posted to the brigade on 18 June.

Anson's Brigade: Anson was absent between 1 March and 15 May, leaving the Brigade under Arentschildt of 1st Hussars KGL.

Long's Brigade: A new brigade was formed under Robert Ballard Long on 13 June, comprising 13th Light Dragoons and 2nd Hussars KGL. On 18 June 13th Light Dragoons were transferred to Slade's Brigade and replaced by 11th Light Dragoons

On 19 June 1811, the cavalry was re-organised into two divisions:

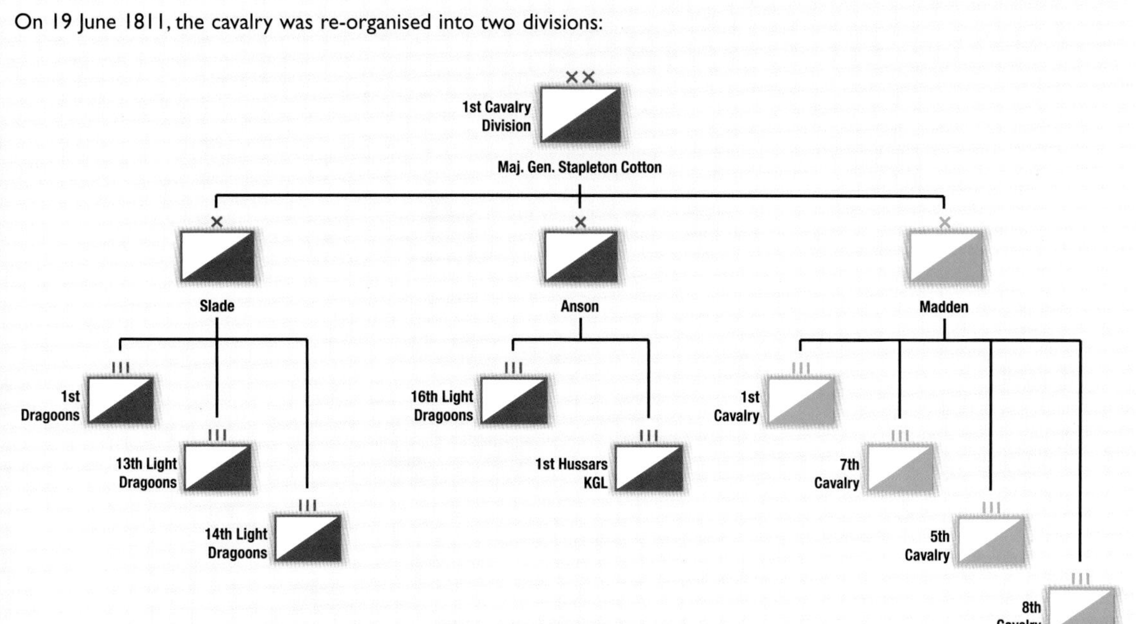

N.B. George Madden's Portuguese contingent was actually organised in two brigades: his own 5th and 8th Cavalry, and the 1st and 7th Cavalry under Loftus Otway.

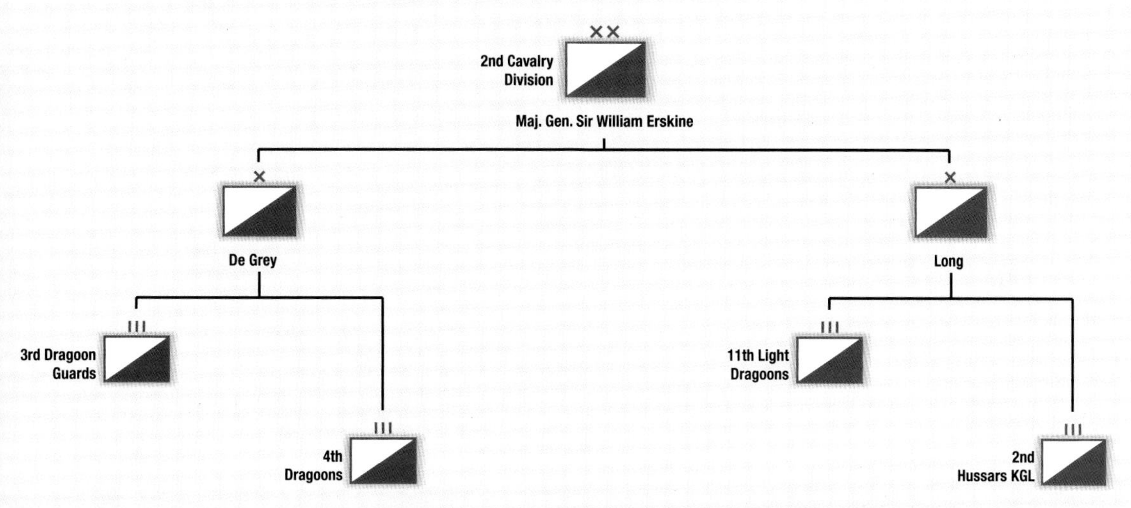

This arrangement immediately proved unsatisfactory and a further re-organisation therefore took place on 19 July.

Sir William Erskine (d.1813)
Sent out to command 2nd Cavalry Division in 1811, but not a success, especially when placed in temporary command of Light Division. Short-sighted, drunken and generally considered mad as well as incompetent. Committed suicide at Lisbon 13 February 1813.

Commissions: second-lieutenant 23rd Fusiliers 23 September 1785; lieutenant 13th Light Dragons 14 November 1787; captain 15th Light Dragoons 23 February 1791; major 15th Light Dragoons 1 March 1794; lieutenant-colonel 15th Light Dragoons 14 December 1794, half-pay February 1796; colonel (brevet) 1 January 1801; colonel 14th Reserve Battalion 9 July 1803, half-pay February 1805; major-general 25 April 1808.

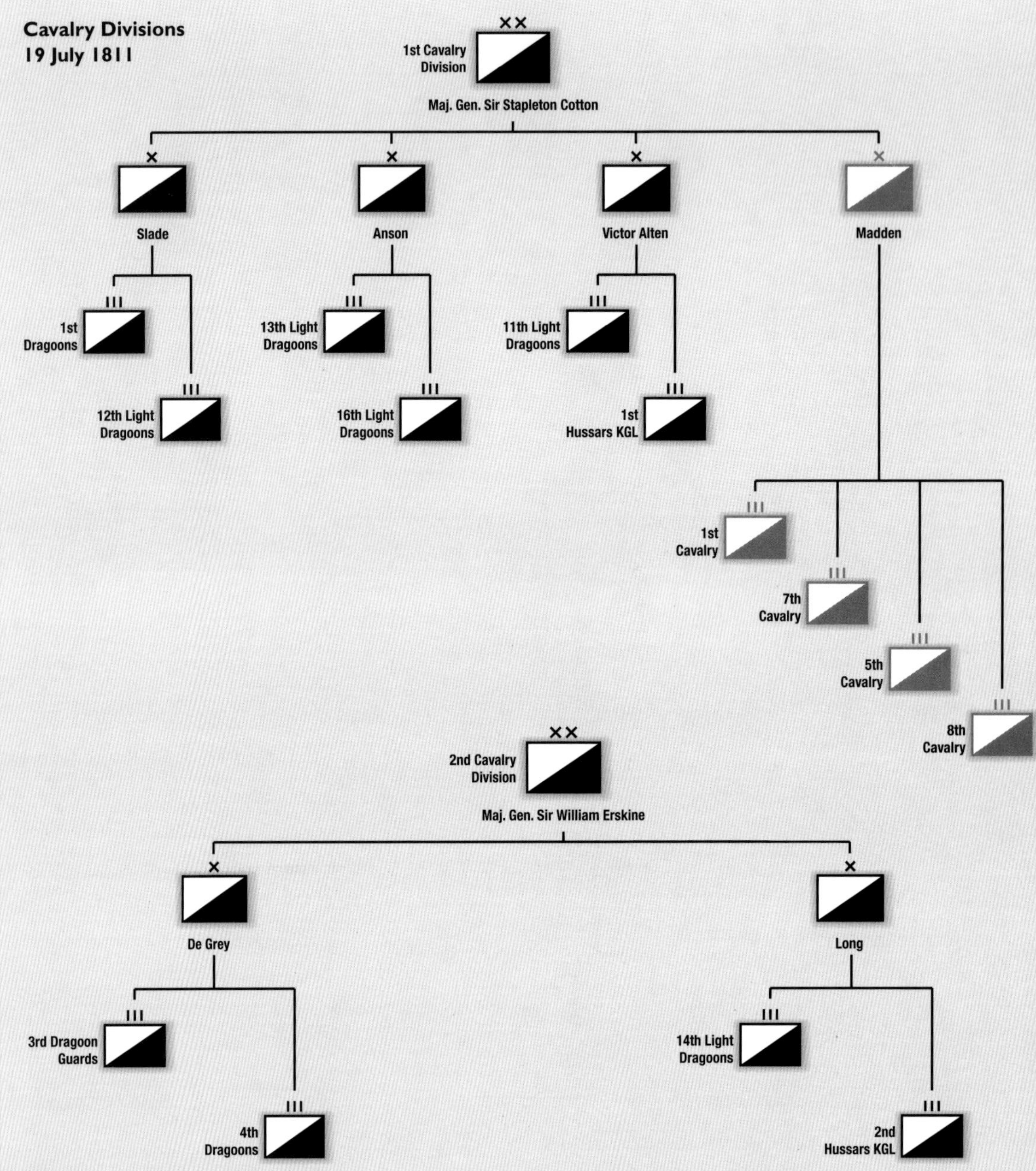

Subsequent alterations:

Erskine was absent between 8 December 1811 and 8 April 1812, but as by that time the 'division' only comprised Long's Brigade this was hardly a matter on any importance.

De Grey's Brigade:	Transferred to 1st Cavalry Division on 5 October.
Long's Brigade:	9th Light Dragoons were posted to the brigade on 1 August. At the same time 14th Light Dragoons exchanged with 13th Light Dragoons from Anson's brigade in 1st Division.
Le Marchant's Brigade:	A new brigade comprising 4th Dragoon Guards and 3rd Dragoons was added on 30 August. On 1 October 5th Dragoon Guards were posted to the brigade, which was then transferred to 1st Cavalry Division on 8 November to replace Madden's Portuguese, who were struck off on the same date.

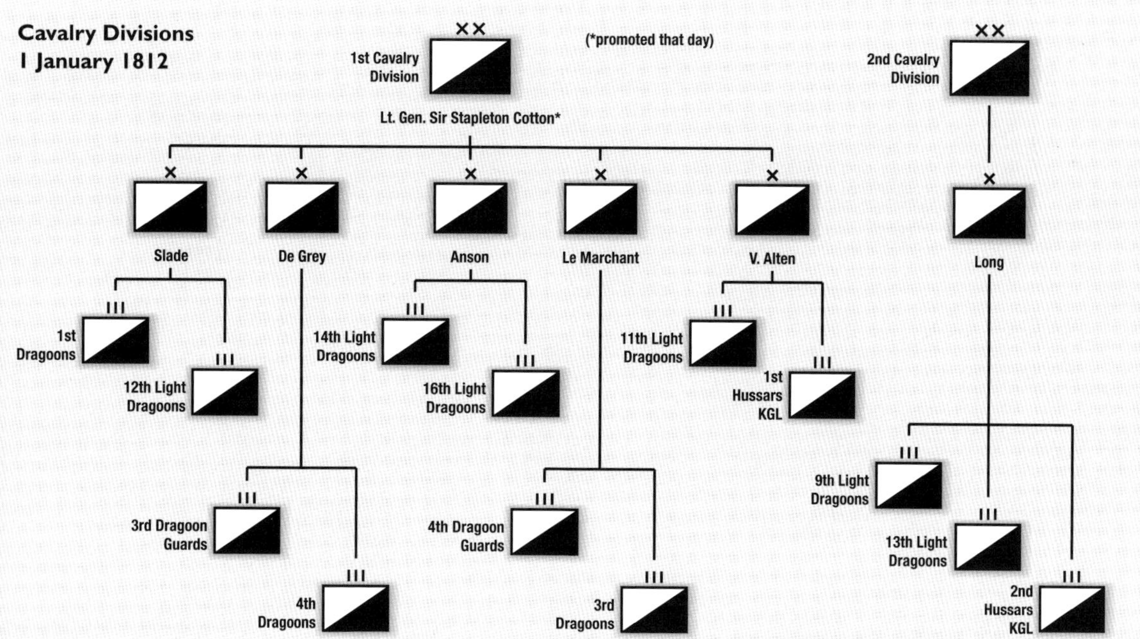

Subsequent alterations:

1st Division

Cotton was wounded at Salamanca and temporarily replaced by Maj. Gen. Eberhardt Otto Georg von Bock of KGL. He returned before 15 October but was invalided home in December.

Slade's Brigade:	On 29 January the 3rd and 4th Dragoon Guards were transferred to the brigade, and in exchange 12th Light Dragoons were posted to Anson's Brigade.
Anson's Brigade:	Anson was absent during the first half of the year and the brigade was looked after by Col. Henry Cumming of 11th Light Dragoons until his return shortly before 1 July. On 29 January 12th Light Dragoons were posted to the brigade, then on 1 July 14th Light Dragoons were ordered to exchange with 11th Light Dragoons from Alten's Brigade.
V. Alten's Brigade:	Alten was absent from 1 August until mid September. On 1 July 11th Light Dragoons were ordered to exchange with 14th Light Dragoons from Anson's Brigade and on 17 October 2nd Hussars KGL were transferred from 2nd Cavalry Division.
De Grey's Brigade:	Broken up on 29 January; 3rd Dragoon Guards to Slade's Brigade and 4th Dragoons to Le Marchant's Brigade.
Le Marchant's Brigade:	Le Marchant was killed at Salamanca and replaced on 23 July by Sir William Ponsonby of 5th Dragoon Guards. On 29 January 4th Dragoon Guards were transferred to Slade's Brigade and replaced by 4th Dragoons.
von Bock's Brigade:	Transferred from 2nd Cavalry Division on 14 April (see below). Commanded by de Jonquiere when Bock took over the Division after Salamanca.

2nd Division

Sir William Erskine resumed command of the division, by then again comprising two brigades, on 8 April.

Long's Brigade:	2nd Hussars KGL were transferred to 1st Cavalry Division on 17 October.
von Bock's Brigade:	New formation comprising 1st and 2nd Dragoons KGL, commanded by Maj. Gen. Eberhardt Otto Georg von Bock – assigned to 2nd Cavalry Division 23 March. Transferred to 1st Cavalry Division on 14 April and replaced by Slade's Brigade.
Slade's Brigade:	Transferred from 1st Division on 14 April.

1st Cavalry Division
1 January 1813

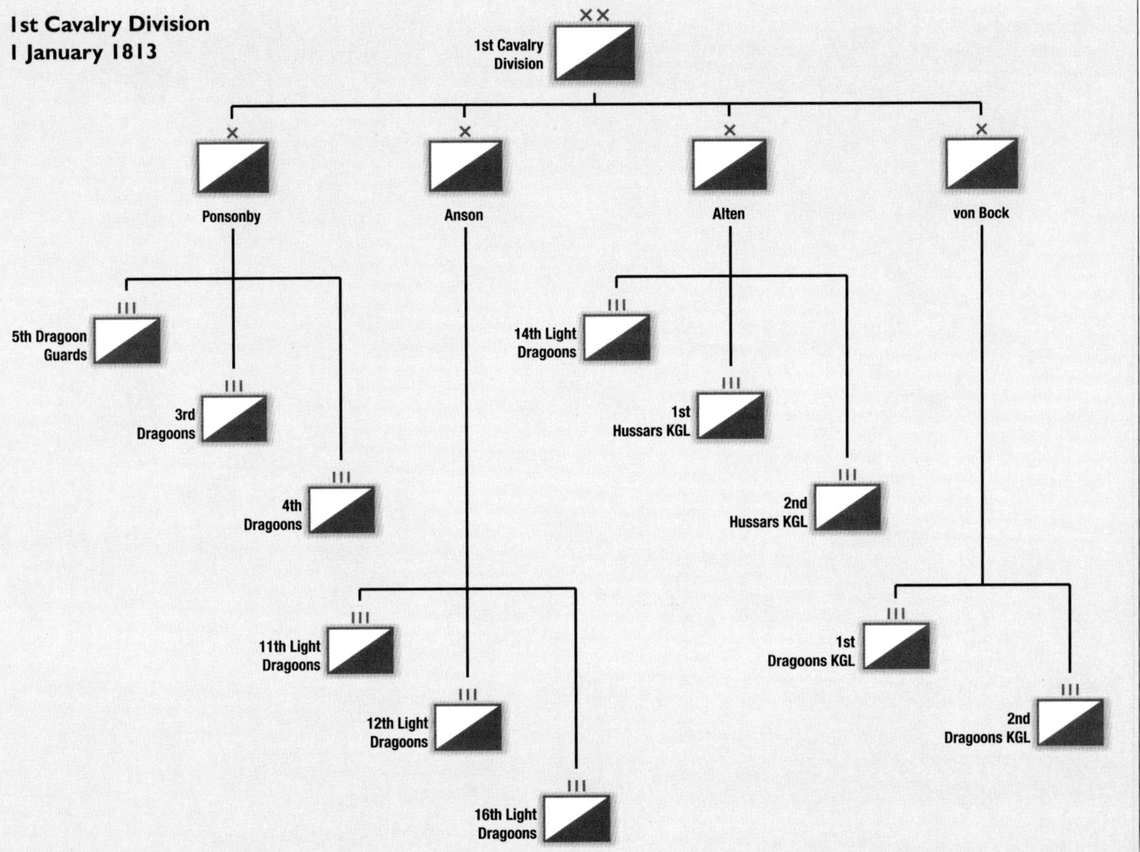

- XX 1st Cavalry Division
  - X Ponsonby
    - III 5th Dragoon Guards
    - III 3rd Dragoons
    - III 4th Dragoons
  - X Anson
    - III 11th Light Dragoons
    - III 12th Light Dragoons
    - III 16th Light Dragoons
  - X Alten
    - III 14th Light Dragoons
    - III 1st Hussars KGL
    - III 2nd Hussars KGL
  - X von Bock
    - III 1st Dragoons KGL
    - III 2nd Dragoons KGL

(See page 85 for notes on subsequent alterations.)

A British heavy dragoon; other than the wearing of overalls instead of breeches and jacked boots, this is a pretty fair impression of one of Wellington's heavy cavalry, although the horse's tail was almost invariably docked.

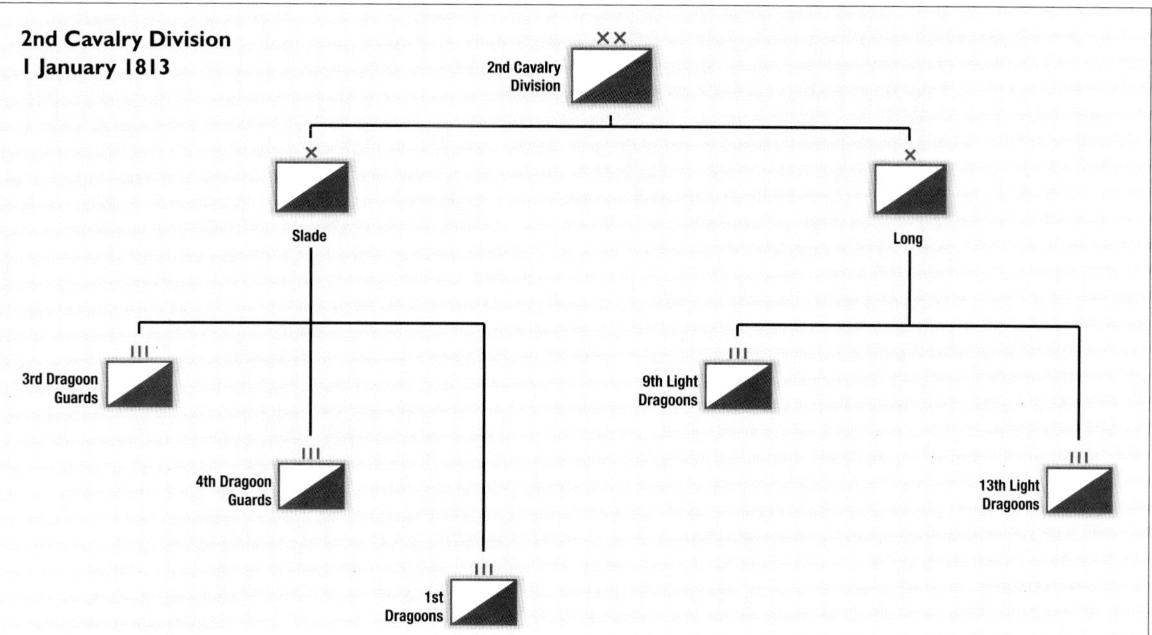

Subsequent alterations:

Neither division had an actual commander at the beginning of the year, although Bock appears to have acted in overall charge of the cavalry until Cotton's return on 25 June. The fact that these divisions were purely administrative was also underlined by their amalgamation on 21 April (see page 86).

Anson's Brigade:	Anson was ordered on to Home Staff on 2 July and replaced by Maj. Gen. John Ormsby Vandelueur. 11th Light Dragoons were ordered home on 13 March.
Alten's Brigade:	2nd Hussars KGL were ordered home on 13 March. 14th Light Dragoons were transferred to Long's Brigade on 2 July, and replaced by 18th Hussars from Grant's Brigade.
von Bock's Brigade:	Commanded in his absence by Bülow.
Slade's Brigade:	Slade was ordered home on 23 April and replaced on 20 May by Maj. Gen. Henry Fane. 4th Dragoon Guards were ordered home on 13 March.
Long's Brigade:	Long was replaced by Colquhon Grant on 6 September, who was in turn replaced by Sir Hussey Vivian on 24 November. 9th Light Dragoons were ordered home on 13 March, but not replaced by 14th Light Dragoons until 2 July.
Rebow's Brigade:	A new brigade comprising two squadrons apiece of 1st Lifeguards, 2nd Lifeguards and Royal Horse Guards (Blues), commanded by Maj. Gen. Francis Slater Rebow. Initially posted to 2nd Cavalry Division on 25 January it was transferred to 1st Cavalry Division on 5 February. Rebow returned home shortly afterwards and by March the brigade was commanded by Lt. Col. Sir Robert Hill of the Blues. In October the brigade was taken over by Maj. Gen. Terence O'Brian O'Loghlin.
Grant's Brigade:	The 'Hussar Brigade' under Col. Sir Colquhon Grant joined the army on 15 April to replace the 4th Dragoon Guards, 9th and 11th Light Dragoons and 2nd Hussars KGL. It comprised 10th Hussars, 15th Hussars and 18th Hussars. Grant was replaced by Lord Edward Somerset on 2 July. On the same date 18th Hussars were transferred to Alten's Brigade. 7th Hussars joined the brigade in October but do not appear in orders until 24 November.

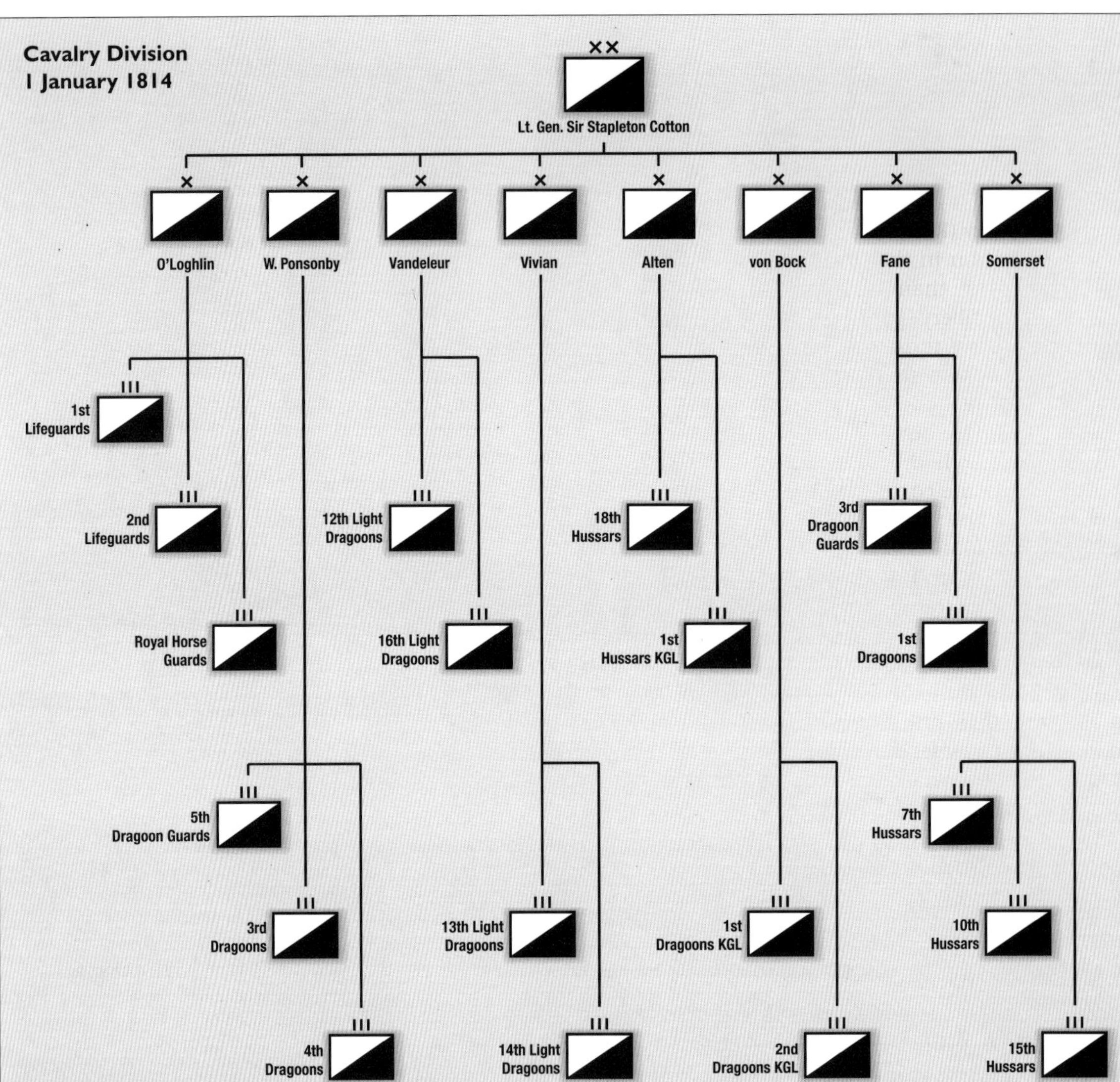

Subsequent alterations:

Ponsonby's Brigade:	Ponsonby was recorded as absent on 25 January, and Lord Charles Manners of 3rd Dragoons had the brigade.
Vivian's Brigade:	Vivian was transferred to the command of Alten's Brigade on 16 January and officially replaced by Fane. In actual fact Fane commanded both this and his old brigade jointly as an ad hoc division. Day-to-day command of the brigade was therefore exercised by Lt. Col. Doherty of 13th Light Dragoons.
Alten's Brigade:	Alten returned to Germany and was replaced by Vivian on 16 January. Vivian was wounded on 8 April and replaced by Arentschildt.
von Bock's Brigade:	Bülow took over the brigade on 16 January – Bock, heading back to Germany, was drowned in a shipwreck on the coast of Brittany on 21 January. Arentschildt was posted to command the brigade on 25 March, but then transferred to take over Alten's old brigade when Vivian was wounded on 8 April. Bülow then took over the brigade again.
Fane's Brigade:	Fane took over Vivian's Brigade on 16 January in addition to his own, and ran both as an ad hoc division. Day-to-day command of the brigade therefore passed to Lt. Col. Arthur Clifton of 1st (Royal) Dragoons.

Artillery

The Royal Artillery (RA) and King's German Artillery (KGA) occupied a slightly anomalous position in that they were ultimately answerable to the Board of Ordnance, rather than to the Army's headquarters at Horse Guards. Consequently artillery personnel are not normally included in divisional morning states, and those returns made to the Board of Ordnance tend to be uninformative as to whether a certain company or brigade was attached to a particular division.

Artillerymen were organised for administrative purpose into battalions and companies, although the former had no tactical significance and the basic combat unit was the company. Terminology was, however, slightly confusing in that Royal Horse Artillery units, numbering about 140 officers and men including the requisite detachment of drivers from the CDRA (or Corps of Drivers Royal Artillery) were designated as Troops. Theoretically they were referred to by letters (as in Capt. Harry Ross's 'A' Troop, and Capt. Robert Bull's 'I' Troop), but in practice they were normally identified simply as Ross's Troops and Bull's Troops respectively.

Foot artillery on the other hand continued to be organised in companies of approximately 145 officers and men, again commanded by captains, for administrative purposes. For actual service in the field these were again linked with quite separate detachments of about 100 men from the CDRA, but in this case the combined units were designated as brigades under the name of the RA company commander. Ordinarily the drivers, who included farriers and other trade specialists, accounted for between 30–40 per cent of the personnel in a brigade, as is usefully illustrated by a return made in December 1809 of the seven field and two garrison artillery brigades then serving in the Peninsula:

Royal Horse Artillery	187 of all ranks, with 106 drivers attached
Royal Artillery	627 of all ranks with 545 drivers attached
King's German Artillery	332 of all ranks with 160 drivers attached

Pulling all the guns, caissons and battery wagons were a total of 951 horses and 132 mules. Ordinarily, as can be seen by the accompanying tables on pages 88 and 89, brigades and RHA Troops fielded six guns apiece and were supported by 11–13 caissons and wagons apiece. RHA Troops had significantly more horses since all of the gunners were mounted.

Initially there were three brigades, commanded by captains Sillery, May and Lawson, of which the first two were equipped with six-pounders and the third with three-pounders, and two King's German Artillery brigades commanded by captains Teiling and Heise, again equipped with six-pounders. From 1809 onwards the six-pounders were replaced by nine-pounders.

The Rocket Troop, which arrived in the Peninsula in 1813, had three heavy limbers, three light limbers, six ammunition carts, and a forge cart, but seemingly no spare-wheel cart or wagon.

Portuguese artillery companies were very similarly organised and initially seven served with Wellington's army, but in 1812 the number of companies was increased to eight, of which three had five six-pounders and a howitzer, and the others five nine-pounders and a howitzer in line with what was then British practice. Ordinarily two or more companies were combined to form a brigade, and as with the infantry included a number of British and German officers.

Sir Alexander Dickson (d.1840)

Third son of Admiral William Dickson. Served Minorca 1798; blockade of Malta and surrender of Valetta 1800. Served Buenos Aires 1807. Served throughout Peninsular War: Oporto, Bussaco, Campo Mayor, Olivenca, Badajoz (twice), Albuera, Ciudad Rodrigo, Badajoz (again), Salamanca Forts, Salamanca and Burgos. CRA at Vittoria, San.Sebastian, Bidassoa, Nivelle, Nive and Toulouse. Served New Orleans and capture of Fort Bowyer 1815. Commanded Battering Train at Waterloo, Mauberg, Landrecies, Phillippville, Marienberg and Rocroi. Director General Field Train Department and DAG Royal Artillery. Married a Miss Briones with issue. Died 22 April 1840.

Commissions: second-lieutenant Royal Artillery 6 November 1794; lieutenant 6 March 1795; captain 14 October 1801; major 6 February 1812; lieutenant-colonel (brevet) 27 April 1812; colonel (brevet) 27 May 1825; major-general 10 January 1837.

Artillery tactics

British (and Allied) artillery tactics were relatively unsophisticated in this period and in large part constrained by the relatively light weight of the ordnance available. Initially the British Army entered the Peninsular War equipped with six-pounder guns which were light and manoeuvrable and well suited to the terrain, but outclassed by the heavier French guns. Although they were soon replaced by heavier nine-pounders, there was little or no attempt made to mass artillery fire. Instead, whilst there was no question of reverting, as the French briefly did, to the old and outmoded doctrine of attaching 'battalion' guns to infantry units, British artillery brigades were invariably deployed individually and almost always in direct support of infantry formations. Indeed Wellington positively discouraged wasting his scant artillery resources on counter-battery fire – especially as the heavier French guns were likely to be superior in any direct contest of this nature.

Ideally the artillery brigades were deployed as complete formations and so sited with neighbouring units to achieve crossfire in front of the infantry they were supporting. At Albuera, for example, an artillery brigade was pushed forward and positioned on the flank of each infantry brigade (see the maps on pp28–29 and 32), but sometimes it was necessary to split an artillery brigade into two sections in order to achieve this crossfire. At Busaco the guns were scattered even more widely across the British front line, although this was dictated by the nature of the ground and the relatively static defence being undertaken on top of the ridge.

A number of different projectiles could be fired, depending on the range ordinary round-shot or cannonballs could usefully be employed out to 600m

A British (foot) artillery brigade.

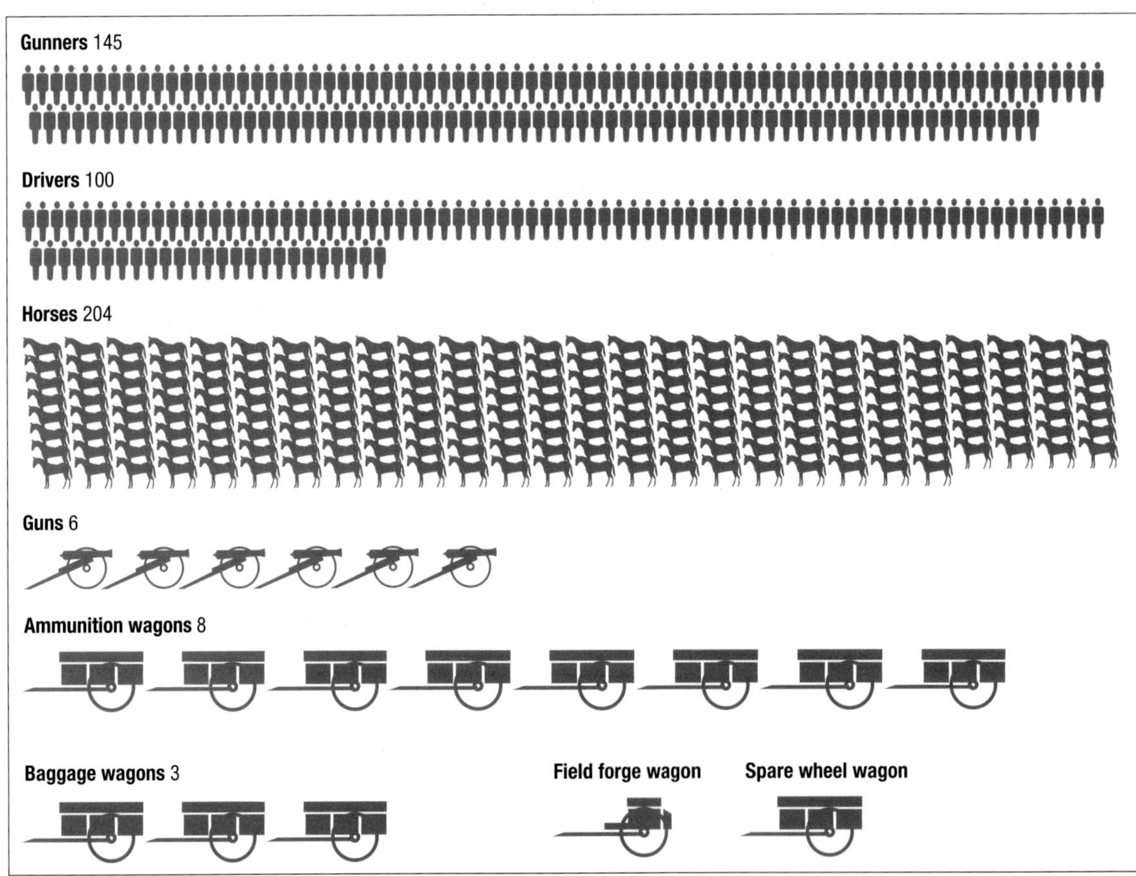

for six-pounders and 800m for nine-pounders (contrasting with 900m for a French 12-pounder); but spherical case could be effective out to about 900–1,000m. The latter, commonly referred to by the name of its inventor – Shrapnel – was peculiar to the British service and effectively comprised a shell filled with iron balls. Its airbursts could be extremely destructive to infantry and cavalry, and in particular against dispersed targets such as skirmishers, artillery crews and headquarters, although its effective use depended on a great deal more skill in estimating the fuse size than did the firing of round shot. At closer ranges, canister (quite literally a tin container filled with musket balls) was effective in both cases out to about 400m, contrasting with the French 12-pounder, which could fire canister out to 600m.

British tactical doctrine therefore envisaged firing spherical case at infantry and cavalry at ranges over 650m – although it needed to be husbanded since only 12 rounds were carried by nine-pounders – roundshot at between 350m and 650m, and canister at shorter ranges. Contemporary calculations reckoned that a battery attacked by infantry from 650m out would have time to fire seven roundshot and ten rounds of canister per gun before the infantry reached the gun-line. No-one, however, was under any illusions that unsupported artillery could actually stop an attack.

Artillery units

The listings that follow on pages 90–91 relate only to troops and brigades actually serving in the field, and do not include units serving in garrisons or forming part of the occasional siege train. It will be noted that in the early years of the war there appears to have been a deliberate policy of rotating units between garrison and field service.

Sir Augustus Frazer (1776–1835)
Born Dunkirk 6 September 1776, son of Colonel Andrew Frazer, Royal Engineers. Educated at Edinburgh High School and Military Academy Woolwich. Served Holland 1794. Appointed to Royal Horse Artillery 1796. Served Helder 1799. CRA Buenos Aires 1807. Served Peninsula from November 1812. Commander Royal Horse Artillery in Peninsula from April 1813 to end of war. Commander RHA at Waterloo. Director of Royal Laboratory Woolwich at time of his death (11 June 1835). Married Emma Lynn 1809 with issue.

Commissions: second-lieutenant, Royal Artillery 18 September 1793; major (brevet) June 1811; lieutenant-colonel Royal Artillery; colonel (brevet) 18 June 1815.

A Royal Horse Artillery troop.

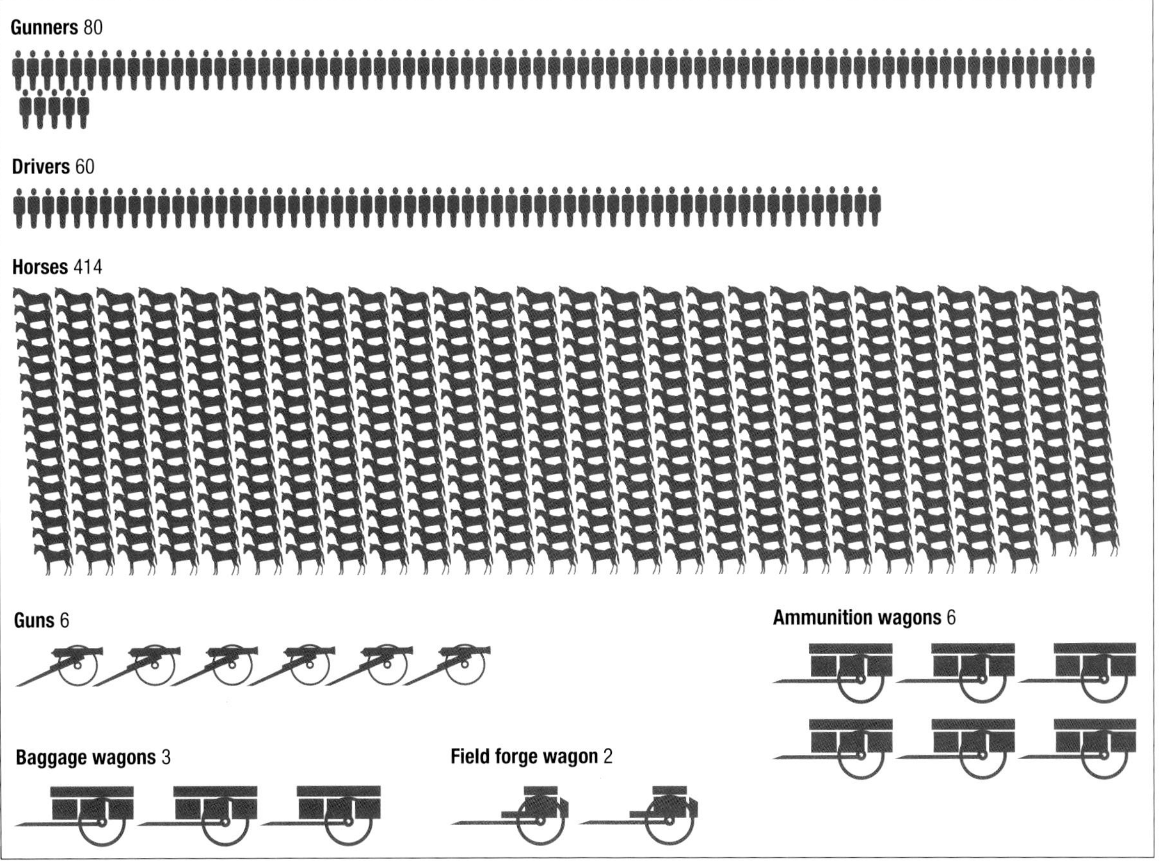

Field Companies 1810		
Royal Horse Artillery	A Troop	Capt. Harry Ross
	I Troop	Capt. Robert Bull
Royal Artillery	Capt. G. Thompson (formerly Sillery's)	
	Capt. R. Lawson (arrived September 1808)	
	Capt. J. Hawker (arrived October 1810)	
	Capt. P. Meadows (arrived October 1810)	
	Maj. A. Bredin (arrived 1809)	
	Capt. H. Baynes (officially May's)	
King's German Artillery	Capt. A. Cleeves (formerly Heise's)	
	Capt. C. von Rettberg (formerly Tieling's)	

Portuguese Artillery 1810	
Maj. Alexander Dickson's Brigade	Capt. Pedro de Rozierres
	Capt. João da Cunha Preto
Maj. von Arentschildt's Brigade	Capt. João Porfirio da Silva
	Capt. Jacinto Friere

Field Companies 1811		
Royal Horse Artillery	A Troop	Capt. Harry Ross
	D Troop	Capt. G. Lefebure*
	E Troop	Capt. R. MacDonald (7th Division)
	I Troop	Capt. R. Bull
Royal Artillery	Capt. G. Thompson	
	Capt. R. Lawson	
	Maj. J. Hawker*	
	Capt. P. Meadows	
	Maj. A. Bredin	
	Capt. H. Baynes (still officially May's)	
King's German Artillery	Capt. A. Cleeves*	
	Capt. F. Sympher* (formerly Rettberg's)	

Portuguese Artillery 1811	
Maj. Alexander Dickson's Brigade *	Capt. William Braun
	Capt. S.J. de Arriaga
Maj. von Arentschildt's Brigade (3rd Division)	Lt. J.C. da Sequira Lt. J.C. Rosado
Capt. F.C. Pinto	(Pack's Independent Brigade)
Capt. João da Cunha Preto	(5th Division)
Capt. Pedro de Rozierres	(6th Division)

* units marked thus served with Beresford's army at Albuera.

Field Companies 1812		
Royal Horse Artillery	A Troop	Maj. Harry Ross (Light Division)
	D Troop	Capt. G. Lefebure (2nd Cavalry Division)
	E Troop	Capt. R. MacDonald (7th Division)
	I Troop	Maj. R. Bull (1st Cavalry Division)
Royal Artillery	Capt. H. Baynes (May's)	Reserve Ammunition Train
	Capt. F. Glubb	Reserve Artillery
	Maj. R.W. Gardiner	(1st Division)
	Capt. S. Maxwell	(2nd Division)
	Capt. R. Douglas	(3rd Division)
	Capt. R. Lawson	(5th Division)
	Capt. J.P. Eligé	(6th Division)
	Capt. H. Owen[1]	
	Capt. R.H. Birch[1]	
King's German Artillery	Capt. F. Sympher	(4th Division)
Portuguese Artillery	Capt. J. da Cunha Preto	(Hamilton's Division)
	Capt. William Braun	(Hamilton's Division)
	Maj. S.J. de Arriaga	Reserve Artillery

[1] These two brigades were initially in garrison at Cadiz, but came up with Skerrett to join the field army in October.

With some minor alterations in personnel (Eligé, for example, was killed at the Salamanca forts) this organisation appears to have been more or less maintained for the remainder of the war. The only real 'innovation' was the appearance in 1813 of a Rocket Troop, though this came under Army command rather than being attached to a division.

Artillery equipment

At the outset of the Peninsular War the field gun most commonly used by the British Army was a brass barrelled 6-pdr with the block trail introduced by the elder Congreve in 1793. (see New Vanguard 60 *British Napoleonic Artillery 1793-1815(1)*). Although the particular model used in the Peninsula was designed by Gen. Thomas Blomefield in the 1790s, the 6-pdr had more or less been adopted as the standard heavy field gun by the Royal Artillery in the 1770s – in preference to the light 3-pdr. Therein lay the problem, for both guns were intended to provide close fire-support to relatively small infantry formations and so had to balance weight of fire against ease of manoeuvrability. So far as minor operations went, it proved to be a very useful and versatile gun and continued to do good service in other theatres throughout and indeed long after the Peninsular War. In this particular theatre, however, it was soon recognised that the larger formations employed by the British Army required far heavier artillery preparations, particularly in opposition to the generally quite heavy guns fielded by the French. It proved necessary to scale the gun up to a 9-pdr, which proved very satisfactory, although it never entirely supplanted the 6-pdr. Conversely the light 3-pdr made a brief return to service in the Pyrenees, as a pack-mounted mountain gun, although it suffered from the usual problem that it was a little too heavy to be transported easily, but not heavy enough to provide truly effective fire support.

In addition, up to one in six guns might be short, stubby-barrelled 5.5in. howitzers, used for lobbing common shell and occasionally 'carcasses' – incendiary ammunition used for setting fire to buildings, or sometimes for providing illumination at night.

Equipping the field brigades and horse artillery troops was straightforward enough, but greater difficulties were encountered in assembling a proper artillery park for siege work. Initially the problem lay in the fact that the army's role was conceived as serving as an auxiliary force in support of the indigenous Spanish and Portuguese armies, who would obviously be far better placed to provide the required heavy guns. In reality of course this notion proved quite illusory and in his early sieges Wellington was constrained to make use of an unsatisfactory collection of antiquated pieces culled from Portuguese fortresses. Apart from the fact that some of the older guns were quite literally worn out, the ammunition supply for these museum pieces was problematical; in the end, though, British guns were provided.

At this time, two heavy guns were in service: an 18-pdr and a 24-pdr. The former proved inadequate for the purposes of breaching modern fortifications, and was quickly retired.

Engineers

John Thomas Jones (1783–1843)
Served Gibraltar 1798–1803 and Mediterranean 1805–06, most notably at Scylla. Appointed adjutant at Woolwich 1807, then served in Peninsula but returned to Woolwich after Corunna. Brigade Major of Engineers at Walcheren then back to Peninsula; Brigade Major at Ciudad Rodrigo and Badajoz. Badly wounded at Burgos 4 October 1812: spent convalescence writing *Journal of Sieges in Spain*.

Commissions: second-lieutenant Royal Engineers 30 August 1798; lieutenant 14 September 1800; second captain 1 March 1805; captain 24 June 1809; major (brevet) 6 February 1812; lieutenant-colonel (brevet) 27 April 1812; lieutenant-colonel Royal Engineers 16 November 1816; colonel (brevet) 27 May 1825; major-general 10 January 1837.

John Fox Burgoyne (1782?–1871)
Served on Malta at blockade of Valetta, then Egypt, Alexandria and Rosetta. Served Peninsula: Corunna; Oporto; blew up Fort Conception; Busaco; siege of Badajoz; Salamanca; Burgos (wounded); Vittoria; San Sebastian (wounded) 31 August 1813; Nive; Nivelle; Bayonne.

Commissions: second-lieutenant Royal Engineers 29 August 1798; lieutenant 1 July 1800; second captain 1 March 1805; captain 24 June 1809; major (brevet) 6 February 1812; lieutenant-colonel (brevet) 27 April 1812; lieutenant-colonel Royal Engineers 20 December 1814; colonel (brevet) 22 July 1830; major-general 28 June 1838; lieutenant-general 11 November 1851; general 5 September 1855.

With the exception of roads and bridges, which fell to the Royal Staff Corps, most military engineering in the Peninsula naturally enough came under the aegis of the Royal Engineers, a small professional corps of officers answering to the Board of Ordnance. Indeed entrants were normally first commissioned into the Royal Artillery before transferring, usually within a year, to the Engineers if they showed a particular aptitude. They were on the whole a well trained and extremely competent body of men and the famous Lines of Torres Vedras are an ample testimony to their skill. Unfortunately, when judged as a whole, their usefulness in the Peninsula was limited by two factors.

In the first place there was seemingly never enough of them, and the shortage of personnel was exacerbated by the fact that in order to carry out their job properly they frequently had to carry out very close reconaissance of enemy positions. This inevitably led to a great many of them being shot in the process – and not always by the French! One consequence was that their uniforms were changed from the traditional Board of Ordnance blue,to scarlet, which both reduced the chances of being shot by nervous sentries, or assassinated by local peasants who mistook them for Frenchmen. Another and perhaps more inevitable consequence was that for want of sufficient properly trained engineers much of the day to day work connected with sieges had to be undertaken by amateurs volunteered from infantry battalions, and even in one notable instance by an East India Company officer, Captain John Blakiston – although he at least was a professional who had served on Wellington's staff in India.

The second factor was an even more serious shortage of competent hired help. In peacetime Engineer officers could call upon the services of a body of skilled craftsmen; carpenters, stonemasons and the like, dignified by the title of the Royal Military Artificers. Most of them, however, were quite sedentary and resolutely attached to their home garrisons with the result that the few who reluctantly made their way out to the Peninsula were quite inadequate in supervising even the basic tasks of constructing hurdles and gabions for entrenchments. Once again, therefore, most of the work had to be carried out by untrained and even less enthusiastic infantrymen. Not only were they unskilled, they detested being employed as labourers and downed tools at every opportunity. Eventually a new corps of Royal Sappers and Miners were raised specifically to address this problem but the first of them only came out in time to appear (much to the fascination of observers) at the siege of San Sebastian.

The consequence was that whilst major projects, such as the Lines of Torres Vedras, could be accomplished to a very high standard, the engineering associated with field operations and siege work was generally very deficient and indeed it is argued that Wellington was forced to incur heavy losses in storming fortresses such as Badajoz precisely because his engineers were incapable of reducing them by more scientific means.

Sir Richard Fletcher (1768–1813)
Son of Rev. Richard Fletcher. Served Peninsula: CRE under Wellington. Substantially responsible for designing Lines of Torres Vedras. Slightly wounded at siege of Badajoz and killed in action at San Sebastian 31 August 1813.

Commissions: second-lieutenant Royal Artillery 9 July 1788; transferred to Royal Engineers 29 June 1790; lieutenant Royal Engineers 16 January 1793; captain-lieutenant 18 August 1797; lieutenant-colonel 24 June 1809.

Medical services

In 1794 an Army Medical Board had been established 'for conducting the general business of the Medical Department of the Army', but it was discontinued four years later and instead the Physician General, Surgeon General, and Inspector of Regimental Hospitals were each to be solely responsible for their own departments.

Of the three, the Physician General was probably the least important in the sphere of military operations, since his duties lay in recommending the appointment of physicians, inspecting (with the Surgeon General) the army's medicines, conducting medical examinations of officers in London requesting sick leave, and presiding over the professional examinations of candidates for regimental or staff appointments.

The Surgeon General on the other hand was responsible for recommending the appointment of staff and regimental surgeons or medical officers, for selecting staff surgeons to be employed in general hospitals, camps and districts, and for assisting in the examination of candidates for Hospital Mates.

The Inspector General of Army Hospitals – in 1807 a Mr Knight – was responsible for the recommendation of Hospital Mates, Apothecaries (druggists), Purveyors, and Deputies 'and the inferior officers' on the formation of a new hospital or establishment. As such he might in theory appear the junior of the three partners, but in fact as his title suggests he was also required to: 'inspect regimental hospitals at home; to correspond with the Regimental Surgeons; and be responsible for all matters relative to the supply of their medicines, and management of their hospitals'. Consequently he was directly responsible for the day to day management of medical facilities and locally this responsibility very naturally devolved upon the Inspector of Hospitals in the Peninsula: Dr James McGrigor.

As it happened Dr McGrigor was a thorough professional and indeed is said to have been the only man who argued with Wellington and got away with it, on the matter of siting hospitals and on the evacuation routes for his medical columns.

General hospitals were more or less permanently established in large garrisons and depots, in addition to the more temporary ones nearer the front as might be convenient for military operations. Each infantry battalion and cavalry regiment should have had its own hospital supervised by the regimental surgeon and his two mates, even if only in a tent set aside for the purpose, but in practice this was only used as a sort of doctor's surgery for the treatment of minor ailments and diagnosis of more serious ones. Those suffering from the first were dosed or patched up and returned to some kind of duty as quickly as possible, while the more serious were passed back to the general hospitals in the rear. A limited number of spring wagons were available for this purpose, but for the most part bullock carts had to be pressed into service.

In the immediate aftermath of a battle the available medical facilities were likely to be swamped since they were essentially geared to providing the ordinary day to day medical cover required by a large body of men. On the whole, though, under Dr McGrigor's superintendence they coped reasonably well, except perhaps in the matter of returning convalescents to their regiments after treatment: the large body of malingerers infesting Lisbon were widely known as the 'Belem Rangers'.

Chronology

John Francis Cradock (1769–1839)
Overshadowed by Wellington's divisional commanders, Sir John Cradock performed solidly as commander of the British forces left behind in Portugal by Sir John Moore.

Served in West Indies 1794 under Grey in command of 2/Grenadiers; Martinique (wounded), St Lucia and Guadaloupe; ADC to Grey; QMG Ireland 1797; served on staff in Mediterranean and Egypt 1801, then successively in Corsica, Madras and in Portugal; commanded British Army in Portugal during period between Convention of Cintra and Wellington's re-appointment to command. Created Lord Howdon on Wellington's recommendation 1819.

Commissions: cornet 4th Horse 1777; ensign 2nd Footguards 1779; lieutenant and captain 1781; major 12th Dragoons 1785; major 13th Foot 1786; lieutenant-colonel 16 June 1789; colonel 127th Foot 16 April 1795 – reduced; colonel 2/54th – reduced; major-general 1 January 1797.

1807
18 October French troops cross Spanish frontier.
30 November Junot occupies Lisbon.

1808
1 August British Army lands at Mondego Bay.
21 August Battle of Vimeiro.
30 August French surrender.
8 November Napoleon enters Spain.
4 December French capture Madrid.

1809
16 January Battle of Corunna.
22 April Wellington re-appointed to command Peninsular Army.
12 May Battle of Oporto.
28–29 July Battle of Talavera (1st, 2nd, 3rd and 4th divisions).

1810
27 September Battle of Busaco (1st–5th divisions, Lt. Division).
10 October British Army retires behind Lines of Torres Vedras.

1811
10 March French capture Badajoz.
3–5 May Battle of Fuentes de Oñoro (1st, 3rd, 5th–7th & Lt. divisions).
6 May First British siege of Badajoz begins.
16 May Battle of Albuera (2nd and 4th divisions).
19 May–17 June Second siege of Badajoz.

1812
8 January Siege of Ciudad Rodrigo begins.
19 January Storming of Ciudad Rodrigo (3rd Division & Lt. Division).
6–7 April Storming of Badajoz (3rd, 4th, 5th & Lt. divisions).
22 July Battle of Salamanca (1st, 3rd, 4th, 5th, 6th, 7th, & Lt. divisions).
12 August British liberate Madrid.
19 Sept.–22 Oct. Siege of Burgos (1st–7th & Lt. divisions).

1813
3 June British offensive begins.
13 June French abandon Burgos.
21 June Battle of Vittoria (1st–7th & Lt. divisions).
25 July Battle of Maya (2nd and 7th divisions).
28 July First Battle of Sorauren (2nd, 3rd, 4th, and 6th divisions).
30 July Second Battle of Sorauren (2nd, 3rd, 4th, 6th & 7th divisions).
31 August Storming of San Sebastian (1st, 4th, 5th & Lt. divisions).
7 October Crossing of Bidassoa (1st and 5th divisions).
25 October Pamplona surrenders.
10 November Battle of Nivelle (1st–7th & Lt. divisions).
9–12 December Battle of Nive (1st, 2nd, 5th, 6th & Lt. divisions).
13 December Battle of Ste-Pierre (2nd Division).

1814
27 February Battle of Orthez (2nd, 3rd, 4th, 6th, 7th & Lt. divisions).
6 April Napoleon abdicates.
10 April Battle of Toulouse (2nd, 3rd, 4th, 6th & Lt. divisions).
30 April War ends with Treaty of Paris.

Bibliography

Adjutant General *Rules and Regulations for the Formations, Field-Exercise and Movements of His Majesty's Forces* (1792)
Instructions and Regulations for the Formations and Movements of the Cavalry (1796)
Fletcher, Ian *Galloping at Everything; The British Cavalry in the Peninsular War and at Waterloo. A Re-appraisal.* (Staplehurst 1999)
Bloody Albuera: The 1811 Campaign in the Peninsula (Marlborough 2000)
Fortescue, Sir John *History of the British Army* (London 1910–30)
Glover, Richard *Peninsular Preparation: The Reform of the British Army 1795–1809* (Cambridge 1963)
Guy, Alan *The Road to Waterloo* (London 1990)
Hall, Dr. John A. *Biographical Dictionary of British Officers Killed and Wounded 1808–1814* (London 1998 – as supplement to Oman)
Haythornthwaite, P. *British Cavalryman 1793–1815* (London 1994)
The Armies of Wellington (London 1994)
Mollo, John *The Prince's Dolls; Scandals, Skirmishes and Splendours of the Hussars, 1793–1815* (London 1997)
Muir, Rory *Salamanca 1812* (London 2001)
Tactics and the Experience of Battle in the Age of Napoleon (London 1998)
Oman, Sir Charles *A History of the Peninsular War* (Oxford 1902–30, reprinted London 1995-97)
Wellington's Army 1809–1814 (Oxford 1913, reprinted London 1986)
Pimlott, John *British Light Cavalry* (London 1977)
Public Record Office: WO12 Regimental Musters
WO25/749-823 Services of Officers
WO25/3998 Field Officers' Commissions
Smirke, Robert *Review of a Battalion of Infantry* (London 1799)
Ward, S.G.P. *Wellington's Headquarters* (Oxford 1957)

Index

Figures in **bold** refer to illustrations